"Edward's *Voices of Innovation* gives us glimpses of the people harnessing unstoppable forces to move the ultimate immovable object - Healthcare."

Daniel Crane
CEO, Modernizing Medicine

"An unparalleled assembly of innovative healthcare IT leaders in one book. Healthcare is a complicated and rapidly evolving industry, and information technology sits as its cornerstone. Whether you are an IT professional, or a layman looking to expand your knowledge, this single source book will serve as your definitive guide to the most contemporary thinking in the healthcare IT industry."

James Merlino, MD
Chief Transformation Officer of Press Ganey,
and former Chief Experience Officer of Cleveland Clinic

"With the cost development in healthcare, things must change. And change depends on Innovation. However, it is not easy to encourage innovation in healthcare. This book addresses this fundamentally important issue for both institutions and ourselves as future patients. Ed Marx is one of the most influential and experienced CIOs in the US, and he has by this compiled a very important book that is a must read for everyone interested in improving future healthcare."

Torbjörn Kronander, PhD
CEO and President, Sectra

"*Voices of Innovation* is a rare collection of real life anecdotes shared by some of the most prominent healthcare informatics leaders without eschewing in technical jargon or banality. Punctiliously arranged in sections following HIMSS's Innovation Pathway, this book will prove to be an essential reference for all Health IT innovators, regardless of areas of interest and proficiency."

Eric Wong
Group Chief Clinical Informatics Officer,
National Healthcare Group, Singapore

"The stories and experiences shared in *Voices of Innovation* allow aspiring healthcare leaders the confidence to challenge themselves to stimulate new opportunities for their organizations but more importantly for the patients and caregivers they serve. The integration of technology into a business model always drives improved quality and better efficiency and this book provides a foundation for the necessary change in healthcare that will occur."

Dr. Brian Donley
Chief of Staff, Cleveland Clinic London

"Marx's writing is always enjoyable to read, and in this book, he's focused on creating a guide for innovation in healthcare to help others start their own journeys."

Judith Faulkner
CEO of Epic Systems

"I had the privilege of witnessing first-hand the development of Ed Marx as a great leader who builds and inspires teams to innovate in serving patients and clinicians. This book is a much-needed compilation of proven techniques to foster and stimulate innovation."

Kevin Roberts
Executive Vice President and Chief Financial Officer at Geisinger Health

"Rising costs are exerting tremendous pressure to change the value equation for healthcare in the USA. At the same time Digital technologies are enabling dramatic changes in healthcare around the world. The timing is perfect of a book like Voices of Innovation that explores how embracing Innovation is required to manage the changes that we know are coming."

Peter O'Neill
Executive Director- Innovations, Cleveland Clinic

"There is no more important role for innovation than to humanize and enhance the delivery of healthcare. The insights from this book serve as an excellent guide to making this a reality."

Russ Rudish
President & CEO of Rudish Health

"Ed Marx has served his country both in uniform and as a civilian. He is my brother and friend. His genius approach of getting a lot of great minds to collaborate and to inspire is innovative by itself. Voice of innovation is about simplicity and collaborative approach to bring value. If I can innovate so can you approach makes it possible to improve humanity and healthcare. This is just the recipe that healthcare needs today."

Shafiq Rab
Senior Vice President & CIO Rush System for Health and Rush University Medical Center

"The electronic medical record is just this one small part of innovation in contemporary academic medical practice. Innovation defined by new ideas, practically deployed, has the potential to reimagine the experience of healthcare for patients and providers as well as organizations, payers and communities. At Cleveland Clinic Abu Dhabi we have leveraged wired and wireless biometric sensors, and artificial intelligence in literally every corner of our clinical, educational and academic mission. Each lightbulb has an IP address and every breath on a ventilator is tracked, analyzed and adjusted with the aid of learning algorithms. Ed Marx's book, fully appreciated has the potential to take us to the next level in the integration electronic innovation into the heart and science of healthcare delivery. Hold onto your Apps - the future has just begun!"

Dr. Rakesh Suri
Chief of Staff, Cleveland Clinic Abu Dhabi

"Kudos to Ed Marx for curating a powerful mosaic of experiences in the pursuit of greater efficiency and outcomes in healthcare. A timely roadmap to navigating the challenges technology brings about but can also solve, *Voices of Innovation* is required reading for those leading the transformation of care around the world."

Carter Groome
Co-Founder and CEO, First Health Advisory

"As we enter a new generation of technology and knowledge enablement, the skill of innovation has become critical to both leadership and organization success. This book highlights both the individual and organization focus on innovation realization. Let us not forget the very reason we innovate: to provide the highest quality care in the safest environment at the most affordable cost while improving the well-being of all. We strongly encourage you to read this book as a spark to light your own innovation journey."

Russ Branzell
CHCIO, FCHIME - CEO/President, CHIME

"Ed Marx, a feet-firmly-planted-on-the-ground legend in healthcare IT, has provided a refreshingly practical guide to innovation. This book could not have been written by anyone who didn't have the deep knowledge, experience and relationships that Ed and those who contributed to this book bring to the table."

Ivo Nelson
Chairman and CEO of Next Wave Health

"Ed Marx has dedicated his career to leveraging technology as a strategic asset in improving healthcare delivery. He has been at the forefront of driving information innovation in a variety of different healthcare institutions and is currently helping enable a digital transformation inside one of the top academic medical centers in the world."

Eric Sigurdson
CIO Practice Leader at Russell Reynolds Associates

"Some of the most important technology innovations for the world center around health and wellness. When people are well, they can work, learn, teach, achieve, take care of families, and contribute to society. Voices of Innovation steps up to the challenge, not only describing some amazing medical innovations, but providing a much needed "how-to" guide for other technology and medical leaders to follow for future advancement. Ed, you've hit the Marx!"

Sue B. Workman
Vice President University Technology and CIO University Technology
Case Western Reserve University

"Leading innovators in healthcare are starting with the needs of the end users — doctors, nurses, and patients — and working backwards to create amazing experiences for each (words not often used to describe healthcare). This is improving communication and delivery of care, both in the hospital and in the home. And when done well, this creates a sustained 'pull' for these solutions rather than the 'technology push' in healthcare that has at times gotten in the way."

Steve Gipstein, MD

"*Voices of Innovation* provides novel insights into the world of healthcare innovation, and how information technologies are transforming our healthcare systems, by improving the speed and quality of care delivery. Written by one of the foremost experts and leading CIOs, Edward Marx, the book provides a compelling look at new types of IT-enabled innovations in healthcare, along with practical examples on how to lead and sustain innovation across organizations, potential outcomes for healthcare transformation, and best practices from case studies of healthcare providers which implemented these disruptive innovations."

Indranil Bardhan
Foster Parker Centennial Professor of Information Technology,
The University of Texas at Austin

"Healthcare has always attracted its fair share of the best and brightest the world has to offer, but when lives are on the line – and the guiding principal is to, above all else, do no harm – many of those best and brightest have shied away from the necessary risk that innovation requires. Fortunately, Edward Marx's new book, *Voices of Innovation*, provides models and blueprints of how those gifted administrators and caregivers can engage in the innovation their industry so desperately needs while maintaining their commitment to the highest standards of safety and quality. Marx's book is the new required reading for anyone who truly wishes to make a difference by doing things differently in the healthcare industry."

Anthony Guerra
Editor-in-Chief,healthsystemCIO.com

"The art of innovation does not mean buying the latest technology from the market. It starts with authentic leadership and understanding how you have to create a culture of creative thinking. The stories in this book highlights those examples."

David Chou
Chief Information & Digital Officer, Children's Mercy Hospital

"The healthcare sector is experiencing digital disruption form all spheres of medicine. The health eco system is now challenged with leaping to new levels of safety, service and cost predictability. Moving beyond digitization into transformation is the new opportunity, and health organizations across the globe are beginning to rally. Voices of Innovation promises to be a guide that will inspire each reader to bulldoze through obstacles and collaborate on all accessible data points, fulfilling the Hippocratic Oath to serve and teach to the best of ones' abilities."

James Peelman
Managing Partner, Blue Chip Consulting Group

"*Voices of Innovation* is the first practical roadmap to Healthcare Transformation bringing the convergence between key elements of Process Management and Innovation Factors. New healthcare leaders will find this Innovation Handbook invaluable and experienced professionals will use it to rapidly deploy technology to enable clinical workflow optimization. This guide will also provide a Data Driven and Workflow Centric Innovation Pathway for vendors to better understand customer challenges, value creation processes and to apply Machine Learning techniques leveraging from the collaborative process that leads to continuous disruption."

Alan Portela
CEO & Chairman, AirStrip

"As the drumbeat for need of healthcare innovation and disruption gets louder this is a great 'How to' book with practical and pragmatic solutions to achieve that."

Ram Raju, MD
Senior Vice President, Northwell Health

"Innovation is a critical contributor to ensuring that we are collectively able to transform healthcare. *Voices of Innovation* is a remark contribution to these efforts, bringing together a diverse array of experiences and insights from leading innovators in the field. This book is both a textbook and a handbook."

John Glaser, PhD
Senior Vice President, Population Health, Cerner

"I've known Ed for many years, and I know one thing for sure. Ed is a transformational change agent who works alongside his teams around innovative healthcare technologies—not just ideas that sit on a shelf, but ones that get implemented on mountain tops and hospital rooms and that ultimately save lives. That said, Ed has high standards—for the organizations with which he works and for himself—so expect some of this to be quite hard. Know that there no silver bullets herein, only golden nuggets of wisdom earned as scar tissue by Ed and his colleagues over time. In short, Voices of Innovation has valuable content that may just save the life of you or someone you love."

George Sheth, MBA
FHIMSS, Managing Partner, Diligent Partners, LLC

"Ed Marx is one of the brightest and most innovative leaders in healthcare. He is passionate, he is smart, and he understand things both technically and holistically. Ed a very gifted speaker and thinker."

Scott Becker
Healthcare Partner at McGuireWoods LLP

"Ed is one of the most experienced technology executives in healthcare so he is a top authority on innovation. More importantly, he applies the personal insight he gained from his own experiences to select a group of people and innovative solutions that provide relief to the frustrations of patients and caregivers. Ultimately, *Voices of Innovation* provides a sense of hope to individuals who interact with the current system."

Jennifer Covich Bordenick
Chief Executive Officer, eHealth Initiative and Foundation

"In *Voices of Innovation*, Ed Marx takes us on an uncomfortable ride that shows the reader where our healthcare information gaps are, and where we have underperformed. Fortunately, it also offers a glimpse into the incredible future that awaits us as we harness the opportunities of innovation. A must read for anyone looking to disrupt the norms in healthcare."

Wael K Barsoum, MD
CEO and President, Cleveland Clinic Florida

"This is a great collection of practical examples of innovation, which reinforces the fact that innovation comes in many forms and can deliver great outcomes. It is a great read that can help anyone make a real difference in their organization and in the mission they serve!"

Rod Dykehouse
SVP and CIO, Penn State Health and College of Medicine

"*Voices of Innovation* is a brilliant handbook on how professionals are leading change . . . and that is exactly what we need in healthcare!! Integrating technology and clinical care is exactly what we need in healthcare. Ed Marx provides inspiring insights that lead us into the next era of change!"

A message to aspiring healthcare leaders ... consider, ponder and absorb the stories and experiences shared in *Voices of Innovation* You will be leading change in the most dynamic and challenging era of healthcare. And the convergence of technology and clinical care will drive unimaginable change. Get ready. Get prepared. And let's get going.

Britt Berrett
Program Director/Faculty, University of Texas at Dallas

"Innovations in healthcare inspire us to do more and to think differently. The day to day can take its toll, but striving for something better through innovation inspires us to think differently and be the change that is needed in healthcare delivery. Finding a new and better way of doing something doesn't always mean finding a new and better technology. Sometimes it's a new approach to an ongoing challenge. This book is a wonderful framework to encourage us all to think differently in our pursuit of better healthcare."

Cara Babachicos
Senior Vice President and Chief Information Officer, South Shore Health

"Leading an IT organization in one of our nation's leading academic medical centers is a privilege I have had for nearly 30 years. We serve amazingly passionate people, who are defined by a purpose, committed to science, discovery and the best possible clinical care. And now, this book challenges all of us to appreciate the fact that we also have the power of data and some of the newest tools and technologies that we must leverage to truly make a difference."

Stephanie Reel
Senior Vice President and Chief Information Officer, Johns Hopkins University and Health System

"Disruptive information technology will be the catalyst for the next wave of healthcare advancement. One such innovation is leveraging the investment that has been made in digitizing medical records to allow pushed interoperability across disparate health systems enabling enhanced provider to provider and provider to patient communication. This digitized healthcare information provides a multitude of opportunities for healthcare advancement, as evidenced in this book.

All successful innovative technology implementation requires first and foremost engaged leadership. Ed Marx is both an outstanding innovator and, or perhaps because, he is an excellent leader."

Holly Miller, MD
Chief Medical Officer, MedAllies, Inc.

"Timely, yet ahead of its time - I can't think of anyone better equipped to put this work together. Ed's professional knowledge, personal experiences, and incredible passion for and commitment to everything he does are palpable and are poured into this book. If this doesn't move the needle on Healthcare Innovation, nothing will!"

Chris Teumer
Executive Partner, Gartner

"Healthcare has entered the digital age where critical thinking using innovation is essential. This book offers us the opportunity to learn from others, to translate their experiences into our environment and to accelerate our journey as innovators. Every day patients depend on us to think faster, react more specifically to their needs and to return them to their lives. Take the challenge to make innovation the way you think and act."

Liz Johnson
Chief Innovation Officer, Tenet Healthcare

"Ed Marx's book addresses the journey healthcare is beginning around digital transformation. While we know almost all other industries have been going through this transition for years, this transformation is just starting in healthcare. Healthcare leaders must understand how to navigate this very brave new world, Ed's book is an excellent guide to those on the journey. A highly recommended read for healthcare C-Suite leaders."

Eric Yablonka
Chief Information Officer, Stanford Health Care

"Positive transformation of healthcare for humankind will be led by the "Voices" of innovators on the front lines caring for patients or working in partnership with those who do. If you are an IT professional, clinical provider or hospital executive interested in leading digital transformation in healthcare, this book is a must read."

Gregory J. Moore, MD, PhD
Vice President, Google Inc, Google Cloud Healthcare and Life Sciences

Voices of Innovation

Fulfilling the Promise of Information
Technology in Healthcare

Voices of Innovation

Fulfilling the Promise of Information Technology in Healthcare

Edited by
Edward W. Marx

CRC Press
Taylor & Francis Group
Boca Raton London New York

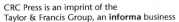

CRC Press is an imprint of the
Taylor & Francis Group, an **informa** business

CRC Press
Taylor & Francis Group
6000 Broken Sound Parkway NW, Suite 300
Boca Raton, FL 33487-2742

First issued in paperback 2021

© 2019 by Taylor & Francis Group, LLC
CRC Press is an imprint of Taylor & Francis Group, an Informa business

No claim to original U.S. Government works

ISBN 13: 978-1-03-209393-2 (pbk)
ISBN 13: 978-1-4987-6968-6 (hbk)

Visit the Taylor & Francis Web site at
http://www.taylorandfrancis.com

and the CRC Press Web site at
http://www.crcpress.com

Contents

Foreword

This is a dangerous book. It's a threat to complacency and the way things have always been done. It provides a direct challenge to all of us who work in healthcare – doctors, nurses, and administrators at all levels.

Why is this? Because, astonishingly, healthcare is the only major industry that has yet to be transformed by the digital revolution. While manufacturing, retail and transportation enjoy gains in productivity from digital technology, some sectors of healthcare are still struggling to adopt the electronic medical record, telemedicine and the host of other game-changing innovations barreling down the digital pipeline.

Voices of Innovation shows us that it doesn't have to be that way. A new generation is taking the helm, energized by the potential of IT to make healthcare safer, more effective and more affordable.

At Cleveland Clinic, our entire organization is moving rapidly to adopt digital technology across all clinical domains. Our surgeons who performed the world's first 100% face transplant planned their stupendously complex procedure using patient-specific 3D-printed models assembled from CT and MRI data. We've partnered with top companies to build powerful databases and systems to enhance the speed and accuracy of clinical decision making. With a variety of hand-held apps, we're monitoring hundreds of patients at home, keeping them out of the hospital, and responding quickly to acute emergencies.

Almost every place evidenced-based digital solutions are applied, providers are seeing favorable clinical outcomes, improved patient satisfaction, and lower costs.

We're rapidly approaching the day when the majority of clinical decisions will be supported by information from wearable devices, imaging, implants, genetic profiles and analysis of the microbiome – with insights from global health and all published research.

This is not a future where doctors are replaced by computers. It's a future where doctors have access to 1,000 times more knowledge than they could ever get from their own reading. It's a future where doctors are liberated from superficial tasks, and can focus their full attention on the patient and the patient's problem.

The people you'll meet in *Voices of Innovation* are at the leading edge of all these trends. They aren't dreaming about the future of healthcare IT: they're making it happen right now. And reading about what they're doing will make you want to jump out of your seat and begin innovating yourself, whatever your sphere.

Digital technology is going to help us do what healthcare does well, even better. We will use it to connect people with people in new ways – to humanize care, and enhance our role as healers.

Dr. Tomislav Mihaljevic,
President and Chief Executive Officer, the Cleveland Clinic

Acknowledgments

No book can be written alone. *Voices of Innovation* is no exception. There are many individuals and organizations who gave birth and life to this endeavor.

First, thank you to the fantastic organizations and teams I have had the honor to serve with. They taught me innovation and allowed me to fail and succeed along the way. It all begins with Poudre Valley Hospital in Northern Colorado, who allowed me to experiment and create unique programs and services for our medical staff, and Parkview Episcopal Medical in Southern Colorado, who gave me my first wings into healthcare technology. We learned that you could flip market share through the innovative application of technology. When I was caught in a long-term project pause at HCA in Tennessee, leadership allowed me to be one of the first in the world to experiment with personal digital assistants, which still informs my thoughts today. University Hospitals in Ohio provided me my first opportunity to collaborate with scientists and providers to co-create and develop repeatable processes along the way. Arlington-based Texas Health Resources was one of the those "right place at the right time" scenarios where we were able to develop life-saving innovation on top of mature electronic health records, moving swiftly into mobile. With New York City Health and Hospitals, we applied innovation retrospectively in order to set the stage to leap frog competing institutions. Cleveland Clinic is the first organization I have served where innovation is part of the DNA of the organization. Surrounded by an innovation superstructure and brilliant researchers, educators and providers, I am learning all over again. Within each of these organizations were mission-driven leaders and teams that inspired me and taught me things I could never get from a book, a speech or consultant.

Second, my contributors. *Voices* is full of global and diverse practical examples of innovation in practice. They each went through a lengthy period to have their work included, some as long as four years! As I read every submission, my eyes were opened and my mind enlightened, leaving me spinning full of new ideas.

Third, my support team has been patient and amazing, including editor, Kristine Mednansky at CRC Press/Taylor & Francis Group. I delayed time and time again as I sought ways to balance the craziness of life and the challenges of writing well. Kris never gave up. HIMSS, who developed the initial idea and asked me to write it, have also been patient throughout this process and were helpful in the solicitation of contributors. The primary reason for *Voices* to finally be published is the tenaciousness of my excellent assistant, Dara Dressler. In addition to her work and in her spare time, Dara served as the project manager and ensured we stayed on track. *Voices* would not have been finished without her.

Finally, my Indian Princess and Wife, Simran Marx: Simran has provided continuous encouragement along the journey. Without complaint, she afforded me the time needed to complete *Voices*. As a healthcare provider herself, Simran understood the importance of this work and the need to help others with all of the examples from our contributors. A goal of *Voices* is to make the practice of medicine easier and less burdensome for clinicians like Simran. She shares in the sacrifice and joy it took to write *Voices*.

About the Editor and Contributors

Edward Marx is Chief Information Officer (CIO) at Cleveland Clinic, an $8 billion medical system that includes a main campus, 10 regional hospitals, 18 family health centers and facilities in Florida, Nevada, Toronto, Abu Dhabi and London. He is responsible for the planning, deployment and execution of technologies to enable the mission and vision of the Clinic. As technology pivots to digitally enable the enterprise, his team's steadfast focus is on developing high-performing teams and maintaining a high-reliability environment, all while delivering excellence in customer service. The vision includes ensuring a seamless and delightful digital patient and caregiver experience.

Prior to joining Cleveland Clinic, Edward served as Senior Vice President/ CIO of Texas Health. In 2015, he spent over two years as Executive Vice President of the Advisory Board, providing technology leadership and strategy for New York City Health and Hospitals.

Edward began his career at Poudre Valley Health System. CIO roles have included Parkview Episcopal Medical Center, University Hospitals in Cleveland and Texas Health Resources. Concurrent with his healthcare career, he served 15 years in the Army Reserve, first as a combat medic and then as a combat engineer officer.

Edward is a Fellow of the College of Healthcare Information Management Executives (CHIME) and Healthcare Information and Management Systems Society (HIMSS). He is on the CHIME Board and serves as Faculty for the CIO Boot Camp, training aspiring healthcare technology professionals. He has won numerous awards, including HIMSS/CHIME 2013 CIO of the Year, and has been recognized by both CIO and Computer World as one of the "Top 100 Leaders." Becker's named Marx as the 2015 "Top Healthcare IT Executive" and the 2016 "17 Most Influential People in Healthcare."

This is Edward's second book. His first book, *Extraordinary Tales of a Rather Ordinary Guy*, was published in 2014. The book was written in response to requests for him to detail the success principles behind many of his experiences. His next book, *Scenes from an Early Morning Run*, is set to publish Spring 2019. It is intended to be a "coffee table" book that showcases unique photos he has taken while running over the last several years. This collage was collated in response to requests to have all these pictures in one volume.

Edward received his Bachelor of Science in psychology and a Master of Science in design, merchandising and consumer sciences from Colorado State University. Edward is married and proud father to five adult children. In his spare time he enjoys climbing some of the world's highest peaks and competing in multi-sport races as part of TeamUSA Duathlon.

Chapter 1   Blend Cultures

Mark Waugh – Murata

Charles Christian – Indiana Health Information Exchange

Charles Christian is the Vice President of Technology and Engagement of the Indiana Health Information Exchange (IHIE), the nation's largest Health Information Exchange.

Prior to joining IHIE, Mr. Christian served as the Vice President/Chief Information Officer of St. Francis Hospital, a free-standing, acute care, community hospital in West Georgia, a position he held for 2.5 years. Before his role at St. Francis, Mr. Christian served as the Chief Information Officer for Good Samaritan Hospital in Vincennes, Indiana, a position he held for almost 24 years. Before joining Good Samaritan Hospital, Mr. Christian worked in healthcare IT for Compucare and Baxter Travenol in both management and implementation roles. Mr. Christian started his career in healthcare as a Registered Radiologic Technologist, serving in various Radiology roles for 14 years. Mr. Christian studied natural sciences at the University of Alabama in Birmingham, and holds a Bachelor of Science in Business Administration from Lacrosse University.

Pete O'Neill – Cleveland Clinic

Pete O'Neill is Executive Director of Cleveland Clinic Innovations, where he manages a group of more than 50 professionals responsible for commercializing Cleveland Clinic's IP portfolio. He has been with Cleveland Clinic Innovations for 13 years, in roles including Director of Commercialization and Senior Officer for commercialization of orthopedic technologies.

Mr. O'Neill is passionate about promoting entrepreneurial efforts within Cleveland Clinic's commercialization ecosystem. Mr. O'Neill was educated as an aeronautical engineer at MIT, and previously held management positions in aerospace manufacturing and technology commercialization.

Chapter 2   Use People with IT

Shawntea (Taya) Moheiser – H3C Chronic Care Coordination

As Advisory Service Directory, Taya is responsible for guiding strategic success with healthcare facilities including guidance on compliance, revenue cycle management, workforce management, planned growth, mergers and contracts. Taya has served in many leadership roles in healthcare and currently sits on the Cross-Specialty and E&M Workgroups with the national Medical Group Management Association (MGMA) that exist to provide feedback to CMS. Taya has spent quite some time in various physician advocacy roles including several terms on government affairs and legislative committees lobbying for physician rights.

John Paganini – Paguar Informatics, Inc

With over 35 years of startups, IT and healthcare information systems experience, John Paganini is a respected authority in healthcare informatics and an industry spokesperson. He is the founder of IoT Directions, which is focused on education on the Internet of Things through event management services and media content. John is also the president of Paguar Informatics Inc., a healthcare IT consulting firm focused on innovation and business development, and the CEO and Co-Founder at DinkerBop, which makes a simple radio for people living with dementia. He previously managed operation and logistics at the HIMSS Innovation Center in the Global Center for Health Innovation in Cleveland, and was the Senior Product Manager at Applied Visual Sciences Inc. for radiology informatics, imaging, computer-aided detection, advanced visualization and digital microscopy. John also co-founded RIS Logic, Inc., a division of Merge Healthcare recently acquired by IBM.

Donna Walker – Revenue Integrity Audit

Juan Luis Cruz – Puerta de Hierro University Hospital

Juan Luis Cruz, MSc, was the CIO at Puerta de Hierro University Hospital in Madrid (Spain) for over 7 years. Named by the Health Information Management Systems Society (HIMSS) as one of the top 50 Healthcare IT leaders in Europe (2018), he holds a Master's degree in Telecommunications Engineering from the Technical University of Madrid and an Executive Program from IESE Business School, among others. He is a member of the American College of Healthcare Information Management Executives (CHIME), CHCIO certified, and founder and member of the board of the HIMSS Iberian Community. At present he is pursuing a PhD in data analytics and clinical decision support in Oncology. Co-author of several peer-reviewed articles, Mr. Cruz's research interests include the application of data science, machine learning and artificial intelligence in the clinical setting to improve outcomes and the value given to patients. Mr. Cruz has extensive experience in the Healthcare sector, working as a Healthcare IT consultant and leading many innovative projects related with the digital transformation of Healthcare, IT strategy and planning and developing and implementation of EMR and digital health solutions at hospitals.

Dr. José Luis Bueno – Puerta de Hierro University Hospital

José Luis Bueno, MD, is the Head of the Transfusion, Apheresis and Non-Transfusional Hemotherapy units at Puerta de Hierro University Hospital in Madrid (Spain). He is a specialist in Hematology and holds a MSc in Statistics and Molecular Oncology. Dr. Bueno serves as a member of the Transfusion Safety Commission at the Spanish Health Ministry and as a reference Spanish member in the European Expert Panel on Ebola Convalescent Plasma Use. Also, he is the transfusion advisor at the National Accreditation Office on Quality (ENAC. Industry Ministry of Spain). Dr. Bueno is an active scientific author, with several publications in peer-reviewed medical journals, and is also a reviewer for Transfusion and Vox Sanguinis, the two most important journals in transfusion medicine. During the 10 years he was the Head of the Apheresis, Collection and Blood Processing Areas at the Red Cross Blood Donation Center in Madrid. Dr. Bueno is also an entrepreneur, founding a Biotech company in 2013 called PRoPosit Bio, dedicated to developing Cellular Therapies in humans and for veterinary uses and IT systems for improving transfusion safety.

Chapter 3   Create Roadmaps

Paul Black – Allscripts

Paul Black currently serves as board member and Chief Executive Officer of Allscripts. As CEO, Paul guides company direction to fulfill its global commitment to build open, connected communities of health. Prior to joining Allscripts in 2012, Paul spent more than 13 years with Cerner Corporation in various executive positions, retiring as Cerner's Chief Operating Officer in 2007. During his tenure with Cerner, he helped build the company into a market leader in healthcare information technology with more than $1.5 billion in annual revenue. Paul also spent 12 years with IBM Corporation in a variety of leadership positions in sales, product marketing and professional services. Paul has served on several private company and nonprofit boards of directors for companies in healthcare information technology, healthcare services and consumer Internet marketing. He is currently the immediate past chairman and an officer of Truman Medical Centers, a 400-bed safety net academic hospital in Kansas City, MO. Paul holds a Bachelor of Science degree from Iowa State University and a Master of Business Administration from the University of Iowa.

Gary Johnson – University of Kentucky Healthcare

Gary Johnson, PharmD, MHA, is the Chief Innovation Officer at the University of Kentucky Healthcare. Dr. Johnson's research interests include the assessment of ambulatory pharmacy services, including quality, access and profitability. His recent work has focused on the expansion of ambulatory pharmacy services. Dr. Johnson received his PharmD and MHA degrees from Mercer University. He completed two postgraduate residency programs, including a management focused residency at the University of Cincinnati. Dr. Johnson served as the Assistant Director of Pharmacy at the University of Kansas Medical Center and the Director of Pharmacy at the University of Virginia Health System. He joined the University of Kentucky in 2011 as the Chief Pharmacy Officer and transitioned to the role of Chief Innovation Officer in 2017.

Paddy Padmanabhan – Damo Consulting

Paddy Padmanabhan is the author of *The Big Unlock – Harnessing Data and Growing Digital Health Businesses in a Value-Based Care Era*, and is widely recognized as an expert practitioner and thought leader on healthcare technology markets, digital transformation and emerging technologies. Paddy's experience includes leadership roles with global consulting firms Accenture and Wipro, and with Silicon Valley startups that went through successful exits. He has published and spoken widely on digital health technologies and hosts "The Big Unlock" podcast featuring C-level executives from the healthcare industry. Paddy is currently the Founder/CEO of Damo Consulting Inc., a healthcare-focused growth strategy and digital transformation advisory firm based in Chicago. Paddy is a graduate of the CMI General Management program of the University of Chicago Booth School of Business, has an MBA from the Indian Institute of Management and a B.Tech (Hons) from the Indian Institute of Technology.

Kristin Myers – Mount Sinai Health System

Kristin Myers is the Senior Vice President in Information Technology who oversees Application Strategy, the Clinical Application and Interoperability portfolio, and the IT Program Management Office for the Mount Sinai Health System. For the last 14 years, Kristin has led the transformation of the Epic clinical and revenue cycle implementations across the health system. Under Kristin's leadership, Mount Sinai was awarded the prestigious HIMSS 2012 Enterprise Davies Award of Excellence for its electronic record implementation. The Mount Sinai Hospital and Mount Sinai Queens have achieved HIMSS Stage 6 certification, and will be seeking Stage 7 certification this year. Kristin, an active member of the Corporate Diversity Council, also leads the Women in IT team, which meets regularly to educate and advocate on gender parity. Kristin previously worked in the healthcare technology vendor and consulting space before joining Mount Sinai Health System.

Bill Russell – Health Lyrics

Bill Russell is the Founder of Health Lyrics, a management consulting firm that moves health systems to the cloud. Bill has served on executive teams in healthcare, higher education and consulting practices over the past 30 years. While Chief Information Officer for St. Joseph Health, a 16-hospital $5 billion system, he rapidly accelerated the diffusion of new IT strategies and methods, and dramatically improved operational effectiveness while also creating new revenue streams by investing in successful startups such as Hart and Clearsense. Bill holds a bachelor's degree in Economics from Moravian College in Bethlehem, Pennsylvania, and has completed executive education courses and healthcare IT leadership training at the Harvard School of Public Health in Cambridge, Massachusetts.

John Guardado – Microsoft

Chris Regan – Microsoft

Chris Regan is a Digital Health Advisor in Microsoft's Office of the CTO. Chris leads customers in navigating the many options and paths to transformation in the Digital Health Era and to leverage emerging technologies to innovate how they interact with patients, how they deliver care, how their clinicians and employees work and make decisions and how they optimize their business and clinical processes.

John Doyle – Microsoft

John Doyle, as a Director within the worldwide health industry team at Microsoft, is responsible for the development of strategy, partnerships and solutions within the health industry, globally. John engages with industry customers and partners, developing strategies and repeatable solutions that harness the power of cloud and Artificial Intelligence (AI) to drive innovation and transformation within the health industry.

Tom Lawry – Microsoft

Tom Lawry serves as Director of Worldwide Health for Microsoft. In this role he works with providers, payers and life science organizations in planning and implementing innovative analytical solutions that improve the quality and efficiency of health services delivered around the globe. He focuses on strategies for digital transformation applied to performance optimization, including Artificial Intelligence, Machine Learning (ML) and Cognitive Services.

Chapter 4   Collaborate and Listen

Helen Figge – MedicaSoft and Health 2.0

Helen is an experienced and passionate healthcare innovator and futurist. She has expertise in partnering with c-suite executives and peers. She has served in three Fortune companies and non-profit organizations such as HIMSS. She has supported, consulted and guided several startup health IT companies to successful next steps. Helen has achieved HIMSS fellow and CPHIMS status, served on several national committees and Boards and has secured service and career awards such as Health 2.0's Ten Year Industry Leader, and was named as Most Powerful Women in Healthcare IT by Health Data Management in 2016, 2017 and 2018. In 2018, Helen was listed on Becker's prestigious Women to Know in Healthcare IT. Helen presents and publishes extensively in healthcare and regularly presents and authors on healthcare technology. She holds several academic appointments; holds a Baccalaureate in Science, a Doctorate of Pharmacy, and an MBA in healthcare administration; completed a drug information research fellowship; and is a Certified Six Sigma Black Belt and Six Sigma Lean Sensei. Helen mentors for organizations interested in positioning product development and go to market strategies in healthcare. Helen is NYS

HIMSS National Liaison, Health 2.0 Chair, Boston, and Chief Strategy Officer for MedicaSoft based in Arlington, Virginia.

Dr. Peter Tippett – Healthcelerate

Stefanie Shimko-Lin – Cleveland Clinic

Stefanie Shimko-Lin, RN, serves as a Clinical Analyst under the Digital Domain Patient Journey and Clinical Delivery Team at the Cleveland Clinic. The team provides innovative solutions to clinical issues using an agile design process. Stefanie's recent focus, the homegrown mobile application Iris Mobile and Epic Mobility, leverages mobile technology to provide end users the ability to review patient data and document on the go. End of life is an area of special interest to Stefanie. The Clinical Delivery Team utilizes existing technology to create tools to visually prioritize patient care and document in real time, improving patient safety and accuracy in electronic documentation. Stefanie has served as a nurse for over 10 years with clinical focus areas of child birth, gynecology, forensics, rehabilitation and end of life.

Danilo Pena – University of Texas Health Science Center

Danilo Pena has a background in chemical engineering, and worked as an engineer for two years. During the job, Pena realized that he needed to make a larger impact on society, and that he also wanted to learn to code. Pena applied to school, got in and quit his job. Pena is currently a Biomedical Informatics master's student at the University of Texas Health Science Center in Houston and an Albert-Schweitzer Fellow. He is interested in entrepreneurship and always finding ways to change healthcare by finding synergies with cutting-edge technologies like machine learning and bioinformatics.

Kathy Ray – Cleveland Clinic

Kathy Ray is a Systems Analyst in the Center of Excellence, Business Relationship Management – Institutes and Shared Services, at the Cleveland Clinic. She serves as a member of the Cleveland Clinic Main Campus Our Voice: Healthcare Partners, and is Co-Chairman for Medina Hospital, a regional hospital of The Cleveland Clinic, Our Voice: Healthcare Partners. She also co-leads the ITD initiative to create IT Our Voice: Healthcare Partner Council in conjunction with IT Administration. Ray is the recipient of the 2011 of the Cleveland Clinic Individual Caregiver Celebration Award, 2018 Candidate for the Business Technology Leadership Academy, a Member of the ITD Caregiver Council, Vice President of Membership of the CCAC Toastmasters,

Innovations project submitted titled "MyRoad", and has been in clinical human research for three years in conjunction with American Greetings.

Amy Szabo – Cleveland Clinic

Amy Szabo, BSN, RN, BSEd, Paramedic, is the Program Manager for the Cleveland Clinic Our Voice: Healthcare Partner program and Human Centered Design. Amy's professional interests include elevating patient and family advisory councils to adhere to collaboration, transparency and co-design. Her recent work has focused on the development and implementation of the Healthcare Partner program at Cleveland Clinic, across the enterprise, as well as to equip council facilitators with the best skillsets to elicit the co-design, transparency and human centered approach to patient experience initiatives. She is an expert in continuous improvement, lean six sigma, and is in her final year at Case Western Reserve University's Executive Master of Business Administration program. Amy received her Bachelor's of Nursing degree from Ohio University, her Bachelor's of Science in Education from Edinboro University of Pennsylvania. She was one of two full-time firefighter paramedics for the City of Mentor Fire Department and was appointed by Ohio Governor Strickland, while in office, to represent union firefighters on the EMS Advisory Board. Case Weatherhead School of Business has approached Amy to continue her postgraduate studies in Business, to the doctoral level with regard to her demonstrated leadership abilities. She has served Cleveland Clinic Medina Hospital as Patient Experience Manager and Lake Health System as Nurse Manager, and Continuous Improvement Facilitator for the Critical Care and Medical Surgical Value Streams. Amy has presented an accepted abstract at the Ohio Hospital Association Summit, regarding Purposeful Hourly Rounding and an innovative education roll out.

Anna Pannier – American College of Healthcare Executives of Middle Tennessee

Anna Pannier is the President-elect of the American College of Healthcare Executives of Middle Tennessee. Anna has over 20 years of healthcare experience and a passion for transformation in healthcare that started with her exposure to influential leaders at Kaiser Permanente. Unique to Anna is her ability to understand and relate to the many areas of healthcare, as she has most recently been an IT and Informatics leader in large regional and national healthcare organizations and has significant experience in product management and sales for various healthcare IT vendors. She received her

Master's in Business Administration from Indiana University Kelley School of Business, and her undergraduate degrees in Economics and History from the University of California at Davis. She is known for asking the right questions to solve complex challenges. She is a silo-buster and process improvement fanatic. She is dedicated to lifelong learning and believes that helping others achieve success also makes her and her organization successful. She currently resides in Brentwood, Tennessee, with her husband Pat and son Patrick.

Chapter 5 Communicate and Eliminate Barriers

Susan deCathelineau – Global Healthcare Sales and Services

With more than 20 years of healthcare technology and operations leadership experience, Susan is a leader in providing management and consulting services for health information management and revenue cycle and electronic medical record strategies. Susan is responsible for developing and implementing a global strategic vision to ensure Hyland Healthcare solutions and services deliver operational excellence and earn customer loyalty.

Amy Scheon, PhD – Case Western Reserve University School of Medicine

Amy Sheon, PhD, MPH, is the Executive Director of the Urban Health Initiative at Case Western Reserve University School of Medicine. Dr. Sheon has worked on a variety of emerging public health issues, from HIV prevention in the epidemic's earliest years to ethical issues in genetics and childhood obesity. Her current focus is on ensuring that advances in health information technology can reduce rather than accentuate health disparities. Thus, she is developing and testing a model of universally screening patients for their digital skills and connectivity, referring to local partners to address gaps and then training patients to use portals, remote monitors, telehealth and apps. Sheon earned her PhD at Johns Hopkins Bloomberg School of Public Health and her MPH at the University of Michigan. Previously, she worked at the National Institutes of Health, the University of Michigan and Altarum Institute.

Leslie Carroll – Case Western Reserve University School of Medicine

Joel E. Barthelemy – GlobalMed

Joel E. Barthelemy is a USMC Reserve Veteran who founded Arizona-based GlobalMed, an international provider of healthcare delivery systems that power the world's largest telehealth programs for payers, health systems, ministries of health, Veterans Health Administration and Department of Defense; even the White House and Air Force One. Since it was founded in 2002, GlobalMed has powered over 15 million consults, improving access to care in 55 countries. Barthelemy was recognized as Global Business Executive of the Year (2017) by the Global Chamber of Phoenix and was elected to Arizona State University's (ASU) Health Futures Council (2018).

Drew Schiller – Validic

Drew Schiller is the CEO and co-founder of Validic, Inc. Drew's mission is to improve the quality of human life by building technology that makes personal data actionable. In service of this mission, and as a patented technologist, Drew regularly speaks and writes on how technology can humanize the healthcare experience and create an invisible, data-driven system. Drew serves as a member of the Consumer Technology Association's (CTA) Board of Industry Leaders, as well as the Vice Chair for CTA's Health and Fitness Technology Division Board. Through his work with CTA, he contributes to moving the industry forward by developing data standards that advance performance benchmarks and consumer acceptance. Additionally, Drew serves as an advisor for the Clinical Trials Transformation Initiative, as a board member for the Council for Entrepreneurial Development, and as a member of the eHealth Initiatives' Board of Directors. Most recently, Drew was recognized by MedTech Boston as a 40 Under 40 Healthcare Innovator for his work to progress the use of data and technology in healthcare.

Rachael Britt-McGraw – Tennessee Orthopaedic Alliance

Rachael Britt-McGraw, CHCIO, is the Chief Information Officer for Tennessee Orthopaedic Alliance. In this role, Ms. Britt-McGraw serves as an innovative change agent and thought leader for the sprawling surgical practice with 21 locations and over 150 providers. Believing that IT projects and goals must at all times be aligned with business strategy and articulated to executives in business terms, Ms. Britt-McGraw has over two decades of proven IT and business success across a wide variety of industries. Ms. Britt-McGraw holds a Bachelor's of Science in Computer Science – Systems Analysis and Design, and a second BS in Management, both earned from the University of North Carolina at Asheville. She currently resides in the Nashville, Tennessee area, where she serves as a speaker on topics of Cyber Security. She is a member of HIMSS, WITT and the Nashville Technology

Council, and holds the CHCIO certification from the College of Health Information Management Executives.

Mitchell Parker – IU Health

Mitchell Parker, CISSP, is the Executive Director, Information Security and Compliance, at IU Health in Indianapolis, Indiana. Mitch is currently working on redeveloping the Information Security program at IU Health, and regularly works with multiple non-technology stakeholders to improve it. He also speaks regularly at multiple conferences and workshops, including HIMSS, IEEE TechIgnite and Internet of Medical Things. Mitch has a Bachelor's degree in Computer Science from Bloomsburg University, an MS in Information Technology Leadership from LaSalle University and his MBA from Temple University.

Rosie Sanchez – Texas Tech University Health Sciences Center

Chapter 6   Stress Simplicity

Daniel Barchi –New York-Presbyterian

Daniel Barchi is Senior Vice President and Chief Information Officer of New York–Presbyterian, one of the largest healthcare providers in the United States, as well as the university hospital of Columbia University and Cornell University. He leads 2,000 technology, pharmacy, informatics, artificial intelligence and telemedicine specialists who deliver the tools, data and medicine that physicians and nurses use to deliver acute care and manage population health. Daniel previously led healthcare technology as Chief Information Officer of Yale New Haven Health System and the Yale University School of Medicine, and earlier as Chief Information Officer of the Carilion Health System. Before those roles, Daniel was President of the Carilion Biomedical Institute and Director of Technology for MCI WorldCom. Daniel graduated from Annapolis where he served as Brigade Commander, began his career as a United States Naval officer at sea, and was awarded the Navy Commendation Medal for leadership and the Southeast Asia Service Medal for Iraq operations in the Red Sea. He earned a Master of Engineering Management degree as he completed his military service.

Marc F. Probst – Intermountain Healthcare

Marc F. Probst is Chief Information Officer and Vice President at Intermountain Healthcare, a not-for-profit, integrated delivery network of 22 hospitals, 185 clinics, a health plans division and other healthcare related services based in Salt Lake City, Utah. Probst is nationally recognized as a CIO and served on the Federal Healthcare Information Technology Policy Committee which assisted in developing HIT Policy for the U.S. Government. For over 30 years, Probst has been involved in healthcare and technology. Prior to Intermountain, Probst was a partner with two large professional service organizations, Deloitte Consulting and Ernst & Young, serving healthcare provider and payer organizations. Probst has significant interest in the use of information technology to increase patient care quality and to lower the costs of care. He is experienced in information technology planning, design, development, deployment and operation, as well as policy development for HIT-related issues. Marc received a degree in Finance from the University of Utah and later a Masters of Business Management from George Washington University.

Richard J. Gannotta – UC Irvine Health

Richard (Rick) J. Gannotta is the Chief Executive Officer of UCI Health. He oversees Orange County's only academic medical center and all clinical and patient-serving operations, including the UCI Medical Center in Orange and ambulatory sites across the county. Prior to joining UCI, Gannotta was Senior Vice President of hospitals at New York's NYC Health + Hospitals, the nation's largest public healthcare system. Before that, he was President of Chicago's Northwestern Memorial Hospital, where he led hospital operations and worked closely with the leadership of Northwestern University's Feinberg School of Medicine. He has also served as President at Duke Raleigh Hospital, part of the Duke University Health System and North Carolina-based WakeMed Health and Hospitals. Gannotta's areas of research interest include the economic impact of alternative models of care, patient safety, high-reliability systems and healthcare disrupters. His academic affiliations include teaching at the undergraduate and graduate levels and he is currently a Visiting Scholar at NYU Wagner School

Adam P. Buckley, MD – UVM Health Network

Adam P. Buckley, MD, MBA is Chief Information Officer, UVM Health Network. Dr. Buckley was appointed to his current position after serving as the interim Chief Information Officer for the Medical Center from mid–2014 until his appointment to the network role in May 2015. Prior to his role as CIO, Dr. Buckley was the Chief Medical Information Officer at the University of Vermont Medical Center. His focus as CMIO was optimization of the medical centers electronic medical record and stabilization of the team that supports the record. Dr. Buckley came to the medical center and health network with 12 years of experience in academic medicine primarily focused on quality, patient safety and graduate medical education. Dr. Buckley served in a variety of leadership roles both at Beth Israel Medical Center in New York City and Stony Brook University Medical Center in Stony Brook, New York. Dr. Buckley received his Medical Degree from George Washington University Medical Center in Washington D.C. and his Master of Business Administration from the Isenberg School of Business at the University of Massachusetts. He completed his residency in Obstetrics and Gynecology at the McGaw Medical Center of Northwestern University in Chicago, IL. He holds two board certifications, one in OB/GYN and a second in Clinical Informatics.

Cynthia Davis – Methodist Le Bonheur Healthcare

Cynthia Davis is the Chief Health Information Officer at Methodist Le Bonheur Healthcare in Memphis, Tennessee. She is a recognized technology strategist with more than 35 years of transformational healthcare experience. Her passion is better as well as failure-free patient care and experience. She has led successful implementation, optimization and customer support efforts for several multi-million dollar fast-track business and clinical transformation projects in single and multi-facility organizations. A registered nurse, Cynthia has been a business and informatics executive in single and multiple facility health systems. She is a Fellow in the American College of Healthcare Executives and a regular speaker at industry associations, including ACHE, CHIME and HIMSS.

Chapter 7   Recognize and Reward

Michael Fey – Symantec

Michael Fey joined Symantec as President and Chief Operating Officer following the company's acquisition of Blue Coat, Inc. completed in August 2016. Fey served as the President and Chief Operating Officer of Blue Coat starting in 2014. In this role, Fey focused on aligning the company's leading web security, encryption management, cloud offerings and advanced threat protection solutions with customer requirements, and was responsible for all aspects of sales, marketing, support, services and product management. Prior to joining Blue Coat, Fey served as Chief Technology Officer of Intel Security and General Manager of corporate products for McAfee, part of Intel Security, where he drove its long-term enterprise strategic vision and innovation in the endpoint, network and security analytics segments. An industry veteran, Fey has held leadership positions with Opsware, Mercury Interactive and Lockheed Martin. Fey graduated magna cum laude with a B.S. in Engineering Physics from Embry-Riddle Aeronautical University.

Steve Trilling – Symantec

Steve Trilling is Senior Vice President and General Manager of Security Analytics and Research at Symantec, the global leader in cyber security. Symantec helps companies, governments and individuals secure their most important data wherever it lives, from mobile devices and the connected home, to desktops and laptops, to enterprise data centers and the cloud. Steve's division delivers Symantec's industry-leading threat protection technologies, advanced security analytics, investigations into new targeted cyber-attacks, and breakthrough innovations in artificial intelligence and machine learning, as well as a variety of shared services including product localization and product security. Trilling holds a BS in Computer Science and Mathematics from Yale University and an MS in Computer Science from the Massachusetts Institute of Technology.

Pamela Arora – Children's Health

Pamela Arora, SVP and CIO at Children's Health in Dallas, is responsible for directing all Information Services efforts including systems and technology, Health Information Management and Health Technology Management (formerly BioMedical engineering). Under her leadership, Children's achieved HIMSS Stage 7 Electronic Medical Record Adoption Model designation, InformationWeek500, InformationWeek Elite 100 and Most Wired designations, and won the HIMSS Enterprise Davies Award for the organization's innovative use of the electronic health record. The organization has earned HITRUST Common Security Framework (CSF) and SECURETexas Certifications, and has won the AHIMA Grace Award for excellence in Health Information Management and the CHIME/AHA Transformational Leadership Award for the organization's work to promote cybersecurity across the continuum of care. Ms. Arora has been named to Becker's 130 Women Hospital and Health System Leaders to know, and, in 2017, she received the John E. Gall CIO of the Year award from HIMSS and CHIME. She also won the 2018 CIO of the Year ORBIE Award under the nonprofit category. She is a member of HIMSS, the College of Healthcare Information Management Executives (CHIME) and the Children's Hospital Association (CHA). Pamela currently serves on the AAMI Board, HITRUST Board, DallasCIO Advisory Council, and Epic's Population Health Steering Board.

Jonathon Scholl – Leidos

Chapter 8   Co-Create Solutions

Paul Nagy – Johns Hopkins School of Medicine
Paul Nagy, PhD, FSIIM, is Associate Professor of Radiology at the Johns Hopkins University School of Medicine. Dr. Nagy serves as the Deputy Director of the Johns Hopkins Medicine Technology Innovation Center (TIC) with the goal of partnering with clinical inventors to create novel clinical IT solutions. This team of designers, developers and data scientists work with inventors to build, deploy and evaluate digital health solutions within the Johns Hopkins Medical System. At Johns Hopkins, Dr. Nagy serves as the Program Director for multidisciplinary leadership development programs in precision medicine, clinical informatics, data science and creating commercial ventures. 360 faculty and staff have taken these programs since 2012. Dr. Nagy is the author of over 130 papers in the fields of informatics and implementation science.

Jasmine McNeil – Johns Hopkins School of Medicine
Jasmine McNeil leads marketing and design work at the Technology Innovation Center, Johns Hopkins Medicine. She holds an MA/MBA in Design Leadership from MICA and the Johns Hopkins Carey Business School. At the TIC, Jasmine runs design thinking-facilitated sessions to gather user requirements for the applications the TIC builds. She also organizes the TIC's accelerator program (Hexcite) for early-stage medical software startup ideas. Jasmine brings Hexcite participants through a series of technical and business design activities to create project teams and startups.

Dwight Raum – Johns Hopkins School of Medicine
Dwight Raum is Vice President and Chief Technology Officer of Johns Hopkins Health System and Johns Hopkins University. Raum has been with Johns Hopkins more than 17 years and is currently serving as a leader in IT infrastructure operations, product innovation, university information systems and precision medicine. His passion lies in challenging the status quo, mobilizing teams to harness technology and championing change. In 2014, Raum co-founded the Technology Innovation Center, which cultivates innovative faculty and teams them with technical experts to solve problems. He now serves as its Executive Director. Raum also leads technical platform implementation of the Johns Hopkins precision medicine initiative called

InHealth, which combines research, data science, technology and clinical disciplines into an integrated program that is transforming the standard of care into precision medicine. Raum holds a Bachelor's degree in Management Science from Virginia Tech.

Emily Marx – Johns Hopkins School of Medicine

Emily Marx serves as a Communications Coordinator for the Technology Innovation Center and holds a BS in Psychology from Towson University. Emily organizes TIC outreach efforts such as e-newsletters, copy writing, events planning and social media promotion. As a member of the TIC design team, she assists in the planning of user research and product marketing. Emily also has a hand in the coordination and management of TIC's leadership development programs focused around entrepreneurship, analytics and precision medicine.

Amy Hushen – Johns Hopkins School of Medicine

Amy Hushen holds a BFA in Graphic Design from the Maryland Institute College of Art. She leads graphic design work for the Technology Innovation Center including branding identity design, print/marketing collateral and user interface design. At the TIC Amy focuses on the functionality and overall visual elements that improve the customer's ability to navigate within a digital product.

Stephanie Reel – Johns Hopkins School of Medicine

Stephanie Reel is the Chief Information Officer for all divisions of the Johns Hopkins University and Health System. She was appointed Vice Provost for Information Technology and CIO for Johns Hopkins University in January 1999. She is also Senior Vice President for Information Services for the Johns Hopkins Health System, and Senior Vice President and CIO for Johns Hopkins Medicine, positions she has held since 1994. As CIO, Ms. Reel leads the implementation of the strategic plan for information services, networking, telecommunications as well as clinical, research and instructional technologies across the enterprise. Ms. Reel graduated from the University of Maryland with a degree in information systems management and holds an MBA from Loyola College in Maryland.

David Rice – USF Health for Bisk

David Rice is a writer and editor working on behalf of USF Health for Bisk, a leading facilitator of online education. USF Health's Morsani College of Medicine, ranked a Best Medical School: Research by *U.S. News and World Report*, offers graduate degree and certificate programs in health informatics and healthcare analytics 100% online. The University of South Florida is a HIMSS Approved Education Partner and HIMSS Academic Organizational Affiliate program member.

Daniel Clark – The Advisory Board and Metro Health Hospital

Kyle Frantz – The Advisory Board and Metro Health Hospital

Dr. Christopher Longhurst – UC San Diego School of Medicine and UC San Diego Health

As Chief Information Officer, Dr. Longhurst is responsible for all operations and strategic planning for information and communications technology across the multiple hospitals, clinics and professional schools which encompass UC San Diego Health. Dr. Longhurst is also a Clinical Professor of Biomedical Informatics and Pediatrics at UC San Diego School of Medicine and continues to see patients. As a result of his efforts to leverage technology to improve patient experience in the UCSD Jacobs Medical Center, he was voted the 2017 Top Tech Exec in the education category for San Diego. He previously served as Chief Medical Information Officer for Stanford Children's Health and Clinical Professor at the Stanford University School of Medicine, where he helped lead the organization through the implementation of a comprehensive electronic medical record (EMR) for over a decade. This work culminated in HIMSS Stage 7 awards for both Lucile Packard Children's Hospital and 167 network practices in Stanford Children's Health.

Marissa J. Ventura – UC San Diego Health

Marissa J. Ventura, MS, is the Communication Lead for Information Services at UC San Diego Health. She is a strategic communicator with experience in the healthcare and pharmaceutical industries, and has worked as a medical journalist and editor. She has an MS from The Graduate School of Journalism at Columbia University.

Laurie Eccleston – Inova Health System

Laurie Eccleston, MPA, BSN, RN, CPHIMS, has over 17 years of IT experience designing, developing and implementing clinical enterprise healthcare information systems that align with organizational goals and strategic plans. She has successfully utilized technology and process re-engineering solutions to maximize business efficiencies and has a high level of expertise in gathering, analyzing, and defining business and functional requirements that deliver quality end-to-end results. Additionally, Laurie has over 28 years of emergency medicine nursing practice. At the time of this writing, Laurie was the Manager of Clinical Informatics at the Medical University of South Carolina (MUSC). She was a co-presenter at the HIMSS 2018 conference of "Bricks and Mortar of a Telehealth Initiative" and is a co-inventor of a mobile remote patient monitoring application. Laurie has since returned to Inova Health System where she is currently the manager of IT clinical enterprise ancillary applications.

Suzanne Richardson – Medical University of South Carolina

Suzanne Richardson, MSN, RN, is the Program Manager for the Structural Heart and Valve Center and Cardiac Surgery program at the Medical University of South Carolina. Her professional interests include clinical care logistics and using technology to improve quality of care and the patient experience. Suzanne has over 16 years of diverse nursing experience in both the private and academic sectors. Suzanne has a high level of expertise in sculpting clinical infrastructure to support concierge service for highly complex patient populations. Additionally, Suzanne is the inventor of a mobile remote patient monitoring application which was highlighted in her co-presentation of "Bricks and Mortar of a Telehealth Initiative" at the HIMSS 2018 conference. She has also presented her patient-facing mobile application and nurse facilitated program as poster presentations at several other local and regional conferences.

Greg Skulmoski – Bond University

Greg Skulmoski is an Assistant Professor at Bond University and leads the Master of Project Innovation program. He has 15 years of project experience and 10 years teaching project management in North America, the Middle East and Australia. He has published over 40 peer-reviewed papers in leading journals. Greg's research interest is in innovation. His PhD is from the University of Calgary.

Gareth Sherlock – Cleveland Clinic London

Gareth Sherlock is the Chief Information Officer at Cleveland Clinic London. He has more than 20 years of experience working in the healthcare sector and completing complex transformation projects across Australia, the UK, the US and the Middle East. Prior to joining Cleveland Clinic London,

Mr. Sherlock was the Chief Information Officer at Cleveland Clinic Abu Dhabi. He has also served as an Executive Consultant for Accenture in Australia and the United Kingdom.

Craig Langston, PhD – Bond University

Craig Langston is a Professor and Team Lead for the Project & Program Management discipline at Bond University, Australia. He has over 30 years of experience as a university educator and manager, and has published more than one hundred peer-reviewed papers over his career. He has a particular interest in measuring project success using an approach that is agnostic to project type, size and location. He is a professional member of the RICS, AIQS, AIPM, CIOB and ICEC, and a Chartered Quantity Surveyor. His qualifications include BAppSc (Hons), MAppSc and PhD from University of Technology Sydney.

Alex Goryachev – Cisco

Alex Goryachev is an entrepreneurial go-getter who loves blazing new trails for innovation. Over the past 20 years, he's turned disruptive concepts into emerging business models. His passion is to create a strategy and then drive it home to "get things done." As Cisco's Managing Director of Innovation Strategy and Programs, he has plenty of opportunities. First, Alex spearheads programs inspiring all employees to share their big ideas, many of which the company helps to codevelop. He carries the torch for co-innovation across the company's partner ecosystem via Cisco's Innovation Centers and Grand Challenges. And he works hand-in-hand across functions to spot and monetize emerging technology and business transitions. Prior to joining Cisco in 2004, Alex consulted at Napster, Liquid Audio, IBM Global Services and Pfizer Pharmaceuticals. Alex was the Emerging Stars Gold winner of Brandon Hall Group's 2016 Human Capital Management Excellence Awards, and his organization also won Golds for best Innovative Talent Management and Employee Engagement programs. A sought-after keynoter and media authority on innovation, Alex has a passion for sharing knowledge, mentoring and guiding innovation programs.

Introduction

I am not sure that I am the best person to write on Innovation, but the idea of helping fill a void in healthcare technology today was something I wanted to have a part in. I was humbled when I was approached by the Healthcare Information Management Systems Society (HIMSS) in 2014, asking if I would take the lead on this important work. Always up for a challenge and passionate on the topic, I agreed. I don't believe anyone needs to be convinced of the acute need for increased innovation in healthcare technology. The gap may be closing, but other industries have certainly benefitted far more than healthcare when it comes to innovation. This book aims to accelerate the closing of the gap.

I have several motivations to see innovation become part of our healthcare technology DNA. The three that stand out the most are highly personal. My mother was diagnosed with stage 4 ovarian cancer in 2002 and after a valiant fight, she died in 2006. Along the way I was engaged in my mom's healthcare as she was shuffled from provider to provider, who all relied on paper charts. I will stay out of the details but the opportunities for disruption were ever present. I always knew of the dysfunction of our industry, but now it was personal. I vowed to make a difference wherever I served to help save lives. My mother continues to motivate me today.

In 2012, after summiting Kilimanjaro with Texas Health Resources colleagues, we traversed to a remote Masai village in the great plains of Tanzania. Several months prior, we had made arrangements with the government to fund, build, and staff the first ever medical clinic. We opened on time and to great fanfare. Our first patient was a young late stage pregnant mother who had not felt her baby in two days. We were not equipped for primary care, let alone trying to deliver a baby in severe distress. Our team of doctors were amazing. They innovated. They created all the tools needed out of our very basic supplies to including a sandwich bag and shoelaces.

The baby was delivered still and brought back to life thanks to the innovation of our providers.

In April 2017 I was completing the national championships to secure my 5th consecutive spot on TeamUSA Duathlon. In the last two miles, I suffered a complete blockage of the left anterior descending coronary artery. I was suffering a heart attack commonly referred to as the "widow maker". In this case, innovation saved my life. When I crossed the finish line I checked myself into the medical tent. The physician did an EKG via smartphone and the strip was read immediately by the interventional cardiologist on staff at a nearby hospital. By the time I arrived via ambulance, the interventionist shared that Cleveland Clinic heart specialists had already conferred with him concerning the treatment protocol. Two days later I was back at work and anxious to heal quickly to race again. Using multiple Bluetooth technologies, all related vitals were transferred to my record and read by my care team daily. As a result, they were able to adjust meds in real-time, no appointment required. This hastened my recovery. Exactly ninety days later, I traveled to Denmark to compete in the Duathlon World Championships as a member of TeamUSA. This scenario would have played out much differently even one year ago. Thankfully there are some companies and organizations innovating. Now we need everyone to join in.

While there are many books written on innovation, including some titles related to healthcare technology, they largely remain theoretical. This is great as we need to proliferate the concepts and need for increased innovation. What is missing is a practical "how-to" guide. Using an established and respected innovation process framework, we wanted to share real stories of how individuals and companies are leveraging those concepts to realize innovation. Theory and frameworks are critical, but real-world examples bring them to life.

Voices leverages the HIMSS innovation framework and supplements each process with a handful of practical stories from people like you and I. They represent innovation taking place around the globe and in all aspects of healthcare to include providers and suppliers. It is my hope that you will find *Voices* to be practical and inspirational. It is designed that any person or organization can take this framework and by learning from other's experiences, bring innovation into your world. If everyone adopts an innovation mindset and way of work, imagine the stories of disruptive transformation we will share with one another as we seek to fulfill the promise of information technology in healthcare (Figure I.1).

Figure I.1   Innovation Pathways Factors of Innovation (HIMSS). Edward Marx, August 2018.

Chapter 1

Blend Cultures

> Include the organization's larger community and ensure that institutional leaders are engaged and supportive of the proposed innovative strategies.

One of the first things you need to do to improve the odds of innovation success is ensure support and engagement from key organizational leaders. Innovation is hard to do in a vacuum. Often it takes a team, some of whom are directly involved and others who provide resources and political cover. As you embark on your innovation, take inventory of key decision makers, influencers and culture. Identify both the individuals who will help you and those who might hurt you. The more organizational community and leadership engagement you develop, the higher the likelihood of overcoming the obstacles that will be on your path to innovation.

Using Blended Cultures for Healthcare Innovation

Mark Waugh

The cost of U.S. healthcare has risen at a staggering rate, nearly doubling between 2001 and 2015. In 2016, it accounted for 17.9 percent of the U.S. gross domestic product. These rising costs are unsustainable. With new technological innovations, these costs can be lowered and change the old healthcare model to a value – rather than the volume-driven system. Value-driven innovation delivers solutions for significant problems affecting many people more quickly and efficiently at a lower cost.

A substantial number of innovations in the healthcare domain come from multi-national companies and are targeted at world markets. These innovations cannot happen without excellent, continuous communication to effectively manage the demands of all stakeholders. Thus, the ability of a company to blend cultures, i.e., hold multiple frames of reference within itself, is a key component of taking an excellent healthcare technology idea from inception to realization.

Murata, Healthcare Innovation, and the Cleveland Clinic

Murata Manufacturing Co., Ltd. is listed by *Forbes* as one of the world's top multinational companies, with sales of $10.38 billion as of May 2017. The Japan-based company started in 1944, integrates established technologies into the transformative world of healthcare innovation, and bridges the divide between a large company and small startups – while addressing global cross-cultural business dynamics. With more than 80 percent of Murata's business outside of Japan, we have to understand what is happening in the rest of the world – and how they do it.

The company is a worldwide leader in the design, manufacture, and sale of ceramic-based passive electronic components and solutions, communication modules and power supply modules. Murata's healthcare technology is derived from our core technology strengths and experience in various fields including PC, smartphone, home appliances, and car electronics. Healthcare technologies produced by Murata include patient monitoring applications, diagnostic and treatment equipment, medical sensors, medical RFID solutions, product distribution and control systems, and pressure measurement applications.

Healthcare technology is a moving target. New sensor technologies, in particular, are poised to change the world's healthcare model dramatically. Wearable health trackers, for example, are designed to help individuals improve their health and fitness levels, and have been found to detect *atrial fibrillation*, a common heart abnormality that can lead to stroke. Thus, new technologies are moving the healthcare sector into a preventative and early treatment mode, rather than treatment after the fact.

Murata began working with the Cleveland Clinic in 2016 when it became a virtual office tenant at Cleveland Clinic's Global Cardiovascular Innovations Center (GCIC). This was the beginning of its on-site exposure and search for collaborative healthcare technology projects. Like the Cleveland Clinic, Murata is focused on putting innovative ideas to work. As an established company, Murata's expertise makes it well positioned to take a great idea from a Cleveland Clinic incubator and help bring it to the marketplace.

Shaze, *Innovation, and Blending Cultures*

The concept of *Shaze*, which loosely translates to company philosophy, is a uniquely Japanese concept. More than a poster on a wall, *Shaze* embodies a company's core values and establishes the mindset each employee should take in their daily activities. It is a vital part of Murata's innovation culture.

Murata's philosophy, fundamental mission, and values, created by the founder Akira Murata in 1954, remains the same: to contribute to the advancement of society by enhancing technologies and skills; applying a scientific approach; creating innovative products and solutions; being trustworthy; and, together with stakeholders, being thankful for increases in prosperity.

Each Murata employee, whether in Japan, the United States, or another global location, is encouraged to exert "innovativeness" in their approach to all tasks; to come up with new and more efficient operational and administrative processes; and to help the company achieve optimum performance. Everyone is seen as contributing to the financial success of the company, its innovativeness and the company's mission to advance society. *Shaze* extends to Murata's approach to working with other companies.

Blending Japanese and American Business Cultures

The differences in business culture between Japan and the United States is so different that, without study and consideration of the other's culture, miscommunication and conflict is inevitable. Communications are subtle and nuanced in Japan, with an expectation that the listener will be reading between the lines. Japanese are more likely to rely on non-verbal cues, and the context of what they say, than the literal meaning of the words they use to say it. American business communications are quite the opposite and articulate intent directly.

In Japan, decisions are reached by consensus (which can take a while). Companies in the United States take more of a top-down approach – the boss or executives decide on behalf of the company.

Even the concepts of taking new ideas to the market are different. Murata looks at how its decisions and methodology will impact the company and its environment 5 to 10 years out. It is a long-term innovation view, not new for the sake of new, and not new for right now. It is creating and introducing new technology to improve and advance society. Further, Murata executives see innovation as a journey involving a constant exchange of ideas and raising awareness of the goal and focus. To be an "innovator" within Murata also means considering how we may be able to improve our society and the environment, and for taking action when these opportunities arise.

Blending Big and Small Company Cultures

While innovative, Murata, like many Japanese companies, is risk-averse. So when it comes to working with a startup, Murata is very diligent and organized in its process, with a focus on how we will work with a company, what we will each bring to the table, and the results we would like to see. We want to build long-term, viable, profitable, sustainable solutions and products. We like to be extremely thorough when evaluating opportunities.

It is a different approach than that of a startup, which tends to be more action-oriented than planning-oriented. Startups are agile and make decisions quickly, often taking greater risks than a large, established company such as Murata would. However, bringing in that careful planning mentality to a startup is helpful for the execution of an idea – even if that path changes.

The careful planning approach also shapes how we track results. Startups want to see an immediate relationship between effort and results. Japanese companies, and Murata in particular look at innovation as more of a journey.

To bridge these cultural gaps – between American startup and Japanese global company – Murata created a strategic marketing group within the company focused on how Murata should collaborate with outside organizations. The team works to bring technology to market while respecting others' viewpoints and ensuring business goal alignments. We strive to get everyone on a project to work as a team.

Part of the mission of the team is a "can do" attitude toward innovation, and a celebration of continuous learning. It is a cross-cultural group, comprised of both Japanese and American employees as well as those with a wide range of technological backgrounds. Team members have an understanding of each other's culture and a goal of fostering understanding between groups, both within the company and between Murata and outside organizations. Murata has other, similar groups with the same mission of bridging cultures in other areas of the world.

Case Study: Prevent Biometrics

Sensing technologies are having a massive effect on patient care – enabling a preventative approach by collecting data in real-time. Patient distance monitoring, behavior modification, telehealth, and other healthcare technology, both software and equipment, is bringing better healthcare to patients at a lower cost.

Prevent Biometrics, a spin-off of Cleveland Clinic is one such sensing technology provider. The Minneapolis-based startup developed a head impact monitoring mouthguard (HIMM). Embedded with sensor technologies, the mouthguard provides real-time feedback on head impacts. Using data from the sensors, an advanced algorithm quantifies the force of blows to the head. When certain thresholds are reached, coaches and trainers are alerted via Prevent's mobile app, so they can immediately monitor the player for a potential concussion or other impairment. A web portal allows for administrative data and analytics on the impact. The system, now commercially available, will have a significant, immediate, and profound effect on helmeted and contact sports.

Currently, the prevalence of sports-related concussions (mild traumatic brain injury) is not precisely known due to under-reporting. An estimated 50 percent of sports concussions go undetected and untreated every year, and estimates from the Center for Disease Control put the total annual number of concussions in the United States at nearly 4 million. Untreated head impacts can result in permanent neurological injury; traumatic brain injuries contribute to about 30 percent of all injury deaths. Conversely, immediately treating head impacts significantly increases the chances of a full recovery and decreases the chances of developing permanent neurological deficits.

Murata began discussions on a potential collaborative approach with Prevent Biometrics in 2015. In 2017, Murata funded the startup in its Series B round and signed a multi-year collaborative technology agreement for the two companies. Murata assisted Prevent in such areas as miniaturization technologies, product engineering, electronics componentry, quality testing and control, and go to market strategies. We intended to provide guidance and help take Prevent's technology to the product readiness level, manufacturing-ready at the right price point with the right form, fit, and function.

Along the way, there were multiple in-person collaborative meetings between Murata and Prevent to understand each other's products, goals and business culture, and strengthen company ties. It took time for Murata to understand the global importance of head impacting monitoring better.

Because of such divergent business communication styles, Murata appointed two "ambassadors" – a Japanese and an American, both familiar with each other's culture and the healthcare sector – to translate and educate everyone on each company's operating style. As one of the ambassadors, I provided primary education on Japanese business style and working with Murata to Prevent executives, because without understanding you cannot have a good relationship.

For example, Murata executives asked many questions to try to understand Prevent's company culture and value proposition. Sometimes this level of detail can be perceived negatively, perhaps as being doubting. However, it is not. It is a method to achieve as much understanding about the other company as possible.

I gave a book on Japanese culture to each of the executives at Prevent so they could understand Murata's culture, particularly to understand that the time to get to commitment is much longer than in the United States. In the case of Murata, we are interested in long-term benefits and growth rather than monetary gains for the next quarter or year.

The benefit of such a deliberate process is a better general agreement between the two companies and within Murata about our collaborative relationship. It has also garnered a broader acceptance of the partnership and Prevent's work within Murata. So, while cross-cultural collaboration can be challenging, achieving mutual trust is the cornerstone of a good working relationship.

Takeaways

1. **Don't underestimate the importance of and challenges with culture blending. Cultural blending is a critical first step for companies to work together successfully.** Mutual respect is essential for successful operations, and there must be a personality match between corporate cultures for joint ventures to succeed. Acknowledging potential cultural issues early and educating employees on such dynamics allows them to appreciate differences that can help build a stronger organization in the long run.

2. **Keep in mind that both parties can learn from each other**. For example, to work with a large company a small company needs to understand what drives the larger company, and big companies need to remember they were a small company once. There are different

challenges at a startup level, such as restrictions on money and time. At a startup, there is typically a small group of high-performing people, whereas at a large company there is a large group of diverse capabilities.

3. **Culture blending is not quick and trying to force it does not work.** In the case of healthcare innovation, some projects take years to bring a great idea to market. However, many startups want quick gratification and returns on investment. These types of projects might not be successful because such a mindset might not understand a slower market and development strategy. In the United States, healthcare equals big money and big potential, whereas the driving forces in other geographies are different.

4. **While you may have a preconceived vision in your mind about the other company, such as what they do and how they operate, you will not see and understand each other until you personally meet and interact with each other**. Japanese companies such as Murata are very interested in a company's background, to understand its business. In Japan, with its high-context culture, successful collaboration is as much about the people as the product or technology.

5. **Keep in mind how you do things at your company and in your country may not always be well perceived by others. It is essential to have "ambassadors" to bridge cultural divides to translate and educate the other company on your company's operation style**. For example, sometimes a Japanese company's, i.e., Murata's, driving need to understand the other company and its value proposition can be perceived negatively, perhaps as being doubting. However, it is not. It is a method to achieve as much understanding about the other company as possible. We ask many questions on our fact-finding missions, and it is a careful process. By contrast, in the United States, many collaborative ventures are based on "gut feelings" and limited, but direct, questioning. Understanding another culture's business etiquette is essential to closing deals.

6. **Remember, it is an innovation journey.** Innovation itself is a process and taking the long view increases your chance of success.

7. **Measure twice, cut once. We believe at Murata that more due diligence up front leads to less confusion and better understanding later.** Of course, questions need to be asked in a way that does not

convey disrespect. Even disagreements can foster mutual understanding by discussing and understanding the issues.

8. **It is not just communication between the companies' executives – internal communications are important too.** Consistent and clear communication with internal stakeholders strengthens the mix, the blend if you will, of the ideas and insights coming in from all members of the collaboration.

Conclusion

Innovation thrives when different knowledge domains come together. Many discoveries have been born following exposure to indirectly related ideas. Similarly, developing relationships is critical to building sustainable achievement. While subjective, cultivating relationships needs to be pursued with the equal discipline applied to pursuing technological innovation. Only by blending cultures can companies leverage each other's core competencies and technologies. World-class organizations understand that great innovation is only achieved through mutual trust in each other's competencies and commitment.

Blending a Revenue Cycle Culture

Charles Christian
Indiana Health Information Exchange

After a long implementation process to replace our revenue cycle applications, I was walking in from the parking lot with our CEO, a longtime friend. We were talking about how long the implementation had taken and the impact on the organization. I was thinking that my team and I might be getting a few kudos from the boss; but that is not what I heard next. In so many words, the CEO mentioned that he had seen our days in accounts receivables climb at a growing rate and he was being told that all signs pointed to the new revenue cycle system; he wanted to have further discussions about what it would take to reimplement the system we just pulled out. Needless to say, the walk in from the parking lot just got a little longer.

Our organization resided in a community that was one of the earliest territorial settlements, therefore, our culture was founded on hard work and trust. We trusted that everyone was working hard to keep the organization successful; which was the case, but as I learned, the assumptions need to be revisited from time to time.

Over the course of the next many days, there were lots of conversations around seeking answers and hard data to back them up. These conversations included the CFO, Director of Patient Accounting, and Internal Audit. Unfortunately, there didn't appear to be agreement on the underlying issues; falling back on what we believed, rather than what we know.

Working with internal audit, we found that we needed to move from a culture of "what we think" to one of "what we know." Working together we quickly completed a detailed analysis of the current state of our accounts receivable (patient claims being processed) and historical data. With this review in hand, we only had a portion of what we needed to work toward the cultural shift. We needed to look at the proverbial "three-legged stool": people, process, and technology. Right now, we were only able to see one side of that triangle.

As part of another cultural shift, the organization was also moving to embrace the tools of continuous quality improvement. Applying these to this issue would be a challenge, but the tools did fit the task at hand.

A cultural shift, especially one of this nature, is not something for which you can stand up in the front of the boat (room) and point the way. The people doing the everyday tasks need the opportunity to engage, understand, unlearn the old ways, and embrace/learn the new. We embarked on a journey that would allow management to learn from their teams; it was a learning experience for everyone.

Over several weeks, each member of each team had the opportunity to map out their current processes with sticky notes, which would eventually cover an entire wall in our conference center. Complex and disjointed don't come close to describing the final resulting "process map," if you could call it that.

Something unexpected occurred during the "mapping" process; those watching their teams describe how the process currently works (for them) realized that each person with the exact same job duties, was going about their jobs differently, with different outcomes. The teams found (for themselves) that the culture of "this is the way we've always done it" just wasn't working and it needed to change for the organization to become successful.

I observed that you can't underestimate the power of allowing people to discover, on their own, something that you may already know to be true. It's a teaching moment that creates ownership in the change or shift; an ownership that needs to be taken, rather than given. Did I mention this was a learning process for everyone?

Armed with an understanding of the present, the teams moved forward with creating the future, the shift to new processes and a culture based on standard processes, metrics/measures, and accountability; a culture of what we know, rather than what we think.

The next question was what to do with this new knowledge and how would the culture be incorporated into the fabric of the everyday. Having addressed the "process" leg of the stool, it was time to add the "people" leg to the stool.

During the process mapping, the teams expressed a concern about their level of knowledge regarding the new revenue cycle application. Management had determined that if they only trained their team members on the specific functions that they thought they would need to effectively do their jobs, it would decrease the total amount of non-productive time set aside for training. In retrospect, this decision had created "process blinders" for their teams; they couldn't see the upstream or down-stream processes, making them blind to the previous and next steps in the very complex process of claims processing. The culture of "what we think" was again at work.

To address this knowledge gap, every member of the claims management team was provided with a comprehensive re-education on all the features/functions of the new revenue cycle solution. Armed with a new level of understanding, the team asked for some time to rework the previously redesigned workflows and processes. The culture of "what we know" was taking root.

Before I add the last leg of the stool, "technology," I need to provide a view of the physical environment that housed the revenue cycle teams. Picture a large, open space with rows of desks and large open filing cabinets lining the walls around the perimeter. Filing cabinets that held the 70,000 to 80,000 open/active accounts (paper records) in various stages of the billing process.

The next step in the cultural shift involved the "technology" leg of the stool, but it also had an associated impact on the "people" leg as well. If we were to leverage the new processes and feature/function of the new revenue cycle solution, we needed to do something about the tsunami of paper that rushed off the printers each day, requiring filing, which delayed the claim submission and follow-up functions. Document/image management was the break waters that we implemented to calm the on-rushing paper waves. The desire was to move from "where did we file that" to "it's here with a couple of clicks of the mouse."

To root the cultural change further into the organization, management also redesign the physical workspace of the revenue cycle team, moving from a large open space with thousands of file folders, to a newly painted and carpeted area that housed individual cubicle workspaces and sound dampening surfaces to create a quiet environment that was pleasant to work in the many hours of the day.

Moving from a culture of "what we think" to one of "what we know" required the development of measures and metrics that allowed us to "know." With any quality improvement process worth its salt, there must be a "check phase" where the assumptions are reviewed and tested, adjustments made, and progress tracked. Do we have strong roots that run deep in the organization like those of an oak tree or are they superficial and easily removed, like those of a corn stalk?

The outcomes from this effort tracked as we had hoped; our days in AR moved in the correct direction, the percentage of claims that had to be resubmitted declined, immediate cost savings occurred with the reduction of filing staff (they were re-tasked to the follow-up team, relieving the need for recruitment), staff turnover declined, while staff morale greatly improved. We declared it a success and continue to monitor progress so that we would "know what we should know."

Finally, the lessons learned were many. First, an issue is probably different than what you think. The real underlying cause or causes require a look at all aspects, especially the culture of the area/department/organization. Second, the work to make modifications to any culture requires a commitment from leadership, good data, partnership with all parties, and a willingness to create the measures and metrics to ensure that you're growing good cultural roots. You have to measure what matters and leverage data to combat emotions that typically come when you try to blend cultures.

Balancing Innovation and Institution

Pete O'Neill

Innovation is one of the pillars of Cleveland Clinic; it is part of our culture. Our hospital was created by doctors returning from World War I who wanted to establish a hospital to deliver the best patient care, and over the next almost-100 years Cleveland Clinic has pioneered incredible healthcare "firsts". Our leaders are innovative people, with a history of delivering innovative solutions to patient care and hospital operations. However, despite our demonstrated organizational and personal interests to be innovative, we still need to be rigorous about how we manage the delicate balance of promoting innovation while running a large, multinational hospital system, and protecting our most precious stakeholders: our patients.

A culture of innovation requires that everyone in the organization feels empowered to open their minds, to identify opportunities to improve what they see around them, and to think about out-of-the-box ways of delivering patient care. At Cleveland Clinic we consider all 55,000+ employees "caregivers"; all of us have the opportunity to improve the way our hospital delivers care to patients. We see innovations, and insights into needs for innovation, coming from all parts of our organization.

However, any effective and responsible organization needs processes to manage innovation. It would be bedlam if every one of 55,000 employees, or individual departments, or any other unit pursued their own healthcare innovation strategies. At the same time, every idea that comes from any part of the organization can't get the full consideration of our leaders. The trick is to find the right balance of nurturing innovation, which is an inherently creative process, with rigorous processes to achieve organizational efficiency.

It's useful to think about our approach to managing innovation as a pyramid. The broad bottom is our sources of innovation, with ideas coming from all parts of our organization. As each innovation is evaluated it gets elevated through the organization (up the pyramid) based on its potential and probability of delivering impact to the organization. Once an innovation reaches its maximum level of impact, an appropriate group of Cleveland Clinic leaders reviews the innovation in the context of our corporate strategy and then decides if the innovation will be "approved" to be pushed down the pyramid to all the areas under the leadership of the decision-making group.

Of course the most impactful innovations are the ones that can improve the entire enterprise, maybe even be scaled so they can be delivered outside our own organization. These innovations rise to the top of our pyramid and are reviewed by our most senior leaders. Some innovations don't have the potential to affect the broad enterprise; they should only rise to the level of their appropriate impact.

One challenge is determining which innovations have limited impact before they get to the highest level. Sometimes the potential for an innovation isn't known until it is shared with leaders with the most strategic perspectives; if these innovations are turned down too soon their full potential will be missed.

Another challenge is making timely decisions about which innovations will be approved to be implemented. All innovations have a shelf-life, influenced by market conditions and the persistence of the source of the innovation; if every innovation is presented to our highest leaders then it will clog and delay their decision-making processes.

To execute on this balance of determining which innovations to push to our highest level, we need to have efficient and trusting communication. We need to be comfortable pushing down as much authority and strategic understanding as possible. We need to recognize that innovation can be messy and risky, and being innovative means being accommodating to working on messy and risky things.

Cleveland Clinic has a wonderful spirit of collaboration among its leadership, and we're always looking for new ways to improve how we incorporate innovation. For example, today we're working on ways to bring more external innovations into Cleveland Clinic. Managing innovation is something an organization probably never gets completely figured out. Being truly innovative requires continuous reflection on and refinement of how innovation is managed, based on external and internal forces.

An organization that desires to have a rich culture of innovation must encourage and nurture all of its employees to be empowered to innovate. A *culture* of innovation can't be nozzled or regulated. We can't tell people we want them to be innovative according to a set of institutional rules. However, we need institutional rules and processes to convert raw innovations into actionable opportunities for the enterprise. Within healthcare, we have the additional balance of managing innovation according to the security requirements of treating patients. At Cleveland Clinic we don't have all the answers, but in our nearly 100 years we've embraced the challenges and look forward with enthusiasm to the opportunities that are in front of us.

Chapter 2

Use People with IT

> Do not create an over reliance on people or on technology; use both resources in concert.

Often we rely too heavily on technology as we embark on innovation. Sometimes innovation starts at the other extreme with people but little incorporation of automation or tools. The best innovations tend to be the result of a strong balance at the intersection of people and technology. Always take an inventory of people and technology to ensure balance. It is the ability to take the best of people and technology, then melding them together, that ignites innovation.

Innovation through Technology-Powered Care Services

Shawntea Moheiser, CMPE, CMOM

Information technology (IT) and artificial intelligence (AI) are entering the healthcare industry in full force causing fear, excitement, and opportunity abound. The idea of treatment decisions driven by AI utilizing predictive analytics and an enterprise data aggregation system sounds both evidence-based and frightening. There is something to be said for the human element. In 1911, Elbert Hubbard was quoted as saying "One machine can do the work of fifty ordinary men. No machine can do the work of one extraordinary man." More than 100 years later this statement still resonates because we recognize that individuals are necessary for the element of treatment.

We are entering a world in which we need technology to *support* us. Alper, Elliott, et al. performed a study in 2004 that found physicians need to read 29 hours a day to remain current in their field[1]. That was almost 15 years ago; those numbers have undoubtedly increased as science and research continue to expand. This is humanly impossible to achieve without support. This is an area in which we need to lean on technological capabilities, and many around the industry have begun doing just that.

At a basic level, we have things like 'clinical decision support software' and 'preventive service reminders.' On a more sophisticated level, we have examples like organizations using IBM Watson to provide a second opinion or AI mining databases to identify diabetic patients and predict which ones are most likely to have kidney damage. This is the more comforting side of technology; utilizing it as a supporting tool. Less comforting would be for technologies to take it a step further by physically speaking to the patient and guiding them through their treatment. Undoubtedly patients in distress would feel more comforted by a nurse than by a robotic voice. Human interaction matters. Inflection and tone of voice, body language, and discrepancies between the two are things that AI is not prepared to emulate.

Two questions make frequent appearances in brainstorming sessions in healthcare technology: "Could we?" and "Should we?" The ability to run algorithms and projections in less than a minute makes technology the optimal resource for answering if something *can* be done. The morality and empathy as to whether something *should* be done will likely always require a human being.

At H3C, our goal is to bridge the gap between providers, technology, and patients. Guided by physicians and empowered by technology, our clinical staff provides the human element that creates the atmosphere for patient engagement. Our technology platform allows us to perform patient risk analyses, predictive risk analyses, patient cohort stratification, and strategic, individualized, and evidence-based treatment plan generation. Our licensed clinical teams utilize this technology to support them as they communicate, educate, and coordinate care. We refer to this as "technology-powered care services."

With our technology-powered care services, we can create strategic, structured, and repeatable care services. We can improve the alignment between provider treatment goals and patient performance and compliance. Cisco Internet Business Solutions released a report noting that "the average person is projected to have between six and seven connected devices by 2020"[2]. Meanwhile, recent JAMA articles have begun to perform studies of stand-alone mobile health interventions. A recent publication[3] focused on the potential impact that could be made by blood-pressure wearables for hypertensive patients. The results were insignificant: "Use of a smartphone app resulted in a small improvement in self-reported medication adherence but did not affect blood pressure; the benefit of this and other stand-alone mobile health (mHealth) interventions on clinical outcomes remains to be established."

How then did Mathematica Policy Research identify patient benefits like decreased likelihood for hospitalization, readmission reduction, and cost savings for the Medicare Chronic Care Management (CCM) program? This program is remote by nature, but it is not a stand-alone mHealth intervention. Simply put, Medicare's CCM program outlines the required participation of actual care staff.

To drive efficiency and stay current on clinical research we need to leverage the benefits that technology can provide, bringing us back to "technology-powered care services." This requires innovation, organizational support, and significant team leadership skills. We have done a few things at H3C to design innovative, technology-powered, care processes into the foundation of our company. Most importantly, we engage in all-hands brainstorming sessions guided by advanced team leaders with cross-functional SME experience alongside full executive support.

All-Hands Meetings

There is a movement in healthcare, meant for patients, referred to as "nothing about me without me." This is present in business as well. If an action is going to affect a specific department, then everyone needs to be party to the discussions.

At H3C, we have taken this one step further with our "all-hands" style meetings and "nothing about us, without us" mindset. Except for HR meetings and board meetings, all of our meetings have an open-door policy. At any time, if I see a meeting of interest or concern for my department, I can invite myself to the meeting. I highly recommend implementing this policy, provided there are ground rules. I cannot take over the meeting; I cannot attend simply to shoot down the suggestions of others, etc. However, I can attend and participate. I can identify potential program hurdles, offer alternative solutions, and volunteer to support within my field of expertise. What drives innovation is personal experience, choice, and the rewarding feeling that you contributed to something that you wanted to participate in.

If you have heard Dan Pink's talk about motivating factors for employees, then you can understand that this process can be highly motivating to employees. Pink notes that monetary rewards for thought-based achievements only incentivize at a small rate. More motivating for employees is the opportunity to do something which they believe is personally rewarding. This falls in line with the top of Maslow's hierarchy of needs, which also defines motivating factors for employees.

Our meetings give every employee, from the front desk up, the opportunity to participate in company-wide change. Getting views and input from all levels mitigates issues before they occur. For example, in 2015 France spent the equivalent of $15 billion updating their railcars. Unfortunately, it was not until after the railcars were created that they realized they would not fit at 1,300 of their existing railway stations. This cost France an additional $55 million and begs the question: how many people could've identified the issue ahead of time, had they been merely included in the conversation?

Cross-Functional SME Leaders

When we first enter meetings, the thought process is to leave your business card at the door. Your title alone does not make anyone else's suggestions immaterial. The goal is to suggest opportunities, ideas, and solutions. So, it is crucial that discouraging language and demeaning behavior is strictly prohibited. Once that is established, a free-flowing brainstorming session can begin. The more variety of participating views, the better. However, these 'all-hands' meetings could quickly get 'out of hand' if we do not have the appropriate leadership in place.

Each meeting has SME leaders that help to define the problem or refocus meeting attendees as needed. They provide the structure of documenting the thoughts, steering conversation in optimal directions, and making sure voices are heard. These are often the people delegated to perform the project management and action-planning tasks. Leadership experts know how to create meaningful thought-exchanges and can observe who has the most to contribute to the project for their planning going forward.

Full Executive Support

The ability to innovate, positively disrupt, and implement systemic change is not possible without the full support of the executive team. Without approval to spend time and resources on an innovation project, any tasks toward it will be viewed as "off mission." One of the primary roles of the executive team is to ensure that organizational goals and operational tasks support programs that are accretive to the mission of the organization. So, it is important for employees seeking executive support to keep the corporate mission in mind.

Experienced innovators know that executive sign-on is mandatory, especially because the executive team usually has a higher-level view of the entire operation and can visualize applications of solutions across other departments. For example, let's say I notice my billing staff makes up 10% of the organization and is experiencing reduced productivity. I have an all-hands meeting, and with our SME leaders, we identify a scrum-style software application that could provide a productivity increase of 15% in my department. I then gain executive support to prioritize with the IS department because this task management program could also be deployed to the clinical staff, human resources, IS, and administration. This changes the projected impact of a 15% productivity increase on 10% of the organization to a 15% productivity increase across 100% of the organization.

When innovation and continuous improvement are part of the mission, resources like staff support, funding, and project managers are allocated toward project achievement. It prompts conversations like, "What do you estimate this would cost to achieve?", "How can we allocate funds?" "How can existing or new staff support this?" When these are not part of the mission, then those resources instead become barriers to innovation and improvement, prompting less encouraging conversations that include statements like "The way we do it is the way we always have" or – the worst I've ever heard – "There is no line item for 'Innovation' in our budget."

Innovation has to be systemic to an organization. This applies to every industry but especially healthcare. Especially right now. Our industry is decades behind in utilizing the integration technologies that other industries rely on daily. Access to care, price transparency, and coordination of care could all be enhanced by the use of supporting technologies.

If Retail Worked Like Healthcare

If retail worked the way healthcare does, Amazon would not exist. Imagine that to buy a new outfit, you first had to sign an agreement to have access to your previous size history. Even though it is your own history, you need permission to access it. You sign permission and complete a few required forms, and a few weeks later you have information on what used to fit. You contact a store that has excellent reviews, and they pencil you in for three weeks from now. You arrive at the store and wait for 30 minutes while filling out forms that are identical to the ones you filled out online when you requested your size history. Finally, an attendant takes you back, looks you up and down, mumbles "Okay, thanks" and leaves. Then a stylist walks in looks at her computer says, "Wear blue" and leaves. You do not have a clue what that means, and you are not sure what anyone typed into the computer. You do know that six weeks have passed and you still don't have a new outfit! This is not the Amazon of today for a reason. People want some element of technology, they want transactions to happen quickly and history to pull up at lightning speed.

People also want people. Amazon had 4% of overall retail expenditures[6] across the US in 2017, but they also had more than 500,000[7] employees dedicated to service delivery, problem resolution, and predicting needs. For healthcare 2.0 to provide shorter wait times, increased visibility, price transparency, predictive analytics, and increased patient touch points we need to support our clinical providers with technology-powered care services. We need to get innovative technological tools in the hands of our clinical staff to enhance how they carry out orders from providers.

How We Do Things Differently

The people who founded our organization were from outside of healthcare. They brought in healthcare experts to explain the primary pain points in trying to manage a practice in this industry. They quickly discovered a few things that to them seemed like "no-brainers," things that change the lives of our clients. As a former practice manager and healthcare consultant, I can tell you the solutions are easy to implement, scalable, and yet radical to the industry.

To provide technology-powered care services, we have clinical staff that operate remotely, licensed in different states to cover the US. They all operate out of a single center in Omaha, Nebraska, where no patient has ever stepped foot. They are the remote nurses and care coordinators of our clients, and though we employ them, they work as dedicated staff to specific providers. In that way, we can extend the resources of each clinic based on their needs and desires.

If one of our nurses calls a patient on behalf of a provider in North Carolina, the caller ID will reflect the name of the clinic in North Carolina. Through an EHR-agnostic approach, we can work with any clinic, anywhere.

As a healthcare consultant, when I first heard the pitch, I hit them with a ton of questions that they hear every day, and there was an answer for every single one:

> *How many more clicks will this be? Is this yet another portal?* No. Our team could work right in the client's EHR with the minimum necessary access privileges.
>
> *What about data analytics? I am not buying another module to add-on to our system!* No problem we can drive analytics with a tool we created that works with all EHRs.
>
> *What about the clinical care? The patients have to be of the utmost concern.* Exactly, that is the whole point. They can have 24/7 access to a dedicated nurse and care coordinator that they get to know well over time. The nurses are triaging with evidence-based tools, etc.

As most would be in healthcare, I was skeptical about these, seemingly mythical, solutions. It was then that they pointed out something I had not considered. These are not new ideas. This technology has been around for decades, but it is never really been deployed to support care delivery. It is never been integrated with clinical staff.

The gas company can read my meter from 300 feet away, issue me a bill within seconds, and identify if my usage is higher than my neighbor's. Why can't my watch report my pulse rates to a dedicated system at all times and immediately notify someone if I am suddenly in A-fib?

Actually, with technology these things can happen, these things are possible. When we open our minds to innovation, obtain executive support, implement new technologies, and focus all of this on a motivation to improve the patient experience, brilliant things can happen.

Today, in less than a minute, I can look at an entire provider roster, identify patients eligible for chronic care management, stratify those with the highest risk of exacerbation, identify likelihood of upcoming hospital admission, sort based on barrier to care, pull appropriate education with patient history, and assign them to a high-risk population for preventive engagement explicitly designed for them. In less than a minute.

I can then have a qualified licensed clinical staff member reach out to the patient utilizing supporting technologies that assist with health literacy education, the social determinant of health solutions, and more. With the technologies we have in place today, each of our care coordinators can have meaningful conversations that improve patient outcomes and increase compliance for over 300 patients per month.

Without technology, this would not be possible. Without people, this would not be possible. Our goal at H3C is to improve this method of continuously providing technology-powered care services. Our patients need it, our providers need it, and healthcare deserves a revolution in technology-powered service delivery.

References

1. Alper BS, Hand JA, Elliott SG, et al. How much effort is needed to keep up with the literature relevant for primary care? *Journal of the Medical Library Association* 2004; 92(4): 429–437.
2. https://mhealthintelligence.com/news/mhealth-interventions-need-care-team-support-to-affect-outcomes?elqTrackId=c7aa805d86964acb8e4f574b74882ad3&elq=0ae1a827a1204382b1acb22c5d3470d4&elqaid=5294&elqat=1&elqCampaignId=4919
3. https://jamanetwork.com/journals/jamainternalmedicine/fullarticle/2678454
4. RSA Animation based on Dan Pink's speech on motivating factors for employees in job design https://www.youtube.com/watch?v=u6XAPnuFjJc
5. "French red faces over trains that are "too wide"" http://www.bbc.com/news/world-europe-27497727
6. "Amazon grabbed 4 percent of all US retail sales in 2017, new study says" https://www.cnbc.com/2018/01/03/amazon-grabbed-4-percent-of-all-us-retail-sales-in-2017-new-study.html
7. "Amazon now has more than 500,000 employees" http://money.cnn.com/2017/10/26/technology/business/amazon-earnings/index.html

Innovation in Radiology over the Decades

John Paganini

Radiology is an area of healthcare that has always been at the forefront of innovation. Ever since Wilhelm Roentgen created the x-ray in the late 1890s, radiology technologies continued to progress at a fantastic pace throughout the 20th century. X-ray film came into usage in 1918; ultrasound appeared in the late 1950s. PET and CT radiologic technology emerged during the 1960s and early 1970s. Moreover, in the 1970s MRI was developed which introduced 2D and 3D images. Looking inside the human body is no longer a mystery.

Enter PACS, RIS, and Voice Recognition

Late 1980s. This is where information technology really kicks in. The radiology department needed to store the digital images. Hence a Picture Archive Communication Solution (PACS) needed to be created to store the volumes of images being created by the various radiology devices (modalities).

With that came the requirement for a standard image format which would also include data about the image itself. The data included the patient name, medical record number, procedure, study type, technical image specifications, and much more. This is generally termed "metadata." Hence, in the early 1990s, the standard "Digital Imaging and Communications in Medicine" (DICOM) was born.

Next on the innovation agenda was to include the images in the overall workflow of the radiology department. We then saw the birth of Radiology Information Systems (RIS). These systems managed the ordering process, procedure scheduling, the management of the patient information, integration with the PACS, and other functionality. Another important aspect of the RIS was to facilitate orders to and from the Electronic Health Record (EHR).

In an ideal world, the patient order information would originate in the EHR and be sent electronically to the RIS. The RIS would facilitate the order, become aware of the images captured, allow for the entry of the radiologist report and then send it all back to the EHR. Note that in some cases, there are specialized radiology image viewing systems which managed the visualization and reporting. These integrations did not happen overnight, and vendors and organizations worked hard to connect them.

It is also important to note that radiologists were among the first in the healthcare enterprise to implement voice recognition. This capability enabled radiologists to speak out loud while viewing the radiology images. The voice recognition technology captured their words and converted them into electronic format as text. This would then become the draft for their radiology report and eliminated the transcription process.

Interoperability

Upon reading the above, the obvious realization is that these systems need to be interoperable. That is, not only do these systems have to exchange data between themselves (bi-directionally), they needed to ensure the data is clearly recognized and understood. It is in the late 1990s that the organization called "Integrating the Healthcare Enterprise" (IHE) was formed. Radiology was in immediate need of standards and required all these modalities, imaging, and information systems to be integrated. Hence the organization Radiology Society of North America created IHE. Note that today, IHE is a collaboration between RSNA and Healthcare Information and Management Systems Society (HIMSS).

Vendors and providers came together and built technical frameworks around existing standards (e.g., HL7 and DICOM) to enable interoperability. This allowed a radiology department to implement various vendor solutions. There are many other benefits of interoperability including patient safety.

Evolving Standards

Standards such as HL7 continue to evolve as integration requirements progress. Currently, many healthcare information systems use Application Programming Interfaces (API). One of the latest emerging standards is called FHIR or "Fast Healthcare Interoperability Resources." FHIR provides an efficient approach to exchanging data between systems while leveraging previous best practices.

Vendor Neutral Archive (VNA)

In the healthcare enterprise, there may be one or more vendor solution used to store images. Ideally, these systems must work and play well with all other systems. Hence, they must be "vendor neutral," and a proprietary solution is not okay. The VNA enables the various modalities and information systems to store their information using non-proprietary industry standard formats. The VNA also provides the ability to reduce costs and facilitates improved workflows. Everyone wins.

Enterprise Imaging

As imaging in the enterprise evolved, it became apparent that radiology was not the only department generating images. Cardiology, dermatology, dentistry, ophthalmology and others also generated images. The concept of "Enterprise Imaging" was born. A VNA would contain not only radiology images; it would store any image from any department. This would provide large infrastructure efficiencies. It also would provide a centralized home for all images across the enterprise. Most importantly, these images could now be made available to clinical personnel and enabled them to be viewed along with the textual report.

The Cloud

As technology advances and the cloud becomes further introduced into healthcare enterprise IT architecture, the storage of radiology images in the cloud is becoming more popular. These images are stored in a secure location remotely. That is, the images are not stored on the premises on the local servers of the healthcare organization. This can be very cost-effective. Some organizations initially implement a hybrid solution. For example, they may keep the seven current years of images on local servers and store all images older than seven years on remote secure cloud servers.

From Computer-Aided-Detection to Artificial Intelligence

During the early 2000s, Computer-Aided-Detection or CAD came into usage. This technology programmatically examines a digital radiology image and identify the area(s) the radiologist should explore further. These computer applications are used to point out unusual characteristics in an image to assist in the diagnostic process. In this case, the CAD (algorithm) becomes a "second observer." For example, CAD is used extensively to identify possible breast cancer on mammograms.

This technology continues to advance rapidly, and artificial intelligence (AI)/Machine Learning is a major trend (movement) in radiology. As continuously increasing amounts of data impact radiologists, there is a requirement to sift through and identify the relevant data needed to make clinical decisions. AI will play a significant role in this area by analyzing the study, providing relevant info, making correlations (e.g., lab test), comparing historical data and images, and much more. These tools provide intelligent assistance to the radiologist by providing (new) knowledge extracted from the volumes of data being analyzed.

The area of AI is one of the most exciting aspects of Health IT. Continuously "feeding" the system relevant information improves the accuracy and capability of the algorithm. Data into Information into Knowledge into Wisdom into Decision.

Radiology and Beyond

The many continued innovations in radiology will continue to improve clinical and operational performance over time. IT innovation will provide incredible amounts of diagnostic, preventative, and analytical information. These will all contribute to better patient care, improved patient experience, and lower costs.

A Two-Way Clinical/IT Bridge

Donna Walker

I am a Registered Nurse (RN) clinical operations analyst and have successfully served on projects as a clinical bridge with IT, obtaining meaningful results and deliverables on special projects. I am sharing some examples in hope that other organizations will replicate them and harvest the rewards.

I was promoted from senior nurse auditor to a management position at a hospital where I previously worked. I was tasked to work with IT to grant access to a group of externally based clinical reviewers who were taking over the work from my earlier role. We had to create unique temporary accesses to certain EMR modules and applications at our hospital; being HIPAA secure, regulation/policy compliant, and having the functionality for the users to perform the work. I was able to effectively communicate the needs between the IT analyst and the clinical review staff. I explained to IT what the reviewers needed in functionality and then explained to the reviewers what IT was doing in the build process behind the scenes. Problems were conveyed to me from both the IT and clinical review sides to assist in developing solutions to resolve them. The IT analyst and I worked together to create training materials for the reviewers. We utilized conference calls, WebEx training sessions, screenshots, and email to communicate and evaluate our progress. This required open communication, translation of technical/clinical terminology from both sides, as well as a lot of tweaking by the IT analyst to finalize the product. The result was a HIPAA compliant electronic system that limited access with temporarily created internal email addresses for the reviewers, and selective unique views created by IT with proprietary templates for review and response letter generation.

I conducted research and educated myself on some basic IT fundamentals to adequately perform in this bridge role. This augmented my communication ability with the technical side, to in turn work with the clinical reviewers and bridge the information back and forth.

The above example led me to continue working as a consultant on security risk assessments for HIPAA compliance for a large group of hospitals and clinics. I served on a diverse team consisting of IT, IT security, clinical, and compliance professionals. We started the process by conducting a situational analysis with the C-suite and then reviewing policies and procedures that the health system currently had in place. We compared the findings against the HIPAA Privacy Rule, 45 CFR 160-164. I again served as a clinical bridge between clinical and IT employees. Hospital and clinic site visits were arranged, where walk-about assessments were conducted, accompanied by local IT management. Observations of the physical environment, including work areas, workflows, and end-user activities, were also noted. Management employees were interviewed facility-wide; inquiring as to what they did to secure protected health information (PHI) and ensure HIPAA compliance, utilizing open-ended questions. The findings were compiled, written up, and presented to the corporate organization with suggestions for process improvement. Follow-up assessments were then arranged with internal management and staff.

Getting buy-in from both sides was found to be a bit challenging, as clinical and IT speak very different languages. Clinicians are a blend of art and science, thinking in creative ways. Medicine is not absolute, as no two patients with diabetes or heart disease are exactly alike, for example. Information technology is more mathematical and linearly thinking linearly, with strict adherence to algorithms. This is necessary in computer science and data analytics. It was found that there was significant opportunity for improvement in collaboration between the two disciplines. I took a helpful approach, attempting to answer the question of "What's in it for me?" for both clinical and IT. Clinical staff are championed with the task of maintaining, improving and optimizing the patient's health. I used the health analogy of the health of the patient's medical record (EMR). An electronic medical record number is more valuable than a credit card number monetarily. Many clinical employees I interviewed were not familiar with this, but were interested, and appreciated the knowledge. EMR safety and health also applies to the employee's own medical record. It was observed that employees grasped the importance of PHI and keeping it secure more readily when they could assimilate an example that also applied to them as individuals. This definitely added value and assisted in effective learning.

Information technology desires accuracy of data and data transmission, with high concern for data integrity. People can help IT with this process and goal. I encouraged IT to collaborate more with the clinical members of the hospital team, advising them that clinical staff would be receptive. I encouraged them to "think different" and not get lost in translation with the end users. Simplicity in communication goes a long way, as sometime less is more. Engage the people, as they are the customers. People are not the problem, they are the solution! Clinicians are helpful by nature and most of them have answered a calling to be a healthcare professional with a desire to serve. They want to help and will help to fulfill the promise of information technology in healthcare, if included collaboratively to care for the health of the EMRs. Healthcare providers want to be part of the cure, not part of the disease!

I have found that some of the best ideas are generated by very diverse teams, where the members have different talents and skills. The members do not all think alike; but, if they can find a common ground to work together as a team, tremendously innovative outcomes can be achieved. That common ground is the desire for process improvement and to find a better way of achieving winning results. I enjoy being a clinical bridge, and though it is a quite a challenge at times, I feel it is my calling to serve in this much needed capacity. Utilizing a clinical bridge breaks down communication barriers and improves understanding not only between clinicians and information technology, but other departments as well. The clinical bridge can also assist in C-suite communication by adding more meaning to financials. What is the clinical benefit of the upgrade in software? Will this save in time and money and improve patient care for our customers? Why are the training costs essential in the implementation process? Are there new, more efficient ways for the clinicians to effectively document, freeing up more of their time for the patient? What does a security breach cost? For example what is the financial impact of forgetting to wipe medical records from a rented photocopier prior to its return? It could be very costly because HIPAA violations are calculated for each and every whose personal health information is compromised.

My suggestion for continued innovation is for healthcare organizations to utilize more two-way bridges between clinical and information technology. This is simplistic, but powerful, and delivers positive results. Maintain these bridges, travel them routinely, and appreciate the culture of both sides as they unite and become strong allies to fulfill the promise of information technology in healthcare.

When People and IT Row in the Same Direction: Patient Safety Innovating in a Public Academic Hospital in Spain

Juan Luis Cruz & Dr. José Luis Bueno

One of the worst things that you can probably experience as a Hematologist responsible for the blood bank in a hospital is receiving a call that a hemolytic transfusion reaction has occurred due to the incorrect identification of a patient. It happened in 2012, and fortunately the patient survived, but the whole team pledged that it had to be the last error they would ever witness.

Puerta de Hierro University Hospital is an academic public hospital located in the northwest of the Madrid region in Spain with over 600 beds and more than 3000 staff. The hospital is a flagship in Madrid's health system, which is an integrated delivery and financing system that serves more than 6.5 million people with 430 primary care centers and 35 hospitals with more than 15,000 beds. Despite being one of the best hospitals in Spain, we make one of those life-threatening errors every 11,000 transfusions, or about one or two per year. About one in ten of those errors results in the death of the patient.

It all started with a patient safety problem and the commitment to solve it; however, that was not the only problem with the transfusion process at the time. Hospital leadership created the Hemotherapy Commission in 2012 in order to oversee the complete process review involving all stakeholders, including prescriptors from the inpatient, surgical, and ambulatory settings, including nurses and hematologists. There were some key aspects that needed to be addressed, such as:

1. Optimizing blood component use. Blood components are a scarce resource that rely on donations. Public policies usually encourage the donation, but few of them are in place to address the need for efficiency in consumption. A good blood donation policy in a country is to get around 8 donations per 1,000 citizens.
2. Improving the detection and analysis of adverse reactions (hemovigilance). Nurses or MDs who carry out transfusions are responsible for identifying and reporting adverse reactions in passive hemovigilance programs. However, some adverse reactions are not recorded, especially those occurring after finishing the transfusion. Despite immediate severe reactions that were usually reported, it seemed many others remained hidden. Regarding late severe reactions, like transfusion

related acute lung injury (TRALI) and transfusion associated circulatory overload (TACO), the hospital reported virtually zero incidents in the period 2010–2012, far different from country-level statistics that set a mean of about one per 1,200 transfusions.

3. Excessive workload for all actors involved due to an incomplete IT supported process, with several systems involved, and reliance on paper and phone. As a non-exhaustive example:

   a. Doctors had to register an electronic prescription with many required fields that made the process painful and slow, and then print it and give the paper to the nurse (or just leave the printing work for the nurses).

   b. Following the prescription, nurses had to conduct a blood extraction (two extractions in case the patient was a new patient for the blood bank, checking to make sure the patient blood type is the same as the one previously extracted so to avoid a mislabeling in the blood tube collected from the patient) and regardless of the availability of a still valid sample for that patient in the blood bank. They had to call the blood bank to ask (slower), or simply do the possibly unnecessary extraction (faster). Also, nurses labelled the tubes and had to call the blood bank several times to inquire where the process was. Once they received the blood components and did the visual checks needed (sometimes in duplicate) they proceeded with the transfusion. When the transfusion ended, they had to write down (by hand) a final report provided with the blood component by the blood bank (called "DCT") including times, identity, numbers of the components transfused, and adverse reactions observed. The empty bags, along with the handwritten document, had to be sent back to the blood bank by means of a hospital porter. This procedure is a mandatory regulation for blood transfusion in most of the developed countries, including European and the United States.

   c. Things were not better at the blood bank. They had to manually register every new prescription using the printed one received with the blood sample, re-label each tube with their own internal code, and register lab tests to be completed in a different system. After the compatibility tests were performed and the blood components were selected, they had to print the DCT, send along the components, and call the ward to announce the arrival of the blood component.

4. Safety for professionals could also be compromised without an adequate traceability, and with the lack of legibility and details in some handwritten prescriptions.

All these problems lead to patient safety issues, unnecessary workload, and dissatisfaction for the professionals.

With the support of the Hemotherapy Commission and the commitment of the whole hospital leadership team, including the CEO and the CIO (Juan Luis Cruz), the head of the blood bank (Dr. José Luis Bueno) led the efforts to implement an ambitious roadmap with an approach based on the following key aspects:

■ Focusing first on patient safety and reducing workloads, reducing costs as a consequence of the former.
■ Using IT as a tool for supporting redesigned business processes.
■ Partnering with all the stakeholders involved in the transfusion process, including not only clinicians and nurses, but also IT and its providers.
■ Considering it not as an isolated project, but as a continuous improvement cycle (Plan – Do – Check – Act) based on data analysis coming from interoperable systems.
■ Thinking big, starting small.

The project was named "OPINTRA" standing for "OPtimización INformática de la TRAnsfusión" (Informatic Transfusion Optimization) and was developed in several phases with these the main milestones:

1. Implementation of a stand-alone transfusion safety system. As a quick win for patient safety, in 2013 the hospital implemented the system that allowed us to:
   a. Verify blood samples collected against the patient, using barcoded stickers and bracelets.
   b. Verify blood components against the corresponding blood samples at the blood bank and again at the bedside against the patient just before the start of the transfusion.
   c. Register electronically the possible adverse events observed by the nurse.

The project implied a change in management and training for more than 800 nurses. The commitment of many nurses, acting as the project ambassadors and elaborating short formative videos, proved itself as a key aspect for the success of this phase.

2. Development of a clinical consensus guide about the utilization criteria for blood components by the Hemotherapy Commission. Published in 2016, it set some key aspects of the transfusion process, such as the appropriate hemoglobin levels for red blood cell (RBC) transfusion and a subtle key change in the prescription process, consisting of implementing a single unit blood transfusion with every prescription.

Transfusión de Concentrados de Hematíes

Umbral transfusional recomendado		
Paciente ESTABLE	**Paciente médico** Paciente en Urgencias, Planta de Hospitalización o Paciente Crítico de larga evolución (incluyendo paciente onco-hematológico ingresado)	Hemoglobina < 7 g/dl
	Paciente quirúrgico (excepto Cirugía Cardiaca) Intra y Postoperatorio	Hemoglobina < 8 g/dl
	Paciente cardiópata	
Paciente INESTABLE	**Signos y síntomas de anemia** Hipotensión ortostática, taquicardia que no responde a la infusión de fluidos o dolor precordial	Hemoglobina < 9 g/dl
	Hipoxia tisular (SvO2, lactato)	
	Hemorragia activa Sangrado mayor de 150 ml/hora	
	Cirugía Cardiaca Electiva	
	Situaciones especiales: SCA/IAM y TCE	No existen Recomendaciones Basadas en la Evidencia

Transfundir SIEMPRE concentrados de hematíes de 1 en 1; y reevaluar al paciente tras el primer concentrado (excepto en hemorragia masiva)

Hospital Universitario Puerta de Hierro Majadahonda

Guía de Transfusión Hospital Puerta de Hierro Majadahonda. Comisión de Hemoterapia. Junio 2016.

Excerpt from the hospital's consensus guide (in Spanish) indicating the appropriate hemoglobin levels for RBC transfusions along with single unit prescription policy.

3. Implementation of a new and tailored blood bank management system, called e-Blue, fully integrated with the rest of the systems involved in the transfusion process, including the Electronic Patient Record (EPR) (Selene from Cerner), analyzers, and the transfusion safety system previously implemented. e-Blue, which was co-created by the different stakeholders involved from the beginning, included these main features:
   a. Integrated with the EPR, so as:

  i. The final transfusion report (DCT) was automatically generated.
  ii. The system could evaluate if there was a valid blood sample for every patient, and automatically cancel the nurse order generated with the electronic prescription, saving unnecessary nursing work and needle sticks for patients.
b. Fully designed to support the reengineered process, so:
  i. Every prescription (request) was linked to only one blood component.
  ii. The information required by doctors while prescribing was reduced dramatically.
  iii. Availability of lab results along with the prescription, so that the blood bank could decide if the transfusion was well indicated according to the new hospital-approved guide and also allowing later analysis about adherence to the guide on a per-doctor basis.
  iv. Integrations with the rest of systems involved and new user interfaces allowed nurses and doctors in the wards and the blood bank staff to know in real time the status of every prescription, in a simple way, without needing phone calls.
  v. A new user interface allowed the implementation of an active quarantine hemovigilance program, so as a nurse could review every transfusion result and record, undetected or not reported, and adverse events.
4. Outcomes measurement and further process improvement. While not totally concluded in its first iteration, we have measured some results so far:
a. Errors avoided: There were 55,636 blood sample collections (SC) and 79,395 blood component transfusions (BCT) verifications using the transfusion safety system during the four years of the study. We found 1,995 (3.59%) SC and 548 (0.69%) BCT incorrect verifications (near-misses). The near-miss rates were broadly different depending on the hospital ward, the user, or the time when the SC or BCT took place. The highest near-miss rates occurred during the night shift. Electronic transfusion safety systems are able to reduce the BCT errors, and also detect the near-misses incidence. They also allow us to detect gaps so as to improve personnel re-training and reschedule not urgent transfusions in those wards where near-misses are frequent.
b. Better management of adverse events: In 2016, only 13 adverse transfusion reactions were reported with the previous passive

hemovigilance system (6.1 incidents per 10,000 blood components transfused); while after carrying out the active hemovigilance process, the number of identified events was 102 (48.2/10,000). Therefore, the number of incidents detected using the new system was 7.9 times higher than those detected by the passive system. In 2017, the number of events detected was 143, corresponding to a rate of 74.8/10,000. This rate is 6.77 times higher than the average rate reported for the last 7 years, which corresponds to 11.05 events per 10,000 transfusions. Thanks to the new systems we could also detect late adverse events that occurred after finishing the transfusion, especially dyspnea or other lung-related adverse events (TACO/TRALI). In 2017, the average time for an adverse event to occur was 5.5 hours from the beginning of a transfusion. In conclusion the system allowed us to increase the number of identified adverse events, especially those that occur after the end of transfusion. The increase does not mean a higher incidence of adverse events, but a better detection of them and better care for our patients.

   c. Blood component consumption reduction: After the implementation, we have experienced a 7.3% reduction in the consumption of red blood cells and a 34.6% of plasma. Apart from implementing the single unit prescription policy, knowing the actual hemoglobin level used for transfusion in different settings will allow us to educate prescriptors proactively.

   d. Avoiding unnecessary work and costs: Paper has been eliminated from the whole circuit, as well as duplicate blood sample collection and analysis at the lab. Less time fulfilling the final transfusion reports, relabeling, or on phone calls has created additional savings, as well as avoiding the need to return empty bags to the blood bank by hospital porters (that is about 15,000 displacements per year!).

Working on this project has generated new, innovative ideas for the future, such as using analytics, including Natural Language Processing and Machine Learning techniques to automatize, find influencing variables and make predictions. As an example, these technologies would allow us to:

■ Identify variables influencing transfusion prescriptions, errors, and adverse events, so as we can establish a risk score for patients and act proactively.

■ Automatize detection and information collection regarding adverse events buried in the free text of the EMR.

To summarize, these are in our view the key takeaways extracted from our experience:

■ Identify an actual and relevant problem and solve it.
■ Focus first on patient safety and secondly on reducing workloads and dissatisfaction for the professionals. Reducing costs will be a consequence of the former.
■ Get your leadership team involved.
■ Use IT as a tool for supporting redesigned business processes, not to impose them.
■ Involve all the stakeholders from the beginning of the project; partnering with IT and its providers is also critical.
■ Measure before and after, and take actions based on data.
■ Despite how we manage specific projects, innovating is a process and as such it should be managed and improved incrementally.
■ Think big, start small. Results take time.

Chapter 3

Create Roadmaps

> Develop a plan for the functions required to innovate and encourage effective communication between functional experts for strategic clarity.

There is an unsubstantiated fear that plans and order run counter to the innovation spirit. Effective roadmaps actually serve as beacons or markers that help innovators navigate their way without being distracted and thrown off course. Plans do not stifle innovation but rather provide necessary guardrails to ensure focus and completion. Too many great ideas were never realized as resources and passion dwindled from an unnecessarily long journey.

Open, Connected Environment Drives Healthcare Transformation

Paul Black

Imagine a world where patients can go anywhere, anytime and know that their healthcare provider is up to date and readily accessible from their mobile device. To achieve this vision, the technology delivering it must contain two key components: it must be open and interoperable. The result of the open-plus-interoperable equation is a new digital health platform: a connected community of health.

Closed IT systems lock important clinical data into silos, making it difficult to share patient information, and hinder point-of-care teams that need complete and real-time information at their fingertips. Open architecture makes it easy to create apps, share data and upgrade individual components of this platform. Open systems also help caregivers extend and scale functionality so that they can meet the unique needs of their patients and their community. When we add true vendor-agnostic interoperability, we enable providers to seamlessly communicate and exchange data with any trusted system and use that data to make better-informed decisions at the point-of-care and beyond.

Open architecture has long been part of Allscripts' vision and culture. In 2007, we launched a research and development group to focus on solving interoperability problems by using Application Programming Interfaces (APIs). The Allscripts Developer Program (ADP) was designed to work with companies and individuals who are creating new solutions to improve the clinician and patient experience, improve clinical workflow, enable interoperability and reduce redundancies.

Building an open, connected ecosystem holds the power to inform and transform the health of populations and individuals. As our nation grapples to contain the deadly opioid epidemic, we can work toward the integration and optimization of data systems already in place to help provide critical information to stem the tide of tragic addiction and deaths. On an individual level, data can provide clues to genetic components of both rare and widespread conditions. Millennials have, in particular, embraced the power of this information that will usher in a new generation of personalized medicine, delivered in a way that focuses on the patient experience – from online appointment scheduling and transportation confirmation to point-of-care, care plans and follow-up. The ability to search and enroll in clinical trials will also be facilitated by this platform, one that grants consent to the patient's record by the person who owns the data – the patient.

Health IT is critical to delivering the right data to the right place at the right time and empowering clinicians and other care providers to make informed decisions based on all the data that exists in the community about the individual sitting in an Emergency Department or the clinic waiting room. Developers will play an increasingly vital role in designing applications that inform and equip providers and health systems as we collectively face complex and costly health issues. Allscripts has uniquely and relentlessly pursued open architecture for more than a decade, believing that individual vendors do not own the data collected by or stored in their proprietary systems, but rather that the data belongs to the patient.

Today, Allscripts continues to cultivate an ecosystem around optimizing information to make it genuinely actionable, delivering better care and more value by focusing on the consumer, interoperability, post-acute care coordination, provider wellness, precision medicine, population health and machine learning. This data-driven, collaborative environment holds the key to unlocking some of the toughest healthcare challenges like prescription pain medicine abuse and opioid addiction. With a public health problem so multi-layered and complex, how can an open and connected environment succeed where so many efforts have failed?

Population Health: How Open, Connected Technology Can Help Combat Opioid Addiction

The Centers for Disease Control and Prevention (CDC) reports that prescription opioid use and overdoses have quadrupled since 1999. An average of 115 Americans die every day from prescription and illegally-obtained opioid and opiate overdose. The CDC estimates that the total economic impact of prescription opioid misuse alone in the United States is $78.5 billion annually, including the costs of healthcare, lost productivity, addiction treatment and criminal justice involvement.

We know that technology can better support and empower those on the front lines, and help to reverse this alarming trend of over-prescription, addiction, overdose and death. Our goal is to deliver a comprehensive solution by shifting the process from being a task – i.e., checking the prescription drug monitoring program (PDMP) – to an actual clinical decision at the point-of-care.

The College of Healthcare Information Management Executives (CHIME) has stressed the need for better electronic health record (EHR)-PDMP integration, combined with data-driven reports to identify prescribing patterns. To that end, many prescribers and dispensers place a high value on the information available to them from the PDMPs, yet they are frequently challenged to access this information given their busy schedules. Recent studies have shown that providers take anywhere from five to eight minutes per patient in the current process of checking the PDMP. Our goal is to eliminate the manual workflow associated with the PDMP check process and implement a solution to avoid system latencies in existing PDMPs.

We have a team of data scientists in Allscripts whose mission is to transform data into insights and actionable information. Their mission is to couple the information that is within the EHR with the data we have in our Clinical Data Warehouse – data that represents millions of patients – and combine it with data that is available through public health mechanisms (such as PDMPs). That "data lake" can then be used to develop algorithms to identify or even predict at-risk patients, and look at prescription patterns that most often lead to problems with abuse and overdose.

Organizations can reduce the risk of addiction before it takes hold by utilizing advanced data analytics technology for real-time monitoring, triggering alerts scores that make it easier to identify potential abuse. In this way, we will be providing information that enables prescribers to quickly evaluate the situation and act upon it immediately, if necessary. This data, viewed as an aggregate, can change the health of a nation. We must never lose sight of single data points, however, the role of the individual as powerful drivers of healthcare innovation.

Individuals Driving Innovation in the Healthcare Experience

As healthcare continues to evolve, individuals are increasingly playing a more significant role in their own health. Consumers are viewing health solutions regarding overall wellness, patient experience and outcomes as an indication that patient-centric solutions will become the norm for all aspects of healthcare. Making sense of the explosion of data that is currently available, or will be soon, requires a strong foundation of open, connected IT solutions.

One example of this is the advent of tech-savvy millennials experiencing healthcare in their new role as parents. Many pediatric practices are discovering that millennial parents (those born from the early 1980s to the late 1990s) have different expectations for their children's healthcare than previous generations. Services, such as online scheduling and email appointment reminders that Gen X parents considered a pleasant convenience, have become an expectation for the generation that grew up with the internet.

Millennial parents expect to be able to communicate with their pediatric providers beyond regular office hours via email or instant messaging. They want the option to see their children's doctor in the evenings or on weekends, so they do not have to miss work. Moreover, they expect the practice to have an online presence, mobile capabilities and flexible payment options.

Pediatricians have used tools like CHADIS and the Allscripts FollowMyHealth® patient portal to help modernize their practices with electronic patient intake and other tech-enabled services that millennial parents have come to expect, including shorter wait times and a faster in-and-out experience when they come to the clinic for care.

Beyond a personalized experience, consumers are beginning to expect a greater emphasis on personalized medicine. Epigenetics – the study of how genetic expression works – will take precision medicine to the next level.

Because there's still much to learn in fields like epigenetics, point-of-care genomic solutions must have placeholders for these larger concepts. We have built the 2bPrecise platform to handle this level of complexity. It is ready to help clinicians navigate the ever-growing knowledge base of genomic medicine today and in the future.

As people continue to share information about their individual healthcare transactions, it will change the overall healthcare consumer experience. For example, patients can now see provider reviews, available options for care and providers, and estimated out-of-pocket costs. Patients will be able to make more informed decisions about their care, which will ultimately result in better quality and lower costs.

The dual demand for solving population-level health issues, while at the same time focusing on patient-centric care, has triggered a call for true interoperability and open health data exchange through Application Programming Interfaces (APIs).

Application Programming Interfaces (APIs) – The Key to Unlocking Interoperability

APIs, or sets of tools and specifications that enable software to interact, are not a new concept, and indeed are not new to Allscripts. Other industries have opened up their APIs to enable innovative data exchange. Think about how any car dealer can pull up your financial information, or how your airline ticket can appear on your mobile phone – open APIs make these capabilities possible.

Open APIs are less common in healthcare, which is part of the reason why our industry lags behind in being able to offer these consumer-centric information exchange capabilities. Allscripts recognized early on how important it was – for innovation and interoperability – to create an environment that makes it easy for applications to take root and delivers what clients need in order to be successful. The demand for interoperability in healthcare is bringing APIs into the spotlight, and it is critical that APIs be open and available to connect disparate technologies to one another.

The Allscripts Developer Program (ADP) helps connect innovative devices, applications and other healthcare solutions with its open platform. ADP was created as an opportunity for companies to help providers improve healthcare by integrating new and existing software applications and devices with the Allscripts solutions they use to treat patients. Moreover, clients can use the same web services and other integration technologies to build integration for use in their own facilities.

Open architecture allows for outside developers to access pathways into Allscripts' systems and creates value by providing clients with the ability to build, develop, grow and pivot as needed — and in the manner most effective for the given situation and set of circumstances. This an important differentiator, because it empowers clients to be innovators by delivering complete and meaningful access to various source data and application workflows, regardless of the vendor.

ADP was set up to work with partners who create new solutions to increase quality and communication, improve workflow and interoperability and reduce redundancies. This, in turn, improves engagement, wellness, outcomes and retention of both patients and staff. Clients and companies participating in ADP have already used Allscripts' intelligent APIs 3.5 billion times to support a genuinely open, connected community of health.

There are three ways to engage with ADP:

■ Developer Open Access – This free option gives developers full access and rights to use new Fast Healthcare Interoperability Resources (FHIR)-enabled APIs with calls to help Allscripts clients meet regulatory compliance.

■ ADP Integrator – Companies signing up to be an ADP Integrator will receive rights to use Allscripts' APIs along with industry standard FHIR APIs. The Integrator category is available for any company that would like to connect with Allscripts solutions, with no required review or approval by Allscripts.

■ ADP Partner – This is best for innovators who want to leverage all the technical functionality offered in the Integrator tier, as well as additional testing, sales and marketing support. The online Application Store makes it easy for clients to access our ADP Partners' certified solutions. To help developers along the way, each will be assigned a designated Partner Manager. Allscripts reviews each partnership application for product compatibility and other factors.

Ten years ago, Apple introduced its first iPhone, ushering in a new era of user-centered technology. This technology made it easy for apps and created a brand-new ecosystem. It is just what healthcare needed.

More than ten years ago, Allscripts was the first in the healthcare industry to embrace an open platform because we recognized this was the only way to achieve the promise of interoperability. Allscripts APIs are open and fully supported, which means that we encourage third-party applications to work with our solutions.

Through our developer network, we have helped healthcare applications exchange data 3.5 billion times in just four years, and that rate continues to climb. In August 2017, Allscripts hit a new milestone by facilitating the exchange of more than 100 million data shares within a single month. Today, more than 6,000 third-party and client-employed developers work with Allscripts to deploy innovative solutions using FHIR and proprietary APIs. These relationships are in addition to the 170+ existing Allscripts developer partners, all currently available through the company's application store (https://store.allscripts.com).

It is not just a concept inside the company, it is a philosophy and a part of our culture. We have a team of people inside the company that help third-party application programmers, and program writers access a relatively deep layer of API. This allows them to build their own ecosystems on top of Allscripts' platforms. These programmers and developers outside of Allscripts, essentially who supplement our own engineering team, and are building solutions that are industry-specific, workflow-specific, disease-specific, and that will allow someone to benefit from this vast investment our clients have made. They add value through other smart interfaces, mobile devices, capabilities around scales or whatever people are looking for from a consumer standpoint. We are creating that ecosystem for entrepreneurs wanting access to this big network, access to a data layer and access to a company that wants to work with them.

Open platforms offer a world of potential for healthcare by smoothly integrating proprietary software or plugging in new applications from the industry's most creative innovators. By giving innovators access to our APIs, we are helping clients integrate the innovations that matter most to their patients. Providers recognize the advantages of using APIs to solve business and clinical challenges quickly. Apps are much faster, cost less and are far easier to deploy than making large-scale enhancements and upgrades to core systems. It enables us to be nimble and keep costs low for our users.

APIs: What Have We Learned?

After more than a decade of exploration and integration of APIs, the following best practices have become a part of Allscripts DNA:

1. Take a top-down approach – Senior management must do more than give lip service to demonstrate commitment through allocating appropriate human and financial resources to build and support the API program.

2. Assign a passionate leader – Very few companies have a dedicated leader to support APIs development and usage. Allscripts has appointed a chief innovation officer, as well as a general manager of its open business unit to demonstrate our commitment from a senior level.
3. Be an advocate for innovation and interoperability – Think outside of your corporate walls to engage with the broader community to promote the benefits of open architecture.
4. Be a good partner – Support customers and your vendors through clear, effective communications. Listen to their concerns and be prepared to respond.
5. Market the program both internally and externally – Ensure employees understand the value of APIs and partners have explored and utilized all of the benefits of your developer program. Broadening the understanding of what you have to offer will build your base of advocates.
6. Pay attention to the market to align cost with value – The cost of building out integration cannot exceed the amount that developers could charge a client for a solution. High-cost integration is not sustainable. Allscripts charges a small usage-based fee that developers pay to access Allscripts' info.

Open, Connected Environments: Just the Beginning

For many years, the conversation around healthcare interoperability was narrow in scope: doctor-to-doctor information exchange. However, as healthcare organizations successfully adopt EHRs, we can see countless opportunities that exist above the EHR. Every step toward greater clarity and consensus enables us to invest confidently in new interoperability technologies and standards, such as FHIR, and helps the industry abandon habits that have been keeping information locked away.

Looking toward the future, challenges include emergency preparedness, cloud-based storage and widespread adoption of technology that enables interoperability. Because of the innovative structure of programs like API, we are looking forward to facing – and solving – those challenges head-on.

There's no question that the cloud is going to be a significant factor in bringing down the total cost of ownership. Practice Fusion (an electronic health record platform) is cloud-based, and many of our solutions are cloud-based. We recently put Sunrise into Microsoft Azure, and we are actively moving applications to their cloud. Cloud-based technology will play a role as systems face the untenable costs associated with natural disasters and emergency preparedness. Hurricanes, tornadoes, nor'easters and wildfires require evacuation of critically ill patients with complex medical concerns, and their medical information will need to follow along. There's no question that in five to ten years, most of the applications that hospitals access will be cloud-based.

An open platform enables a world of possibilities and potential for healthcare. Core systems are open to help providers to extend and scale functionality in order to meet the specific needs of their community. They can easily integrate proprietary software or plug in new applications from the industry's most creative innovators.

Healthcare has not yet achieved the promise of interoperability. To make progress, we must continue to think big and not settle for a narrow perspective. Making life better for clinicians by presenting them with accessible, relevant information is critical to moving forward. When big data and open systems are combined, when talented and innovative developers feel free and even compelled to create, the potential outcomes for robust healthcare transformation are limited only by our imaginations.

References

Centers for Disease Control and Prevention (CDC). Drug Overdose Deaths in the U.S. Continue to Increase in 2016. https://www.cdc.gov/drugoverdose/epidemic/. Accessed March 25, 2018.
National Institutes of Health. Opioid Overdose Crisis. https://www.drugabuse.gov/drugs-abuse/opioids/opioid-overdose-crisis#two. Accessed March 25, 2018.

Sleeping Giant

Gary Johnson

This essay describes the transformative innovation deployed within the University of Kentucky Healthcare (UKHC) system that created a dynamic financial catalyst, which expanded patient access and improved patient outcomes. This innovation was built upon the framework of ambulatory pharmacy services and grew to represent 70% of Income from Operations for the health system while reducing readmissions by 40% and expanding access for insured and uninsured patients.

Health system administrators have been trained to view pharmacy services as a cost center where variable costs can be depressed. This traditional

paradigm is not applicable to ambulatory pharmacy services where growing drug expenditures can generate new income streams. In contrast, out-
sourced or shrinking ambulatory pharmacy expenditures is a strategy of
retreat that atrophies organizational growth opportunities.

UKHC faced these same cultural challenges; however, with innovative
ambulatory pharmacy models, UKHC inverted this cost-containment paradigm. This inversion increased ambulatory pharmacy drug costs by 500%,
resulting in 900% margin increases through care models that expand patient
access, with these financial returns reinvested into UKHC to continue the
provision of services for all patients, including self-pay and indigent patients.
This essay reviews guided efforts to optimize ambulatory pharmacy services,
which include the: (1) optimization of contract pharmacy services via the
federal 340B drug pricing program (2) optimization and expansion of retail
pharmacy services, (3) creation of a prescription delivery service for patients
being discharged from the hospital, which is integrated with medication
reconciliation-related processes, (4) optimization of employee prescription
benefits and (5) creation of a robust specialty pharmacy in collaboration
with subspecialty clinics. The topics reviewed in this essay include how
patient access was expanded, how the fiscal impact was measured, the barriers circumvented and lessons learned were applied to other departments.

Compliance: UKHC spent 12 months focusing efforts on 340B program
compliance as a foundation before moving ambulatory pharmacy initiatives
forward. UKHC now employs multiple analysts to audit various aspects of
the 340B program on a weekly basis. Having a regular cadence of compliance reporting allows for accurate monitoring of the program. For stewards
of the 340B program, a process of baseline assessment and continual reas-
sessment of compliance is essential, as it allows the organization to continue
accomplishing its mission while fulfilling the intent of the 340B program.
This framework of compliance provides scaffolding for the UKHC ambulatory care pharmacy strategy, which includes three distinct operational units:
1) retail pharmacy services, 2) contract pharmacy services and 3) specialty
pharmacy services.

Retail Pharmacy Services: In the summer of 2011, at the beginning
of this innovation strategy, UKHC had one flagship retail pharmacy, which
served multiple clinics, as well as a satellite retail pharmacy in an adjacent
building, which served the UK student population. However, the lack of
340B-qualifying software prevented either of those retail operations from
functioning as an "open pharmacy," which precluded the provision of services to many patients with prescriptions from non-UKHC providers, many

of these patients were employees of UKHC. Until that point in time, hospital leadership was focused on cutting costs in the satellite retail pharmacy, which had lower volumes than the flagship retail pharmacy. The pharmacy department demonstrated that this satellite retail pharmacy generated a modest annual operating margin (i.e., net revenue minus operating expenses). This exercise generated interest in measuring the performance of the flagship retail pharmacy, changed the traditional cost-centric paradigm, and initiated a culture of revenue generation as opposed to cost containment. A pro forma for expanding hours in the flagship retail pharmacy, which entailed increased labor costs but would expand patient access and increase the net operating margin, was subsequently submitted. These experiences facilitated the expansion of five additional retail pharmacies throughout the health system during the next five years.

The flagship pharmacy in the clinic building was across the street from the main hospital, which presented a challenge for patients with discharge prescriptions as well as those with emergency department (ED), same-day surgery and employee prescriptions. To improve services for these patient populations, a business plan for a hospital lobby-based retail pharmacy service with a concierge medication delivery component, termed Meds-2-Beds, for discharge-related prescriptions was created. The importance of this service is ensuring that discharge prescriptions are dispensed to prevent unnecessary hospital readmissions. The added importance of providing this service for a safety net hospital (SNP) is that the discharge process – a critical point in transitions of care (TOC) for any patient – is especially critical for those patients whom, when they reach their home destination, find that they cannot afford their medication from a local or mail-order pharmacy. An SNP is prepared to perform a financial assessment of these patients, provide vouchers needed to dispense discharge medications and serve as a resource for processing prescription refills.

This lobby-based discharge pharmacy generated income more than expenses within the first month of operations. The high frequency of Meds-2-Beds service utilization generated visibility for retail pharmacy operations, which presented unanticipated challenges. One year later a similar hospital lobby retail pharmacy offering Meds-2-Beds services was launched at a sister community-based hospital, with similar success. More recently, UKHC opened a large clinic building at an off-campus location, where retail pharmacy services were initiated in the building lobby. Within a year, expansion plans aimed at accommodating the overwhelming needs of these clinic patients were submitted.

Technology: UKHC replaced the pharmacy management system (PMS) in the retail space with a new vendor product, the pharmacy department partnered with this vendor to create a real-time solution to the above 340B related problem. This new solution combined a PMS with a 340B-qualifying system that determined eligibility in real-time. The PMS interfaces directly with the patient registration file and the eligible-provider file, which eliminated the time lag created by the previous retrospective reporting method. At the point of prescription adjudication, the prescription is flagged for either 340B or WAC billing, which enables more cost-efficient product selection. The new PMS also eliminated the need for a third-party administrator to split-bill the order. Instead, dispensed prescriptions accumulated in the PMS and separate replenishment orders (at 340B and WAC prices, respectively) were placed with the wholesaler. This solution was later launched within the UKHC specialty pharmacy and proved critical, as the differing financial implications of WAC and 340B dispensed prescriptions are more pronounced with specialty medications.

Contract Pharmacy: These services include the health system partnering with external pharmacies to repatriate revenue back into the health system. Traditionally, these partnerships include large chain pharmacies, such as Walgreen's, Walmart and CVS.

However, this presented another innovative opportunity to create contract pharmacy models with nontraditional partners, such as home infusion pharmacies and specialty, mail-order pharmacies located in other states. This process of innovation began in the area of greatest need for UKHC: home infusion pharmacy services. UKHC does not have a home infusion pharmacy and extending 340B participation into this arena was vital given that a large percentage of the patients are discharged with home infusion orders. Since home infusions are billed as medical benefit claims and not as pharmacy benefit claims, UKHC developed a nontraditional contract pharmacy model with a 340B split-billing vendor and a local home infusion pharmacy. UKHC also included provisions in the home infusion contract pharmacy agreement to support indigent and self-pay patients who account for roughly 15% of UKHC's home infusion patients. These contract provisions allowed UKHC to extend its SNP role by providing home infusion pharmacy services to patients who would have difficulty accessing home-based services. UKHC structured this relationship such that 340B program related savings would directly pay for medication vouchers generated by social services staff across the UKHC enterprise, which allowed UKHC to directly leverage 340B program savings to extend to care to the underserved.

Subsequently, in the summer of 2013, as the specialty pharmacy pipeline continued to grow, it was apparent that many of UKHC's patients were being forced to fill their specialty prescriptions through mail-order specialty pharmacies outside Kentucky. In the absence of a UKHC specialty pharmacy, UKHC reached out to the largest mail-order specialty pharmacy that was serving UKHC patients to discuss a contract pharmacy relationship. This concept was unfamiliar. This specialty pharmacy partner and both parties struggled with the many facets of implementation. Ultimately, this model resembled the home infusion contract pharmacy model, accommodating both medical and prescription benefit claims. The contract pharmacy model was activated in the spring of 2014, and this experience provided a foundation for the eventual development of a Utilization Review Accreditation Commission (URAC) – accredited specialty pharmacy at UKHC, which was moved into a dedicated space in February 2016.

Specialty Pharmacy: Specialty pharmacy services provided by UKHC in 2012 were limited to oncology and non-oncology infusions, a hemophilia treatment center, a state-sponsored AIDS Drug Assistance Program and an average of a dozen self-administered specialty medications dispensed weekly through UKHC retail pharmacies. In collaboration with eight large subspecialty clinics, it was determined that the total potential revenue from self-administered specialty prescriptions within these clinics was over $200 million annually. The existing retail pharmacy infrastructure was providing specialty prescriptions for less than 1% of the patient's prescribed specialty medications. Furthermore, the same review uncovered dozens of medication access issues, fragmented workflow, and general patient and clinic dissatisfaction with external specialty pharmacies.

In a validation of the quality of the clinical and technical services provided by the specialty pharmacy, specialty pharmacy accreditation was obtained in 2015, and a dedicated 5,000-square-foot site for the operation was secured in February 2016. This space houses a call center, dispensing and management personnel, a mail-order operation and all related inventory. Accreditation also led to improved access to restricted medications and improved contracting opportunities with Medicaid and commercial payers. Specialty pharmacy services in 2017 included care for patients with nine primary diseases and dispensing of an average of over 2,500 prescriptions monthly, which included specialty and related supportive medications.

Because of the unique role UKHC fulfills as both an SNP and a specialty pharmacy service provider, there is an intrinsic investment in patient care by the pharmacy staff. UKHC pharmacists from the specialty pharmacy meet one-on-one with these patients in clinics to build strong relationships and ensure appropriate access to these medications. Specific pharmacy employees serve as access points for patients who cannot afford their specialty medications – or even the high copayments often associated with specialty medications.

UKHC then pivoted the contract pharmacy dynamic and leveraged the UKHC contract pharmacy as a contract pharmacy partner for health systems throughout the state. This model allowed many small- to medium-sized health systems to generate margins from specialty pharmacy prescriptions which otherwise would have been impossible.

Financial Measures: During the initial year of ambulatory care pharmacy development, effort was expended developing business plans, pro-forma documents and return on investment (ROI) analyses to demonstrate opportunities. This work later translated into developing analytic platforms for measuring performance and growth in each strategic ambulatory care pharmacy program. Over a 5 year period, prescription volumes increased from 223,000 to 450,000 (93% growth) while the associated operating margin grew 538% by 2016 from the baseline of 2011 and 900% by 2018 from the baseline of 2011.

Performance of UK HealthCare ambulatory care pharmacy operations, by annual prescription volume (trend line) and annual percentage increase in operating margin relative to the fiscal year 2011 (FY11) margin (bars).

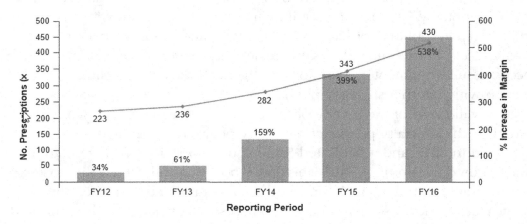

Discussion: This experience demonstrated the value of ambulatory care pharmacy services. However, this experience also demonstrated the complexity of operating a retail business within a highly regulated acute care environment. The complexity of these models extends beyond operations and reflects cultural challenges, which include the need for hospital executives to pivot from acute care to ambulatory care pharmacy services. This pivot is challenging for executives with only acute care experience, who have been trained to assess pharmacy operations as a cost center as opposed to a revenue center. This dynamic requires pharmacy leaders to educate and incrementally demonstrate value associated with ambulatory care pharmacy models.

Another entrenched paradigm is resistance to the propagation of outpatient pharmacy solutions, which include the operating system, automation and tools to ensure regulatory compliance, such as software for managing 340B program complexities. The drug expense for many ambulatory care pharmacy operations nearly equals the drug expense for inpatient operations. As both inpatient and ambulatory care pharmacy costs grow, organizational leaders, including pharmacy leaders, might unflinchingly incur million-dollar software expenditures for inpatient operations, such as an electronic medical record, but grimace at ambulatory care pharmacy infrastructure costs, such as the cost of an operating system that exceeds $50,000 per year. Inpatient pharmacy investments dwarf investment in ambulatory care pharmacy operations. Ironically, in some cases pharmacy directors who are continually pressured to lower drug costs but have minimal capacity to influence utilization to allow opportunities for revenue creation through ambulatory care pharmacy services to be taken away by large retail pharmacy chains situated in and around medical center campuses.

Another challenge to ambulatory care pharmacy development is the lack of competency in that practice area within the pharmacy leadership. Pharmacy directors and managers have long focused on inpatient operations while perhaps failing to recognize the extent to which ambulatory care pharmacy has evolved in both complexity and opportunity. The regulatory environment, specifically within a 340B program model, is particularly onerous and breeds an abundance of caution. This caution and lack of understanding can intimidate pharmacy leaders and retard the development of legitimate opportunities.

A growing chasm between inpatient and outpatient pharmacy operations is being bridged with TOC models. These models, which blur traditional boundaries, include pharmacist-based clinic interventions in targeted populations, such as patients undergoing transplantation, as well as medication reconciliation at admission and discharge counseling about the bedside delivery of discharge prescriptions, which improve HCAHPS scores and rates of completion of medication reconciliation at discharge. Through these models, the discharged patient can be triaged into the ambulatory care pharmacy model to receive prescription services, including specialty prescriptions, as well as various forms of infusion services in the home setting or infusion center.

With the success of the larger UKHC ambulatory care pharmacy initiative, pharmacy services administrators found that opportunities to support the organizational mission in the form of expanded patient care are vast. UKHC expanded pharmacy services by adding more than 30 newly hired clinical pharmacists to inpatient service lines and ambulatory care clinics, such as the cancer center, cardiology clinics and the transplant clinic. Additionally, with the creation of the specialty pharmacy, clinic-based pharmacist roles geared toward enhancing care for patients with ten specialty diseases have been created and filled. The pharmacy department has implemented TOC technician roles that involve 24-7 staffing in the ED and other service lines with a commitment to thorough and accurate medication histories at admission. Inpatient pharmacy services leaders have adopted the Better Outcomes Through Optimizing Safe Transitions (BOOST) methodology, whereby inpatient pharmacy teams have expanded coverage to offer thorough medication reconciliation at admission with the assistance of medication histories captured by TOC technicians, as well as traditional high-quality inpatient clinical services, discharge medication reconciliation, and medication counseling for patients who choose to have their medications dispensed through the Meds-2-Beds program. Also, as mentioned earlier, additional roles were created to assist indigent and self-pay patients with medication access. Without the success of the ambulatory care pharmacy initiative, these additional inpatient services and resources for patients would not be possible.

Conclusion: Opportunities for ambulatory care pharmacy services to provide valuable patient care and improve fiscal performance exist. UKHC expanded patient access to medications while creating a financially viable model that optimized existing retail pharmacy operations and opened additional retail pharmacies, implemented discharge prescription delivery services, implemented contract pharmacy services and opening an accredited specialty pharmacy.

Into the Great Wide Open: Building a Digital Innovation Roadmap

Paddy Padmanabhan

Healthcare is in the early stages of an industry-wide transformation toward digital. What makes it interesting is that unlike other sectors such as retailing, financial services or hospitality, healthcare is insulated from naked market forces – though not for long. Despite all the rhetoric by successive administrations, the shift toward value-based care has been slow – some would even say <u>stalled</u> – as many health systems hold on to the traditional fee-for-service payment model. At the same time, a report by the American Hospital Association (AHA) and AVIA in 2017 indicates that more than 75% of leaders believe that digital innovation is important because it has strong ties to long-term strategy and competitive differentiation.

The question that health systems face is: do we have a burning platform? For those that answer no, the question then is: can we sustain indefinitely with our current business model or are we frogs boiling slowly in the water and we do not know it? It's hard to imagine a health system today operating purely in a fee-for-service model that is insulated from competitive forces and margin pressures. Declining reimbursement rates will eventually force drastic cost-cutting in the face of margin pressures unless the organization transforms its care delivery models. The time to act is now, i.e. while the water is yet to boil because the enterprise can invest in digital innovation to carry the enterprise into the future.

Many health systems have already made investments in "digital" and are struggling to show returns on the investment. For instance, while 87% of Americans had used at least one digital health tool in 2017 (up from 80% in 2015), consumers are yet to demonstrate a sustainable integration of these solutions into their lives. In addition, the adoption rates were for a narrow range of use cases and demographics. Technology firms, for their part, have appended the word "digital" to all manner of offerings, creating confusion and making it hard for enterprise leaders to separate the hype from reality.

In my work with leading health systems and some of the world's biggest technology solution providers and innovative startups, the singular challenge has been to go beyond lip service to "digital" and to lay out a *digital roadmap* that can be executed with *ready-to-deploy* technologies.

Approaching Digital Innovation: Discovery

During the last three years, my firm has worked with leading regional and national health systems on digital transformation initiatives. We have also worked very closely with a wide range of technology firms in helping them position their offerings for digital healthcare transformation and innovation. Some common themes have emerged in our conversations with CIO's, many of whom are also responsible for digital transformation of their enterprises. One of the first issues to address in any digital transformation is who owns and drives the transformation. The CIO's we have worked with understand at the outset that digital transformation needs sponsorship at the highest levels of the organization. They also understand that digital transformation is not an information technology initiative per se, and that it is more about organization and culture change supported by new and innovative digital technologies. This raises questions around who should be involved in developing and driving the digital innovation roadmap. The answers vary from enterprise to enterprise. In one case, in order to ensure that digital didn't become yet another IT initiative, the CIO invited an extended group of leaders across the enterprise to be a part of the digital innovation roadmap process. The response was so overwhelming that we eventually decided to create two groups: the first one would comprise of cross-functional representatives from various functions including the various clinical departments to provide guidance and oversight to the process. A smaller group of a dozen or so hand-selected individuals would be the core team that would be involved in developing the roadmap.

For leaders and teams chartered with driving digital transformation, the initial questions usually are: what is digital? What does digital mean to the CEO and to the Board of Directors of the health system? What does it mean to the broader organization? What does it mean to peer group health systems across the country?

In our work with a nationally known health system, we decided to adopt a three-pronged approach to get an answer to these questions: The first would be to conduct extensive research on published information about digital innovation programs across leading health systems across the country; the second would be to launch an internal survey to gather inputs and views on what digital means internally to leaders across functions; the third was to reach out to peer organizations, leading technology, and consulting firms and industry analysts to learn their views on what digital means to them and to the clients they serve.

Here is what we found:

■ Increasing patient access was key to activating consumers. One of the big challenges was to consolidate all the access points (over a dozen portals and multiple 1–800 numbers) into a single unified interface or a "single pane of glass."

■ Improved use of social media and digital marketing channels to educate consumers was also an essential aspect of engaging and activating healthcare consumers.

- Increasing patient access and engagement, especially through tele-medicine or telehealth programs is a priority for most health systems. Somewhere between 65% and 71% of healthcare providers had deployed sort of a telemedicine program to engage with patients. Our client had already launched a program for advancing virtual care delivery models in the form of e-visits and an urgent care application through which consumers could get access to immediate care through a virtual consultation.
- The concept of a "virtual hospital" was gaining traction. An example of this is Intermountain Healthcare in Utah, one of the pioneers in tele-medicine, that had launched a program titled Connect Care Pro to provide basic medical services as well as stroke evaluation, intensive care, newborn critical care and mental health services.
- Remote monitoring has gained a significant amount of traction as a means to reduce caregiver workload and save costs. California-based Kaiser Permanente has launched Bluetooth-enabled glucose meters to enable patients to have their readings automatically synced to their mobile devices.

The internal survey was designed to elicit answers to a series of questions around how digital transformation could positively impact the work of caregivers, how to implement the transformation, and what kinds of tools and technologies would be required. An important question was whether we had the internal capability to handle the scale and scope of the transformation what kind of partners we would need for the journey.

The survey responses gave us valuable insights about where we should focus our priorities as it relates to the groups we serve. Here are a few ideas we gathered from the responses to the internal survey:

Goal: Engaging Patients

- **Communication:** Easier communication between patients and caregivers; Tools to help patients maintain their care plans and wellness while they are home (engagement)
- **Process:** Simplification of procedures to reduce friction for patients to find a scheduled appointment (access)
- **Care models:** New care models for patients in their homes with ongoing "medical" support through digital interactions (care delivery)

Goal: Enabling Caregivers

- **Remote monitoring:** Enable physicians to engage patients remotely and also train and engage physicians remotely (engagement)
- **Communication:** Easier communication between caregivers (collaboration)
- **Care delivery:** Building tools that allow physicians to practice care when not co-located with physicians or patients (care delivery)

What we discovered were common themes related to the individual *journeys* of patients and caregivers, often from both viewpoints. Access, engagement, collaboration, care delivery – these were core elements that we had to consider in reimagining the future as a digitally enabled enterprise.

The survey respondents saw the best digitalization practices in other industries to be around consumer understanding and engagement in hospitality, retail and financial services sectors. Not surprisingly, they saw opportunities for digitalization in healthcare to be mainly around telemedicine and virtual care. However, there were several essential use cases related to organization efficiencies and community engagement that emerged during our discussions. Over time, we would eventually flesh these out to over a hundred innovation opportunities for digital transformation across the enterprise. We would also develop detailed journey maps and assign each use case to the journey stages for each category of stakeholders.

The final prong of the three-pronged approach was to engage in site visits with some of our peer group health systems and with a select group of solution provider and analyst firms. We found that the range of views on digital innovation varied widely. Many of the health systems we spoke with had a relatively narrow definition of digital innovation which focused primarily on patient access and engagement through telehealth and digital marketing programs. For many of them, their electronic medical record (EMR) vendor had also become their digital innovation platform of choice.

When we spoke with technology solution providers, we discovered, not surprisingly, that each firm had a definition of digital innovation that aligned with whatever they had to sell; the most common themes we heard equated digital innovation with the cloud, analytics or automation. We would learn more about the limitations of these definitions when we dug deeper into the next stage of the process.

Implementing a Digital Innovation Roadmap: Prioritizing, Partnering, and Paying for It

Once we had completed the journey maps and identified the most important use cases, our first step was to prioritize the use cases for the digital innovation roadmap. To do this, we used the prioritization matrix shown in Figure 3.1.

Prioritization: Take a Ticket, Get in Line

Digital transformation is mostly about cultural and organizational change. The prioritization matrix (see Figure 3.1) recognizes the need to show near-term wins, mainly as a confidence-building exercise for the C-suite and the Board. It establishes credibility for the digital innovation team and strengthens their hand when seeking additional investments. Near-term wins in the form of new initiatives with short payback periods are understandably popular with the C-suite. An example of this is a simple virtual check-in application in a pediatric care facility that included a wait-time estimator and ensured that the patient does not lose her place in line if she is running late. Another is a "know-me" feature that allows staff at the patient registration desk to greet individuals by name and pull up basic profile information that reduces the time taken for registering patients for their appointment.

Feature enhancements can often deliver a moderate amount of impact with not much effort, an example of which is voice-enablement of applications that can improve caregiver efficiency.

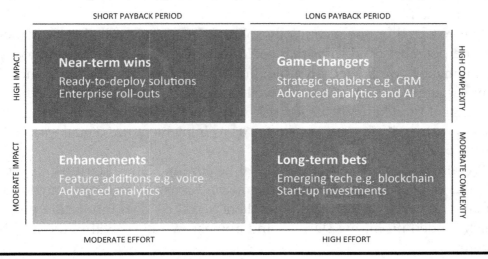

Figure 3.1   Digital innovation prioritization matrix.

Game-changers and long-term bets are typically complex initiatives that require a high upfront investment (e.g., CRM) or have long and uncertain payback, such as emerging technologies or innovative startup solutions.

Once the prioritization matrix is filled out, we quickly did an inventory of "digital" innovation currently in progress within the health system. We found that the health system did have a range of digital innovation programs underway in siloed departmental initiatives. Besides, at an enterprise level, there were many "native" capabilities such as data analytics, systems integration and mobile application development that could be leveraged across the enterprise.

Last, but not the least, the core EMR platform had a range of features and functionalities that we could tap into for many of the use cases.

Partnerships: Custodians, Enablers, Arbitrageurs, or Innovators?

Once the digital innovation roadmap had been established, the big challenge was how to execute such a large-scale digital transformation program with agility and speed.

While the EMR systems were considered foundational for clinical work-flow management, it was clear early on that the health system had to seek out new strategic partners with technology platforms and digital health solutions with superior user interfaces and intuitive experiences to execute on the digital innovation vision. We were tasked with identifying and evaluating potential partners. However, we had to it with the same agility, urgency, and speed with which we wanted to execute on the innovation program itself.

Our research on the technology solutions marketplace had already identified the potential candidates that could meet the client's needs. By process of elimination, we landed on a handful of potential partners which includes some large global tech brands as well as smaller, privately held and venture-capital funded entities. Our task was simple: find out what they have, what is real, and what it will take for us to implement the digital innovation roadmap.

We also looked closely at the digital health innovation startup ecosystem for potential candidates to address some of the use cases, especially for the patient and caregiver journeys. Our client had their own innovation program which funded promising startups and homegrown ideas within the health system.

Figure 3.2 shows the framework we used to analyze the technology vendor landscape.

The *Custodians* were the big EMR vendors who had the data and the workflow. In our client's case, this was Epic, a leading EMR vendor. While they were the foundational system of record, they were also making significant enhancements to their platform, especially with the MyChart™ feature for patient communications and engagement. There was broad agreement that the user interfaces for the Epic platform were not best-in-class and that patient-facing applications had to have a whole different level of design built in for increasing engagement. Despite the shortcomings, the consensus was that Epic would be the choice for any use case for which the platform had an available solution or was going to release one in the next 12 months.

We spent most of our effort evaluating the *Enablers.* These were big technology firms such as IBM, Microsoft, and Google. All of them had invested in building Health Cloud platforms that were a collection of tightly integrated capabilities including cloud hosting, advanced analytics, HIPAA compliance and IT security. The innovators in our consideration set included HealthTap, a Silicon Valley startup that had built a digital health platform with slick interfaces that included many of the tools we envisioned for patients and caregivers.

We knew that none of the tools and platforms would work out-of-the-box, and we would have to engage the *Arbitrageurs* – technology consulting firms – eventually to augment internal resources and develop talent pools.

Our assessment of our technology partnership choices led us to some significant findings.

The custodians
We have the data
and the workflow

The enablers
We built it, you can
rent it

Healthcare
Enterprises

The innovators
We have a whole
new way of doing it

The arbitrageurs
We can do it for you
(and for less)

Figure 3.2   Healthcare IT provider landscape (copyright: Damo Consulting Inc.)

Digital health innovation has a "last mile" problem. Digital innovation ultimately is about reimagining the consumer's experience and enabling that with carefully designed end-user applications delivered seamlessly over mobile interfaces. The big technology firms, for their part, had chosen not to invest in "last mile" solutions. Instead, they were looking to clients and to the startup ecosystem to deploy their platforms and invest in the development work required for building the last mile experiences. We had to assume that the burden of development would fall on us, and furthermore, it would lock us irreversibly to a vendor platform which we were not ready for given the early stage of maturity of the entire digital health innovation ecosystem.

Innovative startups are exciting but risky. While the startup ecosystem was mushrooming with dozens, if not hundreds, of little companies each solving for a specific problem, no company had built out a viable suite of solutions that had been deployed successfully at a major health system. Many startups were in the pilot stage with their early clients and were in a race against time to grow their footprint and revenues before running out of capital. For us, leveraging the startup ecosystem could limit our ability to scale due to the investment and effort in customization and integration for each solution, and deal with contracting and vendor management for a large number of small entities which was unappealing. The biggest challenge for stand-alone startups was that they seldom had robust integration capabilities with EMR platforms. That, and the ongoing challenges of interoperability in healthcare IT meant that we could justify bringing on a startup solution only if their solution was truly unique and innovative.

Technical debt would get in the way of implementing many of the digital innovation platforms. Technical debt refers to the accumulation of underinvestment and short-term fixes that eventually limit an enterprise's ability to grow. As with many health systems, we had been underfunding information technology for an extended period, and we were playing catch-up so that we could have a technology foundation that would enable us to position the enterprise for the future. Our digital innovation roadmap could not be implemented without some essential elements in place: robust IT security, upgraded LAN/WAN infrastructure, cloud enablement, and unified communications to name a few. We were also looking at a significant investment in upgrading our EMR platform and implementing a new ERP system to improve our transaction processing systems, which were the lifeblood of the organization. We had to carefully sequence the implementation of our digital innovation roadmap to keep moving the enterprise forward without getting ahead of ourselves.

Paying for Digital Health Innovation: The Law of Small Numbers

Our internal survey at the beginning of the innovation roadmap development indicated that the top challenges for digital transformation were expected to be funding and technology, followed by culture change and training. As mentioned in the previous section, there was a significant amount of technical debt and the price tag attached to these investments ran into hundreds of millions of dollars for the enterprise. Our original intent was to secure funding commitment from the Board of Directors for the digital innovation program that would allow us to work with an annual budget that we could deploy in implementing the roadmap in a carefully planned and phased manner. As part of the plan, there would be some "game-changing" investments that would lay the digital innovation platform foundation. We anticipated that these upfront investments would enable us to rapidly develop and deploy a wide range of solutions at scale.

While health systems are no strangers to substantial IT investments (considering the tens and hundreds of millions spent over the past decade on just implementing EMR systems), the crucial difference when it comes to digital health investments was that EMR systems were paid for through federally funded Meaningful Use incentives, but there was no such incentive for digital health innovation. For us, this meant that digital health innovation programs had to meet stringent financial criteria to obtain funding approvals, and also compete with other IT and non-IT enterprise priorities for a slice of the funding pie. Many digital innovation programs thus end up starting with a very focused issue and demonstrate tangible returns before qualifying for additional investments – what I refer to as the law of small numbers. An example of this in action is at Providence St Joseph Medical system, where a focus on online scheduling has delivered savings of $3 to $4 per appointment booked, producing over $300,000 in total savings to the health system. The additional insight here was that since labor is typically around 60% of a hospital's costs, any digital innovation solution that has a labor substitution component and increases productivity is appealing for health system executives.

The Solution – For Now

At the time of writing, we were continuing to grapple with the variables and how to optimize for them in our quest to develop and implement a robust digital innovation roadmap. We had a good handle on the moving parts: the digital innovation priorities, the technology solutions landscape, internal capabilities and funding considerations. We had a pretty good idea of what we could do internally, what our current partner ecosystem could do for us, and who our future partners could be. We also realized one very important thing: there is no template out there for a digital innovation roadmap, especially for something as comprehensive in scope and scale as what we were developing. The market was in the early stages of maturity, and each health system had to develop its roadmap based on its own unique set of priorities and challenges. However, build it we must, and build it by leaning on our capabilities and the experience and expertise of our peers and partners. Our healthcare economy will be better for it, and so will the millions of caregivers and consumers who rely on an improved health care system for themselves and future generations.

References

AHA.org. (2017, September 20). American Hospital Association and AVIA Issue Findings from Survey on Health Care Digital Innovation. Retrieved from American Hospital Association: https://www.aha.org/press-releases/2017-09-20-american-hospital-association-and-avia-issue-findings-survey-health-care

AHA.org. (2018, April 12). Fact Sheet: Telehealth. Retrieved from American Health Association: https://www.aha.org/factsheet/2018-04-12-fact-sheet-telehealth

Arndt, R. Z. (2018, July 7). Health Systems Save Money Using Digital Tools for Scheduling Appointments, Administrative Work. Retrieved from Modern Healthcare: http://www.modernhealthcare.com/article/20180707/TRANSFORMATION02/180709982/health-systems-save-money-using-digital-tools-for-scheduling?utm_campaign=socialflow&utm_medium=social&utm_source=twitter

Beaton, T. (2017, April 28). 71% of Healthcare Providers Use Telehealth, Telemedicine Tools. Retrieved from mHealth Intelligence: https://mhealthintelligence.com/news/71-of-healthcare-providers-use-telehealth-telemedicine-tools

Ameya Kulkarni, M. (2018, July 11). *The Future of Medicine*: Remote Patient Monitoring. Retrieved from KPproud Mid-Atlantic States: https://kpproud-midatlantic.kaiserpermanente.org/future-medicine-remote-patient-monitoring/

Padmanabhan, P. (2017). *The Big Unlock*. Archway Publishing. Retrieved from https://thebigunlock.com/

Padmanabhan, P. (2018, May 18). Digital Health's Last Mile Problem. Retrieved from CIO.com: https://www.cio.com/article/3274446/health-care-industry/digital-health-s-last-mile-problem.html

Padmanabhan, P. (2018, July 25). Digital Transformation and the Law of Small Numbers. Retrieved from CIO.com: https://www.cio.com/article/3293056/ehr/digital-transformation-and-the-law-of-small-numbers.html

Padmanabhan, P. (2018, August 15). What My Backyard Squirrel Taught Me About Technical Debt. Retrieved from CIO.com: https://www.cio.com/article/3297743/health-care-industry/what-my-backyard-squirrel-taught-me-about-technical-debt.html

Zweig, M. Shen, J., and Jug, L. (2017). Healthcare Consumers in a Digital Transition. Retrieved from Rock Health: https://rockhealth.com/reports/healthcare-consumers-in-a-digital-transition/

Innovation and Governance

Kristin Myers

As an Academic Medical Center that is part of a large integrated health delivery system in New York City, Mount Sinai Health System has a strong history of innovation, whether it is in our research teams, our physicians, our venture partner's team, our commercialization team, the Institute for Precision Medicine, the data science teams or within our own technology department. At times the challenge can be how do we understand what all of our departments have developed that is innovative as pilots and how do we operationalize and scale this into the workflows for our caregivers and patients across the entire health system to ensure the experience is simple and seamless.

As Senior Vice President overseeing the Application strategy and portfolio, I am honored to work with some of the most creative and bright people in health care and my team's objective is to work with our business partners to support innovation and provide governance to ensure that we are all working with the consumer experience at the heart of our initiatives whether this be our caregivers or our patients.

Governance is not a word typically associated with innovation, however without it, pilots in digital health and other innovations can remain in that state as large enterprise rollouts of major functions such as ERP, Revenue Cycle or Electronic Medical Records take precedence. My objective is to provide governance to support innovation by providing the resources and infrastructure to scale the pilots to health system solutions. I will provide a number of examples of the journey in the last two years to understand the application portfolio and develop roadmaps in relation to the functional strategy, how digital health can be exploited as part of an enterprise strategy, how the technology department can partner with the business to explore new innovative models and how governance ultimately can support, operationalize and scale innovative solutions.

Application Portfolio and Strategy

How successfully adopted an innovative solution is depends on a number of factors: usability, efficiency, ease-of-use and the ability for a particular problem to be solved. It is also dependent on workflow. Can the innovation be embedded into an existing workflow without creating duplicate documentation for our caregivers or asking them to go into a secondary application? Does the innovation create or disrupt a seamless patient experience? Unfortunately, the number of digital health applications or innovations that are developed only address some of the success factors. Others completely fragment a user experience which can be frustrating and ultimately lead to a lack of adoption.

Understanding the overall application strategy which provides a roadmap and direction for each major clinical and business function is critical. In many of the major functional areas there are enterprise systems that dominate the application strategy such as in the EMR/Revenue Cycle functional areas or in ERP; however, there are major gaps in functionality for these enterprise systems that need to be addressed to improve workflows and operational efficiency. The ability to recognize those gaps, understand from the enterprise vendor if this is on their development roadmap in the next 1–5 years and then innovate, or find third-party applications that can be integrated into the workflow if this is not on the imminent development roadmap, is how innovation can be scaled across the health system.

It has taken a large effort to understand the application inventory, develop the functional roadmaps and develop the application strategies that have been vetted and reviewed by the clinical and operational stakeholders. It has provided a level of transparency and clarity around future direction of investments, highlighted gaps that are being focused on from an innovation perspective and the ability to evolve pilots to full-scale implementations at the health-system level.

The key to this alignment has been governance to ensure there is an understanding between all application and digital health teams on future direction and that there is clear visibility into new digital health trends and business requests. The drivers for this were that applications were being piloted or implemented that were not in alignment with the overall enterprise application strategy, there was minimal visibility into business needs and requests for digital health capabilities and there was a lack of understanding of how the digital health trends could impact existing applications.

The objectives were to improve transparency, provide a consistent strategy to all aspects of the business (with the business helping to define the strategy), ensure that there is a minimization of the duplication of efforts for similar digital health needs in different groups and departments and allow early planning and forecasting of investments, resources and support needed to scale pilots across the health system if the pilot is successful.

Telehealth Case Study

The last few years of telehealth experimentation are a good example of how piloting with a number of partners while learning about how this can be scaled for success is how the innovation pipeline works in our health system.

We have many entrepreneurial physicians that work in our health system and a few years ago, before there was commercial reimbursement for telehealth, we surveyed that we had over 20 telehealth solutions across the health system, many of them were low cost or even free that were being used for specialty consults or direct to patients for care. This led to governance across the health system with a business sponsor being supported by the technology team, being appointed to review and vet the technology and the experiences of the physicians and to identify organizational and regulatory barriers to successful telehealth. Over the next few years, some of these technology companies went out of business, the regulatory/reimbursement models changed and ultimately what we found was successful as a pilot was telehealth that was completely integrated within the clinical workflow of the electronic medical record that we are using for physician-to-patient interactions. Once this was finalized, capital funding was approved for telehealth in this model to be implemented health system wide which is currently in progress.

Robotic Process Automation

Another example of piloting innovative technology with the business and then incorporating it as a solution within the technology department is Robotic Process Automation (RPA), which is the use of technology to automate the human element of repetitive and procedure-driven activities. Our enterprise architect had identified RPA as an area that should be explored to automate work in accounts payable, supply chain and after discussion with operations in ambulatory care, identified a potential pilot for the automation of the current manual process performed by Patient Coordinators for loading New Patient Packet data that is received through emails. The opportunity was to reduce the amount of time for the patient coordinator to collect data and manually loading it into the application, improve data loading accuracy and reduce errors. The pilot has been successful and other use cases are being identified with the business. As a result of the pilot success, the applications teams within technology started exploring whether application configuration work could be automated similarly using RPA. Using one application as a pilot, we were able to reduce the manual work on provisioning new users by 90%. Part of the lessons learned regarding both pilots was that the tool chosen for RPA is important as a tool with low accuracy will require human intervention to correct inaccurate data which can add time and cost to the process and detract from the ROI and benefit identified in the business case and cost reduction as part of the business case needs to understood completely as some processes cannot be automated to the fullest potential.

Based on the above learnings, we are now developing roadmaps for full-scale implementation across the application portfolio for our team members to be working on optimization and value-based projects for the business instead of manual, labor and time intensive tasks. This is an example of innovation that was piloted in the business and was applied within the technology department.

Data Science Partnership

Innovation in data science is embedded in our clinical operations team and genomics team which are co-located together to ensure synergy. Members of the technology team that work on these projects will also be collocated with the data science team to increase the collaboration and partnership. Data scientists have been recruited to develop data models in sepsis and other clinical conditions to be able to develop predictive tools embedded into our EMR platform so we can deliver advisories and alerts at the point-of-care for our physicians. Our EMR vendor has a number of predictive models they have developed also, however rather than only using the data models that the Mount Sinai data scientists develop or the vendors' models, we set up governance and an approach that is complementary. We have an approach where requests for models are reviewed against the vendor's models and roadmap, prioritized and resourced from both the data scientists and technology team's perspective. This is an example of collaboration and partnership between the business and technology teams that support innovation and where there is a health system strategy and alignment.

Patient Experience – Access to Care

Healthcare delivery strategy is moving toward a consumer journey which is interlinked with digital strategy and it starts with patient access. There can be systemic barriers that exist at the people, process and system levels of any organization, preventing patients from connection with providers that meets their needs. Creating a seamless patient journey experience which connect, inform, coordinate and communicate referrals from outside the hospital with a transfer center, transparency to patients with regard to future bills, having a single access center for entry for new appointments and future scheduling are key. Patient Access also extends to how organizations connect, engage, serve and ultimately retain patients throughout their journey. Brand competition is increasing and the ability to attract and retain patients is becoming increasingly difficult.

The patient access strategy is complicated by the fact that a hospital or health system's current operational structure and decision making, may involve many stakeholders that are used to making decisions for their departments, rather than taking the enterprise view which complicates strategy, solution design and decision making. The technology team is integral to the strategy; however need to focus on the workflows, process and the problem that needs to be solved first, before defining technology solutions.

This initiative is a priority in our organization and with the hiring of a Vice President of Consumer/Digital that is part of the business operations team, our objective is to partner and support the innovation that is required to support patient access. Bringing talent and experiences in from outside of the provider space is critical for the healthcare industry to evolve. Many other industries such as the payers, travel, retail and the aerospace industry have been through this disruption before and learning from these experiences is key.

The process of understanding current consumer experience based on patient studies and interviews, persona creations, current state patient journey mapping, visioning to define the future state patient experience and then rapidly prototyping with usability testing to get feedback from our patients has not been traditionally work that technology departments in the provider space have been leading or been involved in. However, these are skills along with design thinking that have to be developed as a competency for the technology departments to be able to truly collaborate with the business and support the innovation.

The understanding of our patient population and how they engage with us or do not engage is how we can innovate to serve their needs. Understanding how diverse our population is and why patient portal sign-up hasn't exceeded 30% of our patient population due to the challenges of secure messaging in another language in our patient portal or why the mobile version of the portal does not mirror all the functions of the desktop version when many of our patients do not have internet access but have a smartphone is just the beginning of our journey of innovation in this arena.

The ability of the technology team to expose the data in the enterprise applications using an API framework supports the innovation of the products that will be developed for our patients. Partnering, collaborating and supporting the innovation for patient access is an exciting time and many of our most talented team members in the technology department will work together as part of a joint team with the business to make this successful.

Conclusion

Technology professionals providing support and partnering with the business on innovation need to focus on developing human-centric skills to effectively serve and collaborate in this environment. Skills such as conflict management, cross-functional collaboration, decision making, customer service, teamwork and emotional intelligence are becoming essential skills for those who want careers in technology. A continuous learning mindset to address current and future workplace skillsets, the ability to understand business terms of contracts and oversee managed service agreements and work with applications that are in the cloud will be key differentiators for the future. The ability to apply learnings from outside of healthcare such as aerospace or the retail industry will also be important.

Technology departments risk being regarded as legacy organizations if they do not partner and support the business and clinical operations. We live in a "VUCA" world where there is volatility, uncertainty, complexity and ambiguity. Technology departments need to respond with vision, understanding, clarity and agility by sensing opportunity and responding with action, integrating risk and focusing on simplification. The risk of not being innovative or supporting innovation with our business partners leads to missed opportunities, pilots that do not get scaled to health system wide solutions and low motivation for the technology teams which leads to a loss of talent.

Roadmaps

Bill Russell

> The single biggest problem in communication is the illusion that it has taken place.

> **–George Bernard Shaw**

A story has main characters, a plot, a villain and a resolution to a challenge that the characters must overcome. The development of innovation roadmaps tells a story of a potential future and how a system might organize to get there but it's not the whole story. We tell incomplete stories and in so doing we fail to identify the right challenge and to connect with the very people that are the main characters in the story. In short, we fail to inspire action.

In the fall of 2010 I began work on a 5-year plan to turn around a struggling IT shop for a 16-hospital system as their CIO. We did all the expected activities. We did a listening tour, conducted surveys even organized collaborative sessions to dream about the future and consider the various paths to get to the place that would meet our mission while staying true to our values. We explored the potential of technology and the role and relevance of the IT organization. We believed that a compelling narrative was needed to capture the urgency and potential of technology to address the particular needs of healthcare at this particular moment in time.

We developed a roadmap for transformational change that we believed as an organization was necessary to be prepared for an uncertain future. This roadmap was defined by two core initiatives: a move to the cloud and a data-driven strategy. The move to the cloud represented our belief that a new level of agility was going to be required in healthcare to be relevant in a rapidly changing landscape. Given what is happening in 2018 with new partnerships and business models being introduced almost weekly, that assumption seems to have been correct. A data-driven strategy was recognizing that data is one of the most important assets a company has in the digital world and we believed that healthcare was in the midst of a digital revolution. Data would be the fuel that drove the triple aim in a digital economy. Now we needed a way to communicate the strategy to the stakeholders.

My leadership team did what most would do at this point and we developed a PowerPoint deck and we started presenting our collaboratively developed vision of the future. It is widely recognized today that while PowerPoint may be a good tool it promotes walls of text and bulleted lists which become one of the worst forms of communication. When we were done creating the deck we presented it to a few groups and realized it was uninspiring and didn't motivate action. The message didn't connect with people on an emotional level. If people are expected to act on something they have to know and feel certain things before they will invest emotionally.

We stepped back and retooled our communication, but what follows is more about the mistakes we made and what I've learned since then. For those of us challenged with building a culture of innovation what follows are some lessons for how you can take the elements of your roadmap, organization strategy and technology plan and weave them into something that can motivate people to action.

I would be remiss if I didn't mention that professional story tellers and designers are your friend. If it weren't for Andy Parham, Paul Bussmann, and Jim Fisher and our design sessions I would never have been able to tell our story.

People Think in Pictures

When I say "Red Ferrari" you immediately picture a red sports car, you don't think about the letters "R" "E" "D" that make up the word. Our brains are hard wired to translate words to pictures.

We had several slides which described the challenges that our health system faced in 2010. Every time we started with these slides we noticed that people would reach for their phones to check their email. Spending too much time telling people what they already know is a hallmark of poor communication. We finally enlisted a team of creatives to help us with the process. The result was a single picture that described the state of our system.

In Jonathan Swift's book Gulliver's Travels, Gulliver the giant is tied down by a thousand tiny ropes by the people of Lilliput. The graphic designer told us that as we described the challenges facing healthcare he couldn't help but see this image in his head. The next time we presented we had one slide, a graphic with the image of Gulliver tied down by Lilliputians and no words on the slide. We talked about how healthcare was held back by 1,000 tiny ropes, payment models, culture, interoperability, application sprawl, communication and other factors. We talked about how it wasn't any one problem that held us back but many that work in conjunction to hold us back from being what we could be as a system. And no one reached for their phone.

A Good Narrative Invites People to Step Into the Story as the Hero

We tend to tell the story in a way that doesn't allow people to enter the story. We tell the story where we are the hero, the system is the hero and sometimes even the vendor is the hero. Ask yourself if this resonates. We are buying this new EHR which is going to improve quality, reduce friction and increase efficiency. No one would do this today, but we were reading these stories weekly 10 years ago. The EHR is the hero of this story. It's no wonder it suffers a reputation problem. The EHR stole the lead role in the story from the very people we know to be the heroes of the healthcare story.

How about this well-intentioned narrative: our founders came to this community with nothing but their grit and desire to serve and we stand on the shoulders of their great work. This is the start of a great narrative as we will discuss later, but it needs to invite people into the story. Your founders would want the current generation to put on a cape and solve the greatest challenges of today. I'm not advocating for a rise of individual heroes in healthcare. In fact, our success has been found when we act more like NASA as a group with a shared commitment to a common mission than as comic book heroes. However, even when we lead with our heritage we need to invite people to enter into the story and write the next chapter.

People want to be the hero of their own story. The system, vendor and technology are resources to help them overcome a great challenge. There are many examples of this, but the best one happened on May 25th, 1961. President John F. Kennedy made this declaration before a joint session of Congress:

> *"I believe that this nation should commit itself to achieving the goal, before this decade is out, of landing a man on the moon and returning him safely to the Earth."*

Notice that this was not a call specifically to NASA, it was a call to the whole nation. Everyone was invited to consider how they might be a part of the mission.

Every Story Needs a Villain That Needs to be Vanquished

President Kennedy presented this message in the context of good and evil. To open this section of the speech he framed this work as part of a war between freedom and tyranny. Tyranny and oppression are good villains to the average person. We all know that a common enemy is a powerful unifying force. In this case no one wanted to live under a dictatorship that was represented by communism during this time period. An important step for every organization is to identify the villain in your story.

There are many villains in healthcare in general. The obvious ones are the chronic diseases that threaten the lives of people in our community. In this battle the heroes wear white coats and wage a war on behalf of the patient. The other villains that have been elevated in our national debate and communicated through the quadruple aim are access, cost, quality and experience.

Intermountain Healthcare CEO Marc Harrison, M.D. addressed the villain of healthcare inequalities based on zip code in his comments at the 2018 JP Morgan conference. It has been written about many times that zip code, education and financial standing are more highly correlated to your health outcomes than genetic disposition to disease. Intermountain identified one of these zip codes and is partnering with Medicaid in Utah to take on a risk model that puts them on the hook for improving care in that geography. Health outcome inequalities is a good villain.

Deborah Proctor retired CEO of St. Joseph Health and Rod Hochman, M.D. the CEO of Providence cited a growing concern for mental health and the need for whole person care in the communities they serve on the west coast as one of the driving factors for their merger in 2016. They helped to fund the Well Being Trust in 2016 with an initial investment of $100 million to address mental health shortly following the merger. The previously glossed over problem of mental health in our communities is a good villain.

The role of leadership is to identify the right villains.

Aspirations are Good, Calls to Action Are Better

Our aim is to provide the highest quality care to everyone in our community where both the patient and caregiver have a great experience at an affordable cost. This is a solid aspiration and it helps to frame our activities but it doesn't inspire and motivate to action. A more effective call to action will invite people to step in as the hero of the story, clearly identify the villain that needs to be overcome. Let's examine some calls to action from healthcare leaders.

"Eliminate the waiting room and everything it represents."

David Feinberg, M.D. CEO

Geisinger Health

Dr. Feinberg goes on to explain, "A waiting room means we're provider-centered – it means the doctor is the most important person and everyone is on their time. We build up inventory for that doctor – that is, the patients sitting in the waiting room." The villain in this story is the poor experience that healthcare provides to patients and their family. The symbol of that poor experience is the waiting room. The call to action invites staff to present work and budgets that eliminate every waiting room. Speaking on behalf of all patients, I hope they are successful.

"The future is healthcare with no address, where the patient is in charge."

Stephen Klasko, M.D. CEO

Jefferson Health

This statement is more nuanced. The villain here is the limitations of the healthcare status quo. A health system that requires physical locations will be expensive and deliver a poor experience. This may also represent a culture that is unwilling to be progressive in its adoption of tele-strategies and the use of sensors for remote care. The call to action is to redesign healthcare to be a customer facing organization and not a business-to-business transaction with the payer. Doctor Klasko's call to action invites the healthcare industry as a whole to vanquish the status quo and embrace new methods.

A good call to action, such as Dr. Feinberg's and Klasko's, paints a picture of a potential future. A hospital system without waiting rooms and a health system delivering care that isn't defined by its zip code. People see in pictures. Paint a compelling future picture of what healthcare can be to activate your roadmap.

Use Video to Validate the Vision

I've been particularly impressed by systems that have started to utilize video to tell a story. Kaiser Permanente has cut several videos that imagine a future. One example (https://youtu.be/NZm5gJikhgE) paints the picture of their care anywhere vision. One needs only to watch the video to imagine their place in making the vision a reality. The power of using video to communicate is self-evident: however, the value of the video is far greater than the $20K–$40k investment to create it. You can determine the level of alignment with a broad audience including the medical staff and the community at large. The video acts as a tollgate in validating the vision with your constituents.

There are many examples of the use of video to imagine the future. There are two more that I will highlight, one is technology related and the other was designed to impact the culture. United Healthcare (https://youtu.be/gEybaotgZgc) paints a picture of a future where sensors and technology keep you connected with a trusted care partner. The Cleveland Clinic's empathy video (https://youtu.be/pIGzPsfnpoc) is a powerful message on the role of empathy. A gentle reminder to be present, attentive and compassionate. Once you clearly see a possible future, investing in a video that helps people to see it clearly is money well spent.

Finally, Connect Your Story to the Previous Chapters in the Book

The Sisters of Saint Joseph went into a town that needed education and healthcare with the intent of starting schools. A flu outbreak led them to meet the needs of the community that were most acute, and they started in healthcare. This lesson on its own is powerful, but the story doesn't end there. Some years later the Sisters were the first health system in the region to utilize automobiles in the delivery of care. The automobile is the blockchain of its day. It's a compelling technology that everyone believed had an application for healthcare, but it needs creative people to find the right fit.

The automobile was the connection with our past that we were looking for. Our Sisters were innovative, adventurous and not afraid to try new things. We dedicated one slide to a black and white picture of our innovative Sisters standing next to their ambulance. The result was an unmistakable connection between our desire to utilize the technology of the day to serve the needs of the communities we operate in.

We tend to write a story as if it started with us. The reality is that most health systems have great formation stories. Connect the storylines.

We joke that every movie on the Hallmark channel has the same plotline with different characters, yet if I walk past a screen with one of their movies playing I stop and watch. I try to identify who the characters are, who the villain is and the challenge that they must overcome to find love at the end of the movie. The existence of the Hallmark channel should teach us that there are certain storylines that work no matter how many times you use them. Hero meets challenge that is usually protected by a villain, a guide comes along to help them get past their personal limitations and overcome the challenge which leads to a better future. I know how every Hallmark story is going to end but the predictable nature doesn't detract from my interest, it enhances it.

If you consider yourself to be an innovative person with a technology bent, I wrote this chapter for you. This is my background and bent. What I learned in our process is that you have to invite people on the journey. People have to know their role and the challenge has to be something that resonates with their being. Storytelling is the next step in taking your roadmaps, PowerPoints and project plans and stirring people to action. The more compelling your story, the more motivated people will be.

References

Miller, D., 2017. *Building a Storybrand: Clarify Your Message So Customers Will Listen*. HarperCollins Leadership, an Imprint Of Harpercollins.

Digital Health Transformation: Building Roadmaps from Emerging Patterns and Practices

John Guardado, Chris Regan, John Doyle, Tom Lawry

Innovation from Information Technology can make organizations stronger, faster, more available, more connected, more scalable, more informed and even smarter. Leveraging IT enabled innovation within healthcare has virtually limitless potential, only constrained by the team's visions of how and where to use these evolving portfolios of tools. However, capturing these potentials can be elusive.

When establishing Digital Health Transformation Strategies and Roadmaps it is essential to innovate with a purpose and create predictable, repeatable processes that keep the noise and disruption of the development process to a minimum and the security, quality and confidence of the final solutions at the level needed within the health provider space.

Digital Health Strategies and Roadmaps provide organizations frameworks for innovation, but they must be flexible and learn from the successes and challenges of others. What emerges are patterns of success for capturing some of the potential.

3 Ways Technology Is Delivering on the Promise of Healthcare Transformation

With populations on the rise and resources increasingly strained, health organizations are continually looking to enhance the patient experience and improve outcomes while also driving efficiency. According to the World Economic Forum, the global population will jump from 7.6 billion to 9.7 billion by 2050, and the number of people over age 60 will reach roughly two billion.

To meet the demands of this aging population, the global health system will have to transform. Improving care quality in an era where clinicians and budgets are already spread thin will require providers to implement innovative digital technologies that support multiple goals simultaneously.

While digital approaches are no quick fix, there are multiple scenarios where organizations have an opportunity to achieve gains in patient experience, outcomes and efficiency. Let's take a look at three emerging healthcare application patterns being adopted by providers seeking to harness innovation by creating intelligent feedback loops, infusing AI into clinical workflows and developing interactive health agents.

Connecting with Patients

Personalizing Care and Improving Outcomes with a Greater Understanding of Each Patient

The acute care healthcare delivery model often puts providers in a reactive position when helping patients manage chronic conditions, such as epilepsy. For instance, epileptic patients may visit physicians only sporadically when their condition worsens. As a result, doctors are forced to rely on patient self-reporting and isolated encounters, limiting their ability to optimize treatment plans and prevent conditions from deteriorating. This is an expensive and frustrating model for both patients and providers.

Thanks to a combination of apps, medical devices and sensors, providers can transition from a reactive to a proactive model. By providing ongoing visibility into a patient's status, this digital approach gives providers the comprehensive, consistent insight needed to deliver better outcomes and patient experiences.

For example, at Poole Hospital National Health Service (NHS) Foundation Trust in the United Kingdom, providers have transformed epilepsy treatment with a mobile health app and wearables that enable an intelligent feedback loop – providing real-time insight to the patient and delivering status information in a continuous loop to care teams so they can monitor and take action. Patients wear an activity tracker connected to a mobile app that records data such as sleep patterns, exercise, heart rate and body temperature. These data elements are combined with information regarding the patient's diet, social activity, medications and seizures.

With this ongoing picture, care teams get a better understanding of each patient, enabling them to adjust medications or tailor treatment plans. Over time, this solution has the potential to expand – for instance, by identifying when a seizure is about to occur via pattern recognition and warning patients and their support network before it happens.

Creating intelligent feedback loops supports personalized care, leading to more effective treatments and better patient outcomes. Simultaneously, feedback loops have the potential to lower costs by enabling care teams to keep patients healthier instead of treating them only after problems get worse.

Enabling Faster Diagnoses and Freeing Up Clinician Time through Patient Self-Service

In the typical acute care model, patients go to a hospital or outpatient clinic at the onset of symptoms. They may not know how to describe their symptoms or may forget something that would help clinicians understand their condition fully, yet doctors must triage each patient accordingly. Leveraging interactive health agents combined with validated clinical content could create a more self-service method for patients to triage their symptoms, helping to direct the patient to the most appropriate point-of-care based on their condition.

By mapping patient-reported symptoms to validated clinical information and clinical coding standards, this technology would provide a foundation for the patient-provider consultation. In addition, because interactive health agents can connect to clinical knowledge bases and other machine learning tools, they can reduce the resource overhead involved in the triage process, helping to streamline care.

Interactive health agents have the potential to deliver an enhanced patient experience, as demonstrated by Health Navigator. Health Navigator works with eHealth, telemedicine and other healthcare organizations to deliver the highest quality evidence-based digital health content that improves patient care, promotes patient safety and enhances both the patient and provider experience.

AI-Infused Clinical Support

Detecting Deterioration Sooner by Making Disease Easier to Identify

In many cases, providers miss opportunities to spot deteriorating conditions because they don't have all the information at hand to make accurate diagnoses. This is especially true for conditions like diabetic retinopathy, where tiny clues to future blindness are challenging to discover in occasional specialist visits because the early signs are hard to detect. Using available retina scanners tied to a database, clinicians can detect and prevent disease before it starts. CoxHealth system in Missouri dramatically changed outcomes in their patient population in conjunction with their partner Intelligent Retinal Images Systems (IRIS). IRIS provides an end-to-end diagnostic solution for the early detection of disease, from patient identification to reimbursement and referral, by infusing artificial intelligence (AI) into the clinical workflow.

In the first six weeks of using IRIS, CoxHealth examined more than 1,000 patients and found almost 20% had diabetic retinopathy that would have otherwise been undetected. Within a few short months, more than 300 patients were diagnosed and received care for vision-threatening illnesses that may have progressed untreated.

Infusing AI seamlessly into the clinical workflow surfaces information to providers that could otherwise go unknown, enabling better diagnoses and treatment plans. Earlier interventions, such as those enabled by IRIS, also promise cost savings while improving patient experiences and outcomes.

Preventing Patient Deterioration with Early Warnings and Faster Intervention

In a busy hospital, providers often supervise a diverse range of patients at various stages of acuity. As a result, it can be difficult to know which patients need attention at any given moment and to prioritize care accordingly. By identifying and rating patterns in patient conditions and predicting an elevated risk of deterioration, AI helps providers intervene sooner, enabling them to avoid costly adverse events and adjust the patient's care path as needed, ultimately improving outcomes.

As we begin to realize the benefits of applying AI, there's evidence that this approach is saving lives.

Creating Actionable Insights

Predicting At-Risk Patients and Reducing Costs with Enhanced Chronic Disease Detection

As people live longer, chronic disease affects increasingly more patients worldwide. According to the Kaiser Family Foundation, chronic conditions account for nearly 75% of annual healthcare expenditure in the United States alone. Today's healthcare system is designed and optimized for episodic care instead of long-term delivery, making chronic disease management a priority issue that could rupture the entire system. When faced with such a big burden, it's easy to see how determining at-risk patients and enhancing preventative care represents a tremendous area of opportunity for AI. By predicting and lowering the need for acute care interventions for patients with chronic conditions, providers can decrease costs and minimize hospitalization.

Recently, data science leader and Microsoft partner KenSci partnered with the largest managed care provider in the United States to develop an award-winning platform to address cardiovascular diseases (CVDs). CVDs are the number one cause of death globally, representing approximately 31% of all deaths. KenSci applied machine learning to clinical data to identify patterns that indicated risk and provide predictive insights on care outcomes. Based on early results, the solution has been able to predict early onset of chronic heart failure and identify and stratify patients that may be at risk of readmission or need palliative services.

By helping providers detect and classify patients at risk for chronic conditions, physicians can tailor care plans based on a patient's unique risk factors, turning AI into a powerful tool for treating disease and driving down costs.

Decreasing Hospital Infection Rates and Establishing Best Practices with Actionable Insight

Another way artificial intelligence is lowering costs and improving patient outcomes is by reducing hospital infection rates. The World Health Organization estimates hospital infection rates range between 5–12% globally. The costs associated with these infections in Europe alone are approximately $7 billion euros and 37,000 lives lost annually. Through sophisticated analysis of infection data, AI solutions uncover factors associated with higher infection risk, creating opportunities for mitigation. On the other end of the spectrum, AI-driven analysis also reveals factors associated with lower infection risk – paving the way for organizations to establish best practices.

Hospitals using AI-driven analysis to reduce infection rates are already seeing tangible results. For example, Epimed Solutions, a market leader in clinical and epidemiological information management, recently partnered with Rede D'Or in Brazil to develop a new approach to infection management in their intensive care units (ICUs). Rede D'Or was using an aging, on-premises analytics solution that didn't offer real-time access to data. The new solution empowers clinicians to easily enter patient information at the point-of-care, which is then aggregated for near real-time access by the quality assurance office. With this data, they can generate reports that identify problems and compare quality indicators, enabling clinicians to intervene faster and reduce ICU infection rates.

Rede D'Or used this analysis to determine best practices in their top ICUs and implemented them throughout their network. As a result, hospital infection rates dropped 20%, mortality rates decreased and care quality improved.

By making data easier to capture through mobile methods and applying advanced analytics to determine patterns, organizations can identify areas for improvement and evangelize best practices that keep patients free from infection.

Improving Lives of People

Improving patient outcomes and driving efficiency doesn't mean putting more technology between patients and providers – it's about empowering the people that make healthcare work. Microsoft's approach is focused on enabling the healthcare industry's move to the cloud and helping them use technology to improve the lives of people around the world.

By building digital health strategies and roadmaps on the patterns of connected patients, AI-infused clinical workflows, intelligent feedback loops and interactive health agents, providers can start to develop the foundations for precision healthcare.

Chapter 4

Collaborate and Listen

Listen for ideas that will potentially solve a problem or present an opportunity to collaborate with stakeholders and galvanize your network.

Many innovations started by listening, observing and then communicating ideas and solutions to problems. When you listen, people are more likely to share ideas and provide encouragement. The more you engage others, the more ideas you are likely to catch. Great innovations are typically a result of multiple iterations by numerous individuals invited to participate in ideation and execution. Inviting others to share in your innovation will galvanize support and engagement necessary for success.

One is too small a number for innovation. Innovation is largely a result of a team of teams' approach to solving a problem or exploiting an opportunity. It can be an ego challenge to have a great innovation and allow others to modify and edit your dream. We can take innovation too personally and become captive to the potential and miss out on something greater. Leveraging others actually frees the innovation to grow and expand beyond what you initially envisioned. There is strength in seeking the wisdom of others.

Talk Less, Listen More, but Mentor Most of All

Helen Figge

Listen, learn and listen some more. Being able to articulate a position or vision and having it actually adopted and embraced is invaluable as we build upon the incorporation of technologies and solutions in healthcare. Having the ability to listen and use common terms and definitions for all to use in the workplace resonates best with the success of a project producing timely and valuable results for an organization. For a truly sustainable healthcare IT model, both technologies and the "people factor" will be forever paramount for current and future system successes and wide acceptance; yet without practical frontline input, along with positive coaching of all of the stakeholders and instructional and positive interactions with staff, the various innovations will be nothing more than add-on systems that risk an end result of adoption failure. This, in turn, only equates to more burdensome and cost-inefficient programs and investments that otherwise could have provided monies best spent elsewhere. Given that the practice of medicine changes daily based on new findings for cures and disease identification and even regression, healthcare and its technologies will always be in fast, forward-moving trajectories. However, one common denominator, the "people factor" that supports these nuances, will remain. Those using and implementing these technologies and/or healthcare nuances to better healthcare and its delivery will be the final determinants of either acceptance and adoption or rejection and continued barriers to needed change. Thus, an investment in the "people factor" will become the premier investment in the years to come in healthcare and healthcare IT – to ensure a sustainable healthcare system used for generations to come.

From a dyslexic hyper-insecure adolescent to a healthcare executive – winning several accolades along the way for career accomplishments was a journey that only I could imagine – and that is me. Moreover, as the world of healthcare is forever changing, embracing it and its nuances are the only solution – so embrace it! More than ever we see the healthcare industry adopting various technologies and their components to assist every stakeholder in the system, not only to document, comply and deliver healthcare to the end consumer – us – but also a potential means to an end in a potentially phenomenal career path for all to enter. Take me, for example, starting out as a pharmacy student in Boston, the lowest person on any pecking order in the healthcare arena, yet simultaneously acting as a sponge surrounded by brilliant individuals – some Nobel Laureates wanting to change the way medicine was practiced, delivered and experienced. So, I learned the "tricks of the trade" through watching, observing and doing many odd jobs no one wanted to do. I always struggled with school and reading and I had to take extra hours to read a chapter that otherwise should take someone less than an hour; I always needed a visual aid and could never see or think in the abstract. However, one thing was in my favor through all of these barriers – I was a great listener. I nodded my head a lot and I recall Dr. Eugene Braunwald (he wrote the book "The Heart," the bible for cardiac training) telling me while rounding to stop nodding because I looked like a turtle sticking his head out of his shell. I volunteered to do things others found too demeaning or too much work because the task would yield little reward, so many would say. Those "volunteer jobs" were actually my ticket out of mediocrity. I accomplished things others failed at just by sheer hard work and determination. Moreover, those odd jobs, whether it be compiling data or hands-on, roll-up-your-sleeves work cleaning test tubes for a Nobel Laureate – for free – created a path that today benefits me in my career. I suffered from dyslexia as a child, was a C student in college as I had to work two jobs to pay my bills to survive in Boston and often was too embarrassed to ask a question as I always felt I got the "rolled eyes" reaction. So instead, I learned the art of listening intently. I also spoke only if the words added to the current conversation at hand and worked hard at trying to stand out without being a jerk. If I was to be at work or someplace at 7 AM, I showed up at 6:30 AM and helped the former team end their shift a little quicker and with less hassle. I learned that if people genuinely "liked" you, they gave you a break when you really screwed up – which I did often. If a deadline was for a Friday, I presented the material on a Thursday. I spoke only when I presented the deliverables and only questioned or got redirects and never asked for extensions. I always felt the need to help others and always yearned for people to respect and like me. If someone did not like me or my work, I would go through excruciating lengths to figure out why. I feel people, if genuine, need to be liked and if the liking is not reciprocal then it is not your issue – move on. That attitude gave me the buzz of a person who never complained and delivered to others the materials they asked for way before the deadline. That is what I was known for. And with that, I was rewarded with friends that to this day, I can honestly say are not only my friends but colleagues from all walks of the professions.

I learned to self-educate myself with things that I needed in order to fulfill a job requirement and to be competitive in the workplace. I accumulated most of my degrees on weekends and nights in hotel rooms (if traveling for work) or when I put my kids to bed and was then able to grab a two-hour block to learn something that would help me be better and more confident in the workplace. I learned for me – to build my confidence because growing up I had none and most of the time was picked on for not being as smart or as fast as others. I also was never good at accepting criticism as I received so much of it as a child growing up in a tough neighborhood and suffering from dyslexia. My mom tried her best; my dad was a victim of post-traumatic stress from WWII and he never learned to read or write English very well. So, I overcame every obstacle – personal, social and professional – through acquiring an education.

Today, I take those lessons learned and apply them to the field of health-care and healthcare IT. If you are a hiring manager, you will never find the perfect candidate for any position, but you can find an individual that has skill sets that can be cultivated into a role that fits your desired qualifications for a position you seek to fill. I found my best hires were the "underdogs," those candidates who might not have been my first choice but because I provided them opportunity and were subsequently chosen for the position, their drive to prove they could do a job surpassed any and all expectations, as if they were born for the role.

So, you ask how do you get to this point in a person's career to real-ize the obvious might not be obvious? One word: "listen." Listening comes in many forms, not just the ears but listening to your environment. Listen to what are people asking. What are people questioning? Whom are they speaking about and why? Is there someone in your environment that wants to fit in but cannot because of the environment with which you breed? Listen to what is not being said as much as what is being said. Listen to the noise not the static. Listen to the audience "ask" then decide if the question is something you need to address or if they did not listen to you because of your messaging. Most importantly, NEVER listen to or abide by gossip or innuendos. Form your own opinions about people, places and things, not just the "hearsay" or stories of a person and what someone else's percep-tions are based on another's assessment. Form your own opinions by listen-ing to the pure data and circumstances, not how it is perceived or delivered to you by others. Remember, often times the guiltiest party in any circum-stance is the first one to get the story out. So, remember there are two sides to every story, and a true leader makes an assessment by hearing and listen-ing firsthand from all parties and stakeholders.

Another important point is being able to listen and be a good listener who is respected and appreciated by everybody. Important level-setters include listening to everyone regardless of title, age or position. Listening is an art, and in that, you can learn from so many individuals who are really good at one thing or another. Don't worry about where they are on the totem pole of title, age or position. We can all learn from each other. I learned my best PowerPoint skills from a secretary who did graphic ceramic artwork in her free time; I learned how to book travel from an engineer who developed an app to find the cheap rates because he was cheap at heart; I learned how to run a tight profit and loss from a communications director who had a limited travel budget; and I learned how to be a decent individual from my many bosses that I chose to work for regardless of pay or title. I always chose a job because of what it did for others, not how much I could make in the role. I learned to make my own coffee and carry it in a large travel mug in my trunk while on the road versus buying Starbuck's on the road; I traveled light and always had a bag in my car of emergency essentials – like granola bars and a bottle of water.

For healthcare to be sustainable, we all need to realize that there are different approaches to various problems and some are more orthodox than others. There is no easy "fix" but rather a compilation of several different pieces needing to work together to create a unified and streamlined approach to its delivery. New organizations coming into healthcare, like Apple, Uber, Amazon and others, will need to "listen" to the market, the various stakeholders and its own staff to figure out what is working – and what is not working and what has been done wrong that should not be replicated. We are seeing the world becoming boundary-lessly ripe with novel ideas that, if spoken previously, would have been heckled out of the conversation. No more. The art of "listening" will be paramount as we reshape healthcare and its destiny.

So how do you "learn" to be a good listener? Always set aside time to meet and greet people, places and things. You are never too busy to provide your time to others because if you love what you do, time never stands still. I suggest you also just stand quietly for a few seconds and survey your environment, whether it be in a meeting, in line for food or in the boardroom and just notice people, places and things around you; feel the energy around you and the inhabitants of the room as well. Energy and vibes play a big part in the "feelings" you will encounter when listening; seek out those sitting in corners and engage them; ask others their opinions; confidently look everyone in the eye when speaking; remove all disturbances like social media technologies; and most importantly thank everyone for their opinions. A good listener is genuine and honest and non-judgmental. Be that leader who is a good listener. It made me who I am today against all the odds that I never would get here.

I have a golden test I use in my career and life. It is called the "supermarket" test. Say you are walking down an aisle in a supermarket and you spot someone down the end of that aisle, and you hesitate to continue on your path down the aisle. If you cannot walk down the aisle and feel the need to avoid them, you have done something wrong. So, figure out what it is and go back and fix it. I always instruct my students and colleagues, let the hate and inability to look someone in the eye be on the other side of the fence, not on your side where you live.

Disruptive Innovation in Healthcare

Dr. Peter Tippett

The process of innovation is most simply defined as the "introduction of something new." We often think of the invention of the telephone, personal computer, Internet or other monumental achievements as the embodiment of innovation, but the reality is that innovation happens every day at varying scales and with varying impact.

Personal, Local, and Market-Scale Innovation

On a personal level, many people, especially those of us who like to "tinker," regularly innovate while solving problems for ourselves, our family or others facing a challenge, with a novel twist on something old or by leveraging an existing capability. We might substitute one mechanical part for another in order to create or repair something or use common software to create a purpose-built solution. In many cases, this might only yield "good enough" efforts for a single or limited use, but they are innovations nonetheless.

At a company, local government or on another limited scale, followers of a larger innovation may become the first early adopters, leveraging newly-established technologies or capabilities as-designed and contemplated by the technology. Some recent historical examples include adding online purchasing where it was not previously available or moving manufacturing or customer support offshore to deliver a competitive advantage. Extending newer technologies to adjacencies and/or use cases that they were not designed for, is the other most likely type of innovation at the local or medium scale.

The innovations we all know and love are those that happen at market-scale – in which an entire industry, economy or even the world is transformed because of wide-scale adoption. In the past few years, companies such as Apple, Amazon and Google have delivered this scale of innovation: creating the platforms and tools that are used by personal and local innovators so that they in turn may leverage the operating systems, web or online platforms to deliver on the next big idea. In healthcare, we have long expected that precision medicine, as well as the shift to electronic health records (EHRs) and making meaningful use of health information technology, would also be disruptive. But neither has yielded disruption yet.

How does market-scale innovation happen? First, let's sub-divide large-scale innovation into:

- **Driving** innovation is how established companies continue to evolve, grow and drive new business, typically into adjacent markets. One example is in the next generation of telecommunications, as with the deployment of 4G LTE as a major advancement in mobile digital bandwidth and capability.
- **Sculpting** innovation is how people or organizations use an existing strength to move into a newly-established space in which pricing and other business models are becoming understood and accepted and where the disruptive flux is settling down. An example includes Google, IBM and Microsoft moving into cloud computing after Amazon AWS and others established the concept and market.
- **Disruptive** innovation changes the entire way in which we do things, and also typically lowers entry barriers and price while changing delivery channels, market access and player relationships. Examples in healthcare include the century-old disruption brought by evidence-based care, antibiotics and the pharmaceutical revolution, sterile procedure and the surgical revolution, etc.

For the purpose of this chapter, let's focus on Market-Scale, Disruptive innovation in the healthcare industry, keeping in mind that true disruptors rarely derive from a single person but require the skills and culture of an entire organization to achieve market transformation. In my career(s), I have found that beyond inspired leadership, there are common attributes to organizations that are successful at delivering market-leading innovation, including:

- A passionate and deeply-ingrained vision
- Hiring for strength and diversity

- A culture of empowerment for all
- Both confidence AND doubt (with rewards for open-mindedness)
- Hyper-near-term delivery focus (while never losing sight of the long-game)
- A fanatical focus on and understanding of the customer
- Creating multi-dimensional customer delight
- Unrelenting drive for simplicity
- Willingness (and eagerness) to adapt as the market unfolds
- Solving the surround

Each of these deserves exploration and analysis, but of all of the traits needed to succeed, one of the least well understood and most powerfully real challenges in building a disruptor is in "solving the surround," or understanding and addressing what I like to call the "seven big problems."

Solving the Surround

To explain the concept of "solving the surround", let's consider the evolution of the music industry. The first disruption occurred somewhere in the Middle Ages when concert and opera halls combined with the development of the symphony, powered by new styles of city living. The concert hall model provided scale, reliable monetization and delivery mechanisms, along with a driver for new musical content. Artists and musicians were paid to create and perform and individuals had a reason and a simple way to consume.

The next disruption of the music industry occurred with the invention of the phonograph. This was combined with radio, which provided a second channel of delivery, as well as new opportunities for monetization via advertising revenue. Now music was delivered to people.

Subsequent music innovations, such as LP, Hi-Fi, Stereo, multi-track tape players and CDs were all examples of sculpting innovation. Each of them improved quality and extended the market into adjacent markets, but none of them changed the fundamental model.

The most recent disruption in music was achieved through the success of Apple's MP3 player, the iPod. The iPod did not win the market and drive disruption of the entire industry because it was from Apple or because of its great design, but because the company had also "solved the surround" – to identify and address what would be required for mass adoption and to support new delivery, distribution, monetization and consumption models.

Other well-funded companies, including Microsoft, Creative Labs and Philips, had MP3 players and excellent engineering, marketing and distribution, but never realized the same success. Apple had these capabilities, but also identified and attacked the "surround" problems, such as:

■ software needed to be available for the PC and Mac
■ users needed easy ways to use ("rip") their old CD collection
■ an online store needed to be created along with a
■ huge library to house a wide selection of music
■ without needing to purchase an entire album to acquire 1–2 favorite songs
■ addressing several different licensing issues
■ a way to synchronize and backup music across devices and more

In other words, Apple broke down most of these barriers at once as part of their "product" to enable broad adoption of their device and platform and deliver rapid revenue during a period of continued innovation and growth for the company. By taking this approach, Apple was the one to successfully disrupt the music industry.

But, disruption cannot happen in a vacuum. The market needs to be "ready" for disruption to be successful so that the old way of doing things is replaced by something new or is supplemented by a new model that is much larger than the old. In music, the success of the concert hall model didn't come solely from the building of symphony halls. It only worked because the new model of urban living was taking hold. And the iPod needed the Internet, online payment systems, ubiquitous home computing and much more. The success of the iPod wasn't the result of Apple building all of the things required for the market to be "ready." Instead, Apple identified the few additional "surround problems" that could be leveraged and accelerated for the otherwise-ready market to complete the puzzle and enable the disruptive market shift.

The Revolution that Missed Healthcare

To understand market readiness, let's step back and consider the path that healthcare has taken thus far. In many respects, healthcare IT never had its "PC revolution." We all use personal computers, but in healthcare enterprises, there has not been much individually driven business use to solve our common healthcare delivery problems. Consider what "personal" meant for the adoption of PCs in most other sectors:

When the PC was born, and long before the Internet, the CFO and the finance staff in many large organizations had projects waiting in the IT queue. Perhaps one was related to understanding different pricing models, another might have been related to planning the budget for the next year or maybe something around new expansion or an acquisition. Whatever they were, the finance staff was beholden to the IT staff to get the project planned, scoped, vetted, priced and staffed, then tested, trained and deployed.

Then came the PC. The CFO or an other finance leader went out and bought one. After a few days of trial and error, he/she realized that with the PC and some personal software and a few thousand dollars, they could do their own analysis of pricing models, budgets or expansion or acquisition analysis without any help from the IT staff. They simply bought PCs and software for their team and told IT to spend their energies on bigger problems. And the same scenario played out in law firms, engineering companies and other innovative groups seeking to improve how they got their jobs done. The spreadsheet and word processor were the "killer apps" of the PC era.

Together, the PC, Internet and mobile revolutions led to the biggest expansion of workforce productivity since WWII. Productivity in *nearly* all industries soared. The biggest exception was the healthcare sector, which did not participate in that productivity revolution – or at least did not realize anywhere near the same benefits as other sectors like finance or retail. Whereas the constant-dollar prices for product and services in most sectors leveled off or declined, the cost of healthcare continued its inexorable rise and health IT largely kept to the IT-centric model; EMRs and related software were planned centrally and driven out as a formal IT project.

Bringing Disruption to Health IT

In the 1990s, some doctors and other healthcare professionals began using PCs and dabbled in using them to help with clinical work. They were often worried about the privacy and security of these new technologies and especially about using email to share dictations and other medical patient information. At the same time, electronic communication of medical billing information within the payer sphere was beginning to evolve.

William (Bill) Braithwaite, MD, PhD, then Senior Advisor on Health Information Policy at the U.S. Department of Health and Human Services (HHS), recognized these problems and authored the Administrative

Simplification Subtitle of the Health Insurance Portability and Accountability Act of 1996 (HIPAA). He was not aiming to restrict data sharing, but to help enable it (remember the "P" stands for portability) by showing how to address the privacy and security problems. I was fortunate to sit on the President's Information Technology Advisory Committee (PITAC) with Bill, which closely coincided with the creation of the Office of the National Coordinator (ONC) at HHS. As part of that group's mission, I became invested in helping the healthcare industry achieve the "Triple Aim": Improving the patient experience of care (including quality and satisfaction); improving the health of populations; and reducing the per capita cost of healthcare.

Most of the PITAC members and I (and many, many others) thought that the physician and hospital markets "were ready" for both widespread adoption of EHRs and for widespread digital communication of both medical messages and electronic versions of medical records. We anticipated the future that EHRs would enable, and that doctors and everyone else would embrace EHRs just like the business and academic world had adopted word processors and spreadsheets. And we believed that records would be shared between and among care teams in larger health systems and smaller practices and include "ambulatory islands" like physical therapy groups, ophthalmologists and skilled nursing facilities. It appeared the adoption would mirror the way in which email and text were used by professionals in other industries.

Of course, HIPAA and PITAC begat ARRA, HITECH, Meaningful Use, MIPS/MACRA and more, which strongly incentivized the deployment of EHRs and the sharing of digital medical records. The drive for broad deployment of EHRs was effective, but the widespread sharing of digital medical records among caregivers in different organizations largely has not come to pass.

"Fast Forward" 20 Years

In late 2017, I had lunch with David Blumenthal, M.D., former National Coordinator for Health Information Technology, and current President of the Commonwealth Fund. We spent much of the time reflecting and discussing why modern digital communication and medical record sharing is still so abysmal in healthcare. He acknowledged lots of inhibitors but focused primarily on the competitive business issues between health systems, and also among health IT vendors.

After that lunch, I was inspired to write him a lengthy email with a list of potential inhibitors and later tried to distill our shared beliefs into a blog post that provides insight into some of the "surround problems" restraining healthcare data sharing:

> *Most people working in the healthcare system are interested in tools that help in getting their job done and in providing quality care. Therefore, most people relish easier digital medical communication. Most scientists, policy makers and regular citizens are Connectors [those seeking to ease data sharing also include independent physician practices, specialists, clinics and probably smaller hospitals]. And with the shift to quality and accountable care, along with incentives from payers and evolving regulations, even some of the Resistors [those organizations who fear the sharing of patient records conflicts with their broader business interests] are getting on the Connector band wagon. So why is the sharing of medical records and messages still so difficult? I see several primary drivers for this market "conflict":*

1. ***Market Competition*** *– One of the dominant early reasons for the lack of easy health data communications has been business resistance by large providers and health IT companies as a competitive maneuver. By seamlessly sharing digital patient records across town with competing facilities, the hospital potentially dis-incentivizes a patient from remaining within their own system. Similarly, the EMR vendor, seeking to become the dominant system in a region, benefits from volumes of patient data staying within their domain to prompt market demand and expansion to neighboring facilities.*
2. ***The Ubiquity Problem*** *– The value of any network to its users is a function of the number of users cubed. We wouldn't find phones or email addresses to be particularly useful if we couldn't reach the right people, because a communications network that does not include nearly all appropriate users isn't likely to succeed.*

   EMR adoption has generated exactly this type communication challenge because as an industry, we have created fairly closed user groups for each enterprise, when one of the largest values to clinicians, to patients, and to the market is in the secure flow of medical information where it is needed. Where we are now is like having computers before the internet. They were useful, but adding ubiquitous access and sharing brought by the internet (with proper privacy and security) led to multiple orders of magnitude of expansion, along with numerous extensions of entirely new value.

3. ***High Costs*** *– Healthcare is a business, and across the industry, providers invest heavily each year in modernizing systems, equipment, personnel training, and related operational areas. Since 2009, technology costs at physician-owned multi-specialty practices have increased by more than 40%...After investing so heavily in IT requirements, the industry is understandably fatigued... Until the industry creates truly turn-key secure communications capabilities, resistance will remain.*

4. ***Enterprise Focus*** *– In healthcare, the dominant adoption models and drivers over the past 20 years have been focused on business-to-business (B2B) value propositions, sales strategies, and implementation methods rather than personal value needs.... Broad cultural shifts rarely take place without the buy-in of individuals en masse, and to secure the future of communication and the flow of digital health information, the individual will need to play an active role in market adoption so the technology itself needs to be tailored to the individual.*

And there are many more surround problems, such as the challenges of arriving at consistent data formats and labeling, managing hundreds-of-thousands of unique data elements, the complex relationships between the numerous data elements and the need for contracts and Business Associate Agreements to share information. Clinically speaking, the patient's story or narrative is at least as important as anything in a database. In order to change behavior or create a viable treatment plan, doctors need to understand the "nuance" and the "why" at least as much as the "what." And there is the elephant in the room: the need for security, privacy and compliance to be both effective and universal to protect patient health information.

So here we are, decades past the PC revolution, with a combination of industry standards, regulations, clinician and consumer demand and even tens of billions in EHR incentives, but not yet able to truly disrupt healthcare IT and communications. We have neither a 'killer app' nor ubiquitous medical communications, and as a result we don't have the efficiency nor ease-of-use benefits from our EHRs, nor do we have repeatable examples of improved quality or lower errors.

I am confident that we don't have a market readiness problem. We have more than ample electricity, distributed computing platforms, ubiquitous broadband communications and both consumer and clinician demand. We have strong security and the legal, privacy, compliance, data format, interoperability and related standards to move forward. So I would contend that our biggest innovation inhibitor is our collective misunderstanding about how to solve the surround. Once we do that, we will unleash market disruption and find success.

Bedside Nurses Use Their Experiences in Patient Care to Drive IT Solutions

Stefanie Shimko-Lin, RN

> *"We are useful supernumeraries in the battle, simply stage accessories in the drama, playing minor, but essential, parts at the exits and entrances, or picking up, here and there, a strutter, who may have tripped upon the stage."*

I am a registered nurse (RN) and clinical analyst at the Cleveland Clinic, one of four RN's and a flight paramedic who work in this role in the Digital Domain of Information Technology. Before becoming a clinical analyst, I became a bedside nurse. I've been a bedside nurse for 10 years of my career and have witnessed births, held the hands of the dying and all that is in between. Every patient I've cared for has touched my heart deeply and I have a story for all of them. Not all nurses have a chance to work in IT and not all IT personnel get to step into the shoes of a nurse. I'd like to share a patient story with you for which I remember every detail. It led me to the William Osler quote above and has shaped my career ever since.

I was a night shift nurse on a cardiac step-down unit, mostly postoperative or preoperative open-heart patients. I vividly remember a woman who passed away on our unit, two days before Christmas. It was the first time watching a life slip away in front of me after the valiant fight to save it. My personal goal as a nurse was to know the person I was caring for before the end of my shift. I knew this particular woman's family, how they would spend Christmas and the hopes that her surgery would give her the energy to enjoy her life, children, and grandchildren. She was in her late 60s with happy years to live, or so I'd thought at the time. I'd met some of her family members and knew a bit about her as a person. We were unable to save her.

One moment she was using the bathroom and the nurse was walking her back to her bed when the patient reached her hand out in front of her and went limp. An alarm sounded and we all ran in to help. We got the patient into her bed and began CPR and called a code in an effort to restart her heart. A cardiology fellow and friend of mine ran the code that day. We tried our hardest for 40 minutes to revive her but were unable. The feeling is one of a deep pit in your stomach. Doing all you can, only to fail to bring back a life that existed only moments before. We readied her to have her family come and say goodbye to a mother they hoped would be there for Christmas, for weddings, for births – now gone. We cleaned up the patient and combed her hair, changed her gown and sheets. It was surreal watching the physicians call and ask the family to come to the hospital, watching the family arrive thinking their mom was still alive and seeing the face of the physician with tears as she walked down the hall to break the news that their family member had died.

The physician breaking the news was a resident and she said, "Oncology patients are easier to do this with. At least then you know it is coming and it's not a surprise." I'll never forget that statement as my mother died from stage 4 uterine cancer a few years later and I believe it is a little easier knowing, but not by much. I remember the scene as if it were yesterday, though it happened almost 10 years ago. The fellow came out to the nurse's station and we were talking about what occurred during the code. He had been remarkably calm and never raised his voice once. Anyone having been in a code might tell you that is not always the case. It's stressful and lives are literally at stake and it can be chaotic at times, but not that night and not that physician. I asked why he was able to remain so calm and he said he'd graduated from John Hopkins and part of their training was to remain calm in the storm… Aequanimitas. He had a pin he wore on his lab coat which had the word on it. He told me to read William Osler's essay 'Aequanimitas.' I urge you to read it if you never have. The quote above is one I have taken to heart and feel I have completed my role as a nurse and then some and know my purpose.

After reading the quote by Osler, I realized there was a correlation between my patient in the scenario I described and Osler's quote. My patient's life was the play and I was merely playing my part in her story. Many other families have had similar stories and other nurses and physicians played their parts in those stories. As direct care providers in a clinical setting, you pay attention to the details no matter how minute and develop an urgency for how the storyline will play out. We are trained to take responsibility for others' lives in healthcare and it can be a heavy weight to bear at times. But with that responsibility comes the ability to see clearly what's important and what to prioritize. One small change in the storyline and the whole play changes.

If we are stage accessories in life's play, then the medical record is the script for each player's life. As a clinical analyst working in information technology, it is of utmost importance to me and to other clinical analysts on my team to make sure the script is written in the best and most efficient way and that the information is used to provide the best care possible for our providers and patients. Our team of analysts and developers have created tools that help tell the patient's health story and surface information which was already recorded in medical records to enhance outcomes and patient safety, as well as provide comfort and meet patient requests, even at the end of life.

Vital Scout[SM] is one such tool, created to help identify patients whose health is subtly deteriorating and surface the information in a way that nurses and providers are able to clearly see there is a problem and intervene as soon as this is noted. Vital Scout[SM] was the brainchild of one of our nurse clinical analysts. Her background is critical care and pediatrics. The patient stories she knows and has heard led her to do research on early warning systems and the information they use to identify patient deterioration. As part of her master's degree dissertation, the early warning system was used and she felt it was an important part of the patient's chart. It would help nurses and physicians intervene sooner for our patients and identify problems early on. Her passion for patient safety and nursing drove her to create a risk-stratification tool based on five pieces of patient care information discretely documented within the EMR. Vital Scout[SM] provides users on medical-surgical floors with a visual cue for subtle changes in a patient's vital signs and correlates the changes with a stoplight color scheme. Users can escalate a patient when the patient is doing poorly. Interventions are performed based on which criteria are considered out of normal limits, then assessments are required within a specified time frame. A report within the EMR is used and seen by nursing as well as physicians, and providers are able to see what vital signs are changing and causing a score change. All patient care providers are now on the same page when caring for patients.

IT included nurses from pilot units in building the user interface for the tool. The lead clinical analyst met with users in a medical-surgical unit to get their feedback on what would be useful to them in reacting to a patient who is decompensating. Feedback was obtained by finalizing a pilot version of Vital Scout[SM] used in one of our regional hospitals. The pilot confirmed the ability for an early warning risk-stratification tool to decrease admissions to ICU's from medical-surgical units. The tool includes a screen-saver that shows a visual representation of patient scores on each unit without jeopardizing patient privacy. It provides situational awareness and helps nursing become a team sport. Now, nurses on every unit have eyes on their patients. From those in environmental services to physicians, nurses and anyone seeing the screen saver, they can identify patients with changes and speak up so that problems can be corrected before a patient declines to the point where a patient might need an admission to an ICU might be required or ends in death.

Vital Scout[SM] ended up being a particularly important part of the caregiver/creator's life when she found herself in the hospital as a patient. She had an infection and caregivers reacted when her Vital Scout[SM] score turned to blue after a blood pressure had been recorded low and out of the norm for her. Immediately her nurse received orders from a physician and started IV fluids to correct the problem and her BP was restored to normal limits after the intervention. Once again, a project generated by a nurse in collaboration with nursing informatics and bedside nurses improved the outcomes of a patient and, in this instance, not only a patient, but the patient who created the tool. The early warning system exists because of the passion generated by the experiences of our nurse analyst.

Iris Behavioral Health was a project created in collaboration with Nursing Informatics and bedside caregivers. At the time it was created, all behavioral health units had their safety round documentation performed on paper. Real-time computer documentation was needed. A previously created application called Iris was used in a past documentation pilot with the iPhone. Nursing Informatics was familiar with Iris and requested assistance with creating an application on a mobile device. Specifications for the information needed were provided to our team. The team building the app consisted of two RN/clinical analysts, a systems analyst and a software developer. Because we were familiar with nursing workflows, we were able to make suggestions to the systems analyst and developer and create a unique application which improved the safety of both care providers and patients alike. Iterative development between nursing informatics, our team and bedside staff took place and the final solution was created. It is currently used in all behavioral health units in our hospital system.

Nurses have a lot of tasks to do during any given shift. The final application included a color-coded timer indicating how long it has been since the last safety round and served as a reminder for the nurse/care provider to check on the patients every 15 minutes. One of the nurses working on our pilot units made suggestions based on how they do things on their unit. Thanks to this floor nurse, the application was approved to have one question, requiring three taps on a phone screen per patient, one to open the patient, one to select the patient's location on the unit and one to save. During training, buy-in from staff members was increased when we introduced ourselves as active nurses. As nurses, we know how new workflows are received by staff and we were able to incorporate those concerns into our training. The outcome was a successfully used application that increased patient safety. During a staff meeting in early 2018, one of our nurse leaders relayed a story about a patient who was admitted to one of our behavioral health units. This patient's life was saved when a staff member performing safety rounds entered a patient's room and the patient was actively attempting to take their own life. The caregiver entered the room because according to their device timer, rounds were due. Currently, the application has increased patient rounding from every 15 minutes to an average of every 10–12 minutes. The decreased time between safety rounds limits the opportunity for patients to perform self-harming behaviors. The success of this application is a direct result of different parts of nursing and information technologists working together to make one solution.

The EOL (End of Life) project in particular is very near and dear to my heart. Our team was contacted by the Organ Donor Coordinator for the Cleveland Clinic. She educated us on the need to call organ procurement with each patient expiration in the hospital setting and how organ donation affects lives. One donor has the ability to save 8 lives and affect up to 50+ more with tissue donation. She asked that we help surface basic information already documented in the EMR by nursing and physicians in order to better serve dying patients and their families at the end of life. In addition to patient concerns, CMS requires that organ procurement agencies be called after all hospital deaths. Without a way of pulling information into a report or filter, there was no way other than manually searching each patient's chart for information regarding their status and making the call after the fact.

Three documented pieces of information are used to identify potential donors: two missing brain stem functions, the patient is on a ventilator and the patient has a life-limiting diagnosis. Each referral only allows the family liaisons to discuss organ donation with the family and provide information for informed decisions as well as find out if a patient wanted to be an organ donor. It also allows Lifebanc to review a patient chart and see if they are a potential organ donation candidate based on their medical history. As a former hospice nurse, I have a great respect for end-of-life care and giving each patient the dignity and considerations to make their final wishes a reality. Organ donation is a last request of sorts and if we fail to meet that request, then we fail the patient. This is another example of how the passion for patient advocacy sets the stage in IT. The tool we created efficiently surfaces information considered when making a candidate known to Lifebanc and our coordinator/family liaison team.

Call information can be seen by all care providers, allowing us to make calls sooner and give families more time to consider donation as an option if the patient did not explicitly state their intent to be an organ donor. Currently, if a patient wants to be a donor, the team at the hospital only has an hour to contact Lifebanc for a referral and only three hours once a patient is pronounced brain dead. Time is of the essence when these patients are identified, and our workflow is important to meet the time constraints of the process. In another situation of life imitating art – in this case the artful care of a dying loved one – I had the honor of witnessing the referral process for organ donors firsthand when a family friend passed away suddenly a few months before writing this essay. The family had some closure and comfort knowing their daughter helped save seven people with her organs and will help many more with her tissue. My experience with the patient's family also shaped my approach to the project.

Sir William Osler had this to say about nurses and I believe it applies to those of us in healthcare who put our heart and soul into caring for others whether at the bedside or behind the scenes in IT: "There should be for each of you a busy, useful, and happy life; more you cannot expect; a greater blessing the world cannot bestow. Busy you will certainly be, as the demand is great, both in private and public, for [those] with your training. Useful your lives must be, as you will care for those who cannot care for themselves, and who need about them, in the day of tribulation, gentle hands and tender hearts. And happy lives shall be yours, because busy and useful; having been initiated into the great secret—that happiness lies in the absorption in some vocation which satisfies the soul; that we have here to add what we can *to,* not to get what we can *from,* life."

As a nurse and an analyst in information technology, my soul is satisfied from the work I've done and continue to do. My experiences at the bedside shape the way I approach any clinical tool we develop. I know I speak for those in my division and in the organization when I say that if our work saves one life, touches one family or makes the end-of-life process less pain-ful for our patients and those they leave, then everything we've done has been well worth the effort. And for me, I am proud of the work we've done and those I've done it with. The IT world is ever-changing and I don't know what will be around the corner, but I know as long as I work with those who have the patient needs at their core, the changes will only bring new and exciting solutions for clinical care providers and more comfort in some shape or form for our patients.

Reference

Osler, William (1999). 'Aequanimitas – The first essay.' The John Hopkins Health System – The John Hopkins University. Retrieved from http://www.medicalar chivves.jhmi.edu/osler/aequessay.htm (Accessed July 2018)

My Click Moment

Danilo Pena

The doctor stopped the small truck in the middle of the rocky road to take in the amazing view.

A rural family physician, my partner who was finishing up her second rotation and I, someone who wanted to help, were trekking down the scenic route of the Pinto Canyon road in West Texas. We were on our way to the Candelaria, Texas, a border town with less than 100 inhabitants.

There, the family doctor, with the help of a couple medical students, would take care of the Mexican population in Candelaria to ensure continu-ity of care free of charge. I, the biomedical informaticist, would do what I do best: observe and think.

I wanted to bring this recent experience up not because of the innovation that surrounded us (trust me, there was none), but because I actually wanted to highlight the amazing work that healthcare professionals do. It is coura-geous. It is the notion of continuity of care. It is the going out of your way to help others in one of the most important facets of life – health. Those few moments we shared with the patients, whom the physician saw only a handful of times a year, were special. I could tell they trusted him, and their interaction was more of a symbiotic relationship that reminded me of a close friendship.

Throughout the several hours, though, I could not help but think about ways that this population could be better served through innovation and technology. That is just how my mind works.

Many of today's experts in the business world tout the need to be data-driven and *innovative*. This concept of being data-driven has gained significant traction over the last decade, especially with the advances in statistical and data visualization tools.

However, as with many things that are done in excess, negative consequences start to emerge. The over-reliance on data, through interpretation and action, has allowed our instinctual nature to sort of get left behind. Mistrusted even. However, I believe there needs to be a healthy balance between being instinctual and being data-driven – a yin to the yang, the head versus the heart, the idea versus the process, the human patient relationship versus the technology to improve care.

Instinct cannot be taught. It is something that is learned through watching people fail, through mentors, and most importantly, through going down the rabbit hole of your own beloved idea.

Unlike the other physicians, educators and innovators that are within this larger piece of work, I do not have a long track record of success that can be listed on my resume. I did not go to medical school, complete multiple fellowships or lead teams of academics. My current position is best defined as someone who simply wants to make a difference, who, every day, is trying to build that dream one conversation, one failed idea, one opportunity at a time.

I am currently a graduate student passionate about innovation in the healthcare space. Coincidentally, I have been pouring over books, articles, meetups, classes and of course projects that will get me closer to creating something that will improve the healthcare system. My fascination and, quite frankly surprise, with the talent and thought leadership in healthcare was fulfilled.

My new sense of the click moment with healthcare and innovation reminds me of someone I met at a meet-up where he confided, "I didn't know how much innovation there was in healthcare."

"I didn't know either until about a few months ago, either. Welcome." I replied.

The first 9 months of interaction with healthcare and my passion for innovation has taught me several key points I would like to highlight. Let's dig in:

Address a Need

From my early encounters with entrepreneurs and healthcare leaders, I have learned that innovation is born out of a need. Needs can be defined as pain points with a current product or service, a work-around in a common workflow, or they can be large gaps in industries that leave customers lost and confused. The best innovators turn these *problems* into *opportunities*.

However, when we start to develop the mental model of looking at problematic processes in a more positive light, we may overwhelm ourselves with the plethora of needs. This is where collaboration and listening plays an important role. An innovator's ear must listen closely to the words, tones and emphasis on the problems their prospective customers are using. These moments are key indicators for early adoption and success. We must train ourselves to think empathetically and with an open mind to disallow our biases from coloring what we think the perfect solution may be.

Once we get this down, we can begin to build our grand solutions and *iterate.*

Iterate

Evolution in nature has taught us that the species who survive adapt best to their ever-changing environment. Bringing this to healthcare, our environment can be the morphing marketplace, the difference between targeting a patient versus provider versus payer or the increasing demand to lower cost while delivering better care. These are all hard constraints and will only get tougher as time flows on.

However, we must not get bogged down with the details. As you already have met the need by listening carefully to your target population, what your job now consists of iterating on the solution you and your team came up with. We sort of know the principles of developing lean projects that this iteration is modeled after.

Build. Measure. Learn. Repeat.

The faster we get through this process as innovators, the quicker we will learn where our pitfalls are and how to avoid them the next go-around. This rapid iteration between cycles will then allow for more click moments to occur during our journey.

Click Moments

Technologies like the telephone, internet and smartphone all made it easier to connect with our friends, families and people we would have never thought of meeting. To extrapolate, we can safely assume that technology will continue to increase the complexity of interaction which can uncover solutions to our everyday problems.

Beneath complexity, lies a variety of moving parts that are interdependent and interrelated. As innovators, we realize this amalgamation of cultures and blending of ideas is a great breeding ground for disruption. It is why the open-workspace has gained popularity, it is why the network effects of blockchain have reached impressive highs, and it is why collaborating with those who do not think or look like us has been the theme among major institutions for the past decade. Innovators understand that with greater interaction and touch points, there is a greater the probability of a *click moment*.

I first heard of this phrase after reading Frans Johansson's book *The Click Moment*. From it, I learned that innovators need a healthy mix of letting inspiration come to you and searching tirelessly to find it. This combination of different approaches will radically change the space in which innovators think. We must realize that prediction is a fool's game, and we must trust that complex forces can be used for our advantage if we spot signals like traction, momentum and moments of success.

Find Needs to Solve. Iterate. Click.

This was meant to be an overview of my early understandings with innovation in healthcare. It is not exhaustive; it is only my subjective view. However, it should be noted that this essay is a result of a click moment. These words brought to you today were the result of my passion for innovation in healthcare, my love of writing and finally, my stumbling upon this opportunity shared by a friend on LinkedIn. You can't make this stuff up, and I am sure you can relate.

Tune into the moments that can change the course of your day, week, year or life. I urge you to gather the experiences you have from work and home and piece them together to solve new, pressing problems. We need your ingenuity. Who knows, your experience may just be the foundation for ideas that will result in the disruption of healthcare for the better.

Thank you for reading.

Our Voice: Healthcare Partner Council for Cleveland Clinic Information

Kathy Ray and Amy Szabo

Cleveland Clinic Information Technology Division has been able to engage patients directly into our daily work, staff meetings and projects.

I am a Cleveland Clinic Regional Hospital Systems Analyst. Several years ago, I joined the Cleveland Clinic Main Campus Voice of Patient Advisory Committee (VPAC) to represent my mother. My mom is 83 years old, has multiple diseases and had been a patient at Main Campus so I felt that I could represent her and be her voice. I participated in monthly meetings with other patients across the enterprise. We collaborated – sharing our patient stories with one another. A unique perspective to our VPAC was that not only did we have patients sitting at the table, but we also had leadership representation from all levels. The co-leaders were from the Office of Patient Experience. This was such a rewarding opportunity as I got to share not only the patient's side but also a caregiver's perspective as well.

As I participated on the Main Campus VPAC, my hospital president found out and asked me to co-chair a council at the regional hospital and I did. Working with the Office of Patient Experience and Volunteer Services, we were able to invite 8 patients to our council meetings. We always had leadership present for our meetings. We would provide food, a meeting room and would collaborate with one another. Often, we would have guest speakers attend and would begin gathering suggestions from our patients on how to improve service, processes and communications. It was at this time we received a new co-chair from the Office of Patient Experience, Amy Szabo. Amy was awesome and brought so much value to the group! The value added was a deeper connection between patients, and what mattered most to them, and caregivers/leaders.

Voice of the Patient Advisory Councils were re-imagined with the voice of many patients and became Our Voice: Healthcare Partners program. Our Voice grew across the enterprise into many different councils. Amy and I were seeing such huge value in asking our patients to express themselves and offer solutions. It only seemed natural to spread Our Voice to the Information Technologies Institute. We presented the idea of forming an Information Technologies Healthcare Partner Council to Ed Marx and Maureen Sullivan, leaders of the Institute. Ed Marx championed the Our Voice mission, vision and values by engaging a patient to serve the Digital

Global Advisory Council. That relationship was one that was sustained over time.

The IT Healthcare Partner Council kicked off with the strategy and forming session at a regional hospital with 35 caregivers and patients from across the enterprise. It was an interactive session where discovery and human centered relationships were built. Collaboratively, what matters most to patients and caregivers was discussed in small groups and later shared with the larger group. As time passed and the relationships and inquiry maintained the Our Voice: IT HCP. The Council is moving forward with engagement from across the enterprise, including distance relationships in other states.

The IT Healthcare Partner Council is embedding patients at the onset of design and project work in the following IT areas: finance, electronic health record, digital platform, population health, imaging, clinical domain, security, infrastructure/network and project management.

When patients and families are empowered to become partners in all aspects of their healthcare, many improvements occur: outcomes are better, patients and their families are happier and treatment can become more meaningful and understandable to patients.

Innovative Collaboration: Applying Success from Outside Healthcare

Anna Pannier

I am starting to envision a reality where healthcare is unable to navigate the future without engaging significantly with new types of partners. This is tantamount to admitting that we are unable to face the future alone. Instead, we must look outward for new mindsets, skills, methods and experience. While adopting these, we must join with nontraditional and innovative partners to remain relevant in future models of health and wellness.

A CIO colleague once passed on a phrase regarding a misaligned sense of urgency. He said, "You are looking at your calendar, and I am looking at my watch." Healthcare organizations are largely looking at their calendars, imagining they have months and years to address change. Healthcare executives speak out and make posts lamenting the challenges: drug price increase, complex consumer trends, growing uncompensated care burdens and the expanding chasms in wellness and chronic illness. While these are problems for us to solve and threats to the norm we have become accustomed to, these are also *opportunities* in the eyes of innovators and entrepreneurs.

Healthcare Leaders Must Stop Whining and Begin Winning!

The good news is that these last two decades have also delivered an amazing technology revolution, one that is on the cusp of yet another transformative change. Enabling technological capabilities continue to advance, propelling virtuous exponential progress. Vast data growth is ripe for testing and harvesting. Machine learning has grown past adolescence, rapidly enabling automation and creating insights that we could not have imagined. The mass adoption of wireless and smartphones has enabled an entirely different personal dependency on technology. Adoption models of the past are no longer relevant in the age of frictionless sharing of information and ideas. Previous privacy and security expectations have been relaxed in exchange for a customized and simplified experience. Imagined requirements of physical presence and niche expertise are being progressively challenged.

So, where can healthcare organizations turn to dive into these turbulent high waters of innovation and transformation and remain seaworthy? The first step is admitting we have a problem.

> We must abandon the security of the lifeboats attached to our huge ships. We need to step away from the academic/expert arrogance of healthcare professionals, starting with any assumption that we have an advantage or superior perspective than others who are not on the "inside."

While healthcare leaders have an advantage in the current model by understanding the layers and complexity that impact care delivery, Tom Goodwin from Havas Media shared these sobering thoughts in 2015: "Uber, the world's largest taxi company, owns no vehicles. Facebook, the world's most popular media owner, creates no content. Alibaba, the most valuable retailer, has no inventory. And Airbnb, the world's largest accommodation provider, owns no real estate."

Entrenched service providers, such as higher education, retail stores and libraries, have been upended by the technological transformations of the past decade. The survivors have had a wide variety of approaches, but none of them have remained the same. Furthermore, *surviving* is in stark contrast to *thriving*, and we should be seeking the higher value.

When I see the local news story of the Main Street store closing after decades of service to the community, I have mixed emotions of sadness for a bygone era, but also acknowledgment that things are simply too convenient and cost-effective to purchase through Amazon Prime, eBay, Zappos, etc. And these companies are continuously evolving without preconceived notions (also in stark contrast to heavily layered healthcare organizations). I recall, years ago, seeing friends use the Amazon Dash buttons to order home staples like detergent. The products were co-branded to put Amazon in the middle of every consumer need, helping get any product into households faster. It's as easy as pressing a button. In addition to not needing to drive anywhere, they got rid of the need to get to a phone or computer. Manufacturers that didn't jump on the "Dash" wagon were left behind by busy moms and dads looking to simplify their lives. Not everyone adopted the Dash buttons, but enough did. And now Alexa and Dash are working together!

So, just think about this for a second in comparison to wanting to get some medical help. In healthcare, we break this down into our inward-focused model: Do you want to find a PCP? What insurance do you have? Are we in your plan's network? Do you want to schedule an appointment? How much of the experience have we defined in our own terms and processes versus thinking about the very basic experience of getting the help one needs or wants by simply pressing a button? We play twenty questions in most customer interactions. Sometimes we are even satisfied when we are simply above average with patient experience scores (again in stark contrast to the Dash!).

Healthcare has begun to respond to consumerism, but again, in an inward manner. Time and money are spent on web advertising and on understanding and influencing online impressions. Consumers are increasingly basing their decisions on online feedback. Soon, pricing transparency won't just be based on niche solutions offered on healthcare provider websites; individuals will post details and images online, bringing real clarity to the problems in back offices. While healthcare organizations try to improve access through online scheduling, e-visits, more care site options and elongated hours, other companies will figure out how to overlay the complexity with smarter searches. These smarter searching capabilities may know the consumer better than we do, perhaps even predicting the consumer's need based on previous searches and purchases. These new solutions will present consumers with best options, closest locations, ratings, even consumer-validated current wait times so the "buyers" can pick what fits best for them.

And don't think that the current insurance model with narrow networks will help for long. If Amazon started offering total knee packages tomorrow, how long would it take for a consumer to buy it and Amazon to line up a top 10 provider to deliver it?

Yes, we need to admit that we don't know as much as we think we know. We need to look outward to reimagine the experience that consumers want, even if the consumers themselves haven't imagined it!

After admitting we don't have all the answers, the logical part of my brain wants to find the infographic or structure that will perfectly help me plan the future. But that is missing the point entirely. The future is developing and fluid. We do not know where it is going, and anchoring any fixed mindsets is dangerous. Instead, we can adopt some skills from Comedy and Design that open us up to becoming collaborative innovators.

Apply Learning from Comedy

Most business leaders engaged in developing a service have a set thought process for working through the data and facts needed to establish a planned, accurate and committed financial return. We follow recipes: a scoop of capital dollars, two scoops of operating dollars, a dozen FTEs and voilà, here is the cost model with planned revenue and a three-year return on investment (ROI). This model structure becomes mostly irrelevant when we are creating something new or innovative.

Have you ever watched "Whose Line Is It Anyway?" My son and I love to watch this show. It started in Britain and came across the pond in 1998. In this show, some staid comedians combine with some revolving ones, and they engage in a series of improvisational (improv) sketches. Though it is structured like a game, it is the creative and fluid improv experience that makes it fun.

In the "Props" sketch, the comics take turns with a prop, imagining all the ways it can be used to tell a story. A blow-up ball may take one turn as an oncoming boulder and its next iteration as a yoga chair. A key facet of improv is the "yes, and how about" conversation model. This follows true brainstorming models, meaning we don't criticize any ideas and just keep them flowing and coming out. Why no criticism or questioning of an idea? In improv, if a comic were to say, "that won't work," it stops the creative flow. Instead, if something didn't work as intended, you just go on to the next thing in an additive, positive way.

As we embark on creative conversations, it is especially important that we not panic about how large or complex something may seem. Overthinking the details too early slows things down by adding unnecessary friction to communication. Trust that there will be time later to plan details.

Another aspect of comedy is the use of stories. This is something most healthcare executives have grown accustomed to, and often have their own story of how they started in healthcare in an entry-level role and came to see healthcare as their calling. These stories help us identify with people and fit our internal culture of being purpose-driven.

In my local volunteer roles within American College of Healthcare Executives, I often meet people considering healthcare careers. In recent years, I'm struck by the number of people from totally different fields now interested in joining healthcare. Their stories are different. These new, non-traditional entrants span a wide age range. Some come from different professional backgrounds, the military or trades. Some college students are interested but don't have a sense of a calling. This diversity, in and of itself, can produce new perspectives. New perspectives can drive innovation. If we are open to these new stories and avoid turning talented people away because they do not fit the traditional model, it can help us develop innovation capability.

Adopting this openness of improv and expanding our stories are two skills that can better prepare us for innovative collaboration.

Apply Learning from Design

Design also offers us some wonderful adaptive models to learn from. Design has many definitions, but one of my favorites is: purpose, planning or intention that exists or is thought to exist behind an action, fact, or material object. When we experience an inspired design, we feel it, we connect to it. It could be as simple as a pen that fits perfectly and comfortably in your hand. Perhaps it is the visual and auditory experience of a waterfall that makes you feel at peace. Or maybe it is a new electronic gadget that inspires you.

Architecture and landscapes are also examples of Design. When I lived in Milwaukee, I enjoyed visiting and walking around the Milwaukee Museum of Art. The Museum is an architectural landmark, comprised of three buildings designed by three legendary architects: Eero Saarinen, David Kahler and Santiago Calatrava. All aspects are examples of inspired Design, but Kahler had a unique role of creating an outside space that unified and accentuated the best of the other designs, tying it into the city and surrounding area. Like the improv tool of "yes and how about" he was additive, but also selective in execution. When you can do anything, it is extremely important to develop requirements and constraints. This may seem opposite of the improv discussion, but it represents the yin and yang of key skills and timing is critical. It is critical to know when to start invoking the design principles that set up constraints.

This selective aspect is a Design method enshrined by Dieter Ram, a German-born industrial designer and academic closely associated with designs from Braun and modern industrial design. His famed "10 Design Principles" serve to streamline our creations, making them sleek and purposeful, and adapted and adopted broadly.

1. Innovative – Technological development is always offering new opportunities for original designs. But imaginative design always develops in tandem with improving technology, and can never be an end in itself.
2. Useful – A product is bought to be used. It has to satisfy not only functional but also psychological and aesthetic criteria. Good design emphasizes the usefulness of a product while disregarding anything that could detract from it.
3. Aesthetic – The aesthetic quality of a product is integral to its usefulness because products are used every day and have an effect on people and their well-being. Only well-executed objects can be beautiful.
4. Understandable – It clarifies the product's structure. Better still, it can make the product clearly express its function by making use of the user's intuition. At best, it is self-explanatory.
5. Unobtrusive – Products fulfilling a purpose are like tools. They are neither decorative objects nor works of art. Their design should therefore be both neutral and restrained, to leave room for the user's self-expression.
6. Honest – It does not make a product appear more innovative, powerful or valuable than it really is. It does not attempt to manipulate the consumer with promises that cannot be kept.
7. Long-lasting – It avoids being fashionable and therefore never appears antiquated. Unlike fashionable design, it lasts many years – even in today's throwaway society.
8. Thorough down to the last detail – Nothing must be arbitrary or left to chance. Care and accuracy in the design process show respect toward the consumer.

9. Environmentally friendly – Design makes an important contribution to the preservation of the environment. It conserves resources and minimizes physical and visual pollution throughout the lifecycle of the product.
10. As little design as possible – Less, but better – because it concentrates on the essential aspects, and the products are not burdened with non-essentials. Back to purity, back to simplicity.

Once we have opened our minds to new possibilities, adopted new skills for openness and ways of evaluating innovation, we are well positioned to expand our relationships in order to increase our access to innovation. Thomas Watson is attributed the quote, "If you want to increase your success rate, double your failure rate." This can be done in many ways, but I propose one specific approach that may feel a little uncomfortable to traditional healthcare leaders, "every patient, every time, 100% accuracy."

In past cycles, organizations would consider that they had significant proprietary expertise. They would be thinking about how they can financially benefit from an innovation before it was even created. Contracts, intellectual property (IP) and investment arms would be engaged. And often little came from the effort. With all this weighing down the process, healthcare organizations often found themselves being very selective about the partners with whom they partnered. This selectivity could have meant picking only a single vendor within each functional space, preferred vendor status, long and arduous contracting processes, complex technical sign-offs and basically making sure that everyone in legal, risk management, compliance and a myriad of committees all signed off on it before it even began or got off the ground.

An alternative, equally ineffective approach is panic and quick partnerships that are defensive-oriented and fear-based, hoping to stave off competition. However, these organizations may not be approaching this with the new mindset, skills and model necessary to co-develop innovation. It is a lot easier to issue a press release than it is to develop and deliver solutions.

Partially due to this construct, most healthcare organizations are not innovation factories cranking out novel approaches and solutions at a fast pace. Following the HIMSS Innovation recommendations, some organizations have created idea intake models, indicated a willingness to fail more and dedicated personnel and financial resources toward this end. Meanwhile, non-healthcare companies with innovation track records have accepted a complex landscape where companies are competitors and collaborative partners in different areas, concurrently. This is the new normal for companies that are expected to innovate. This means less clarity in relationships, IP, rights, etc. However, the reason it works is also because iterations must be launched quickly to see what works. The open world of innovation means that someone else is right behind you, ready to deliver something better, faster, cheaper and/or safer. And you may not have ever heard of them before.

What does this imply for healthcare executives? It reminds me of the homespun phrase, "You have to kiss a lot of toads to find a prince charming." No offense to partners being toads, but the idea is that we must widen the net and get into many relationships, fostering them. Even if they fail on one project, they may be a perfect partner for something else down the road. We need to be connecting with startups all over the globe. Everyone on the executive committee is responsible for connecting with new people, from new backgrounds, with innovative ideas, all the time.

Interested in innovation? Start playing the field. Use the Waze app or something like it, start up a conversation with them about how that might fit into urgent care and ED wait times. Working with Uber or Lyft on patient transportation? Maybe expand it to also think about how you can harness this for your workforce to make an impact on traffic. If you are spending millions on recurring purchases, do you think your GPO has an advantage over Amazon or eBay in the long run? Thinking of automation, why not talk with those delivering on robotic efficiencies right now in warehouses or container shipping ports. Want to see how fast you can develop a solution or harness your data? Consider ways to make it open for innovators to get involved without entrance fees. Stop talking about how we "do more with less" and how to decrease cost and increase revenue. Don't shun prospective partners that lack typical credentials. Remove superiority phrases such as "it's ok if your shoe order gets messed up but, you really don't want your healthcare experience messed up," as if we knew more or caused no harm today. Start talking about our challenges with new and different people who may have new insights, and be open to whatever may come of it.

This is an exciting time to be in healthcare, but we are at an inflection point. Becoming a collaborative innovator is required to stay relevant. Becoming a collaborative partner will take a new mindset, new skills, new models and new partnerships. Let's go!

Chapter 5

Communicate and Eliminate Barriers

Cross communication is essential to promote innovation. By stripping virtual or physical barriers to communication, ideas have a better chance of being realized.

Transparency is a key to effective relationships which are required for innovation to thrive. The depth and width you share will determine the size of your success. Look for every opportunity and platform to share while actively eliminating barriers to communication. Effective communication will make or break innovation. If active or passive resistance rises, so must your communication. While technology provides great tools to reach many, do not neglect the power of in-person eyeball-to-eyeball dialogue.

Fostering Data Liquidity for Modern Day Healthcare Delivery

Susan deCathelineau

The convergence of unstructured patient content with the EMR using Content Services is crucial to building a foundation for interoperability and providing a comprehensive data set to feed emerging AI, analytics, and population health initiatives.

Read almost any article or report on the hottest technology trends in healthcare and a few topics pop up again and again—AI (Artificial Intelligence), machine learning, data analytics, and population health. Many industry pundits believe these technologies are ready for prime time, and indeed these tools have matured to a point where they can transform healthcare for the better by automating clinical information analysis and streamlining workflows, thereby improving patient care and outcomes.

However, it is important that healthcare providers not rush into implementing these solutions. Like many technologies built to harness the power of digital clinical data, they are only as useful as the data that feeds them. Applying AI, machine learning, analytics, and population health tools to partial or inaccurate data sets will yield less than optimal results. And, the unfortunate truth is the clinical data that resides in most health systems today is woefully incomplete and disjointed.

More often than not, digital clinical information is locked away in several proprietary and unconnected siloes. In many instances, the critical clinical stakeholders in an institution are not even aware much of this information exists. Investing in advanced data analytics and AI technologies without first getting your health data house in order is akin to purchasing a sleek new sports car without having the proper fuel to put in the tank. In short, you're not going to get too far.

Gaining optimal results from any analytics, AI, or machine learning initiative requires comprehensive clinical content, and that means a thorough information discovery, consolidation, and integration effort.

There are several principal sources of vital clinical information in today's healthcare organization. Let's review the existing state of these repositories and examine how each must evolve to remove barriers and enable digital healthcare transformation indeed.

Electronic Medical Records

Without question, EMR (Electronic Medical Record) systems have become the single most significant source of digital clinical information in most hospitals and health systems in the United States. Spurred by federal incentives from the ONC, the proliferation of EMR use has been remarkable. In fact, according to HealthIT.gov, 96 percent of hospitals and 78 percent of physicians currently use EMRs.

EMRs are designed to capture and manage structured clinical information (i.e., data that can be entered into discrete data fields) and most do this job exceptionally well. However, the capabilities of these systems are limited when it comes to handling unstructured and semi-structured patient information. This is problematic when you consider that the vast majority of a patient's medical history isn't inherently captured or stored in an EMR. In fact, according to analysts such as Gartner and Merrill Lynch, approximately 80 percent of patient data consist of unstructured or semi-structured information that lives outside the EMR.

This issue is exacerbated when you consider how many healthcare providers fail to look beyond the EMR when it comes to evaluating a patient's medical history. These significant investments, while transformative, have become the end-all-be-all source for health data for too many healthcare organizations, and important clinical content is being overlooked as a result.

Enterprise Content Management

A primary source of unstructured clinical content is ECM (Enterprise Content Management) systems. These systems have historically been used to capture and manage a wide array of clinical documents, emails, faxes, photos, and more. Much of this historical content is valuable when viewed in the context of the overall patient history. These systems have also been leveraged to automate both clinical and administrative document workflows, which have been used to reduce manual labor and process errors, thereby increasing productivity and efficiency.

The problem is ECM systems were often deployed departmentally, meaning that several different ECM repositories may exist throughout a health system. Furthermore, these systems are often disconnected from core clinical systems such as the EMR, which obstructs enterprise access and review, essentially limiting the benefits of these systems to the departments in which they are deployed. Working to consolidate and connect this disparate ECM system for enterprise use can enhance these advantages exponentially.

Enterprise Medical Imaging

Medical images are likely the biggest source of semi-structured clinical content that exists within a healthcare organization. Currently, most healthcare organizations manage these assets using PACS (Picture Archiving and Communications Systems).

PACS are designed to manage large volumes of medical images based on the DICOM standard (e.g., MRIs, CT scans, X-rays, etc.). These systems have served radiology and cardiology departments well for the better part of two decades and, until recent years, have encompassed the vast majority of imaging assets within a healthcare organization.

The problem with a PACS-only strategy in today's healthcare environment is the technology is often ill-equipped to manage the growing number of images that are not based on the DICOM standard. These assets include surgical video, endoscopy, dermatology photos, wound images, pathology studies, and more, whose native formats range from JPEGs to TIFFs to MP4s. PACS was developed more than 20 years ago before any of these image types were even a thought. Many PACS have tried to accommodate non-DICOM specialty images by wrapping them in a DICOM format – a time-consuming, costly, and often inefficient process. As such, many healthcare providers have opted to keep specialty images siloed in multiple departmental systems, unconnected to a PACS or other enterprise systems such as an EMR. This is a growing concern when you consider that an IHS VNA study estimates that upward of 75 percent of the medical imaging assets in healthcare would be non-DICOM as soon as last year (2017).

Another issue with a PACS -focused strategy is that most of these systems are built using proprietary designs and code sets. While PACS are all based on the DICOM standard, many vendors continue to use proprietary extensions to make sharing medical imaging assets outside of the PACS complicated and costly.

Clearly, PACS alone is no longer enough. Today's healthcare facility requires an accurate EMI (Enterprise Medical Imaging) framework that consists of not only a PACS, but complimentary VNA (Vendor Neutral Archive), enterprise imaging, and image capture and connectivity tools. This approach will enable the centralized management, access and sharing of all types of images – regardless of format and source – and allow these images to be easily integrated with core clinical systems such as the EMR.

Through standardized data formatting, enterprise imaging provides organizations with all-encompassing ownership of their imaging information, removing the vendor lock-and-block of proprietary systems. It leverages advanced technologies like enterprise viewing to support the management and sharing of imaging data across the enterprise and beyond, empowering clinicians with near real-time image access and collaboration.

This same principle of leveraging open, enterprise-wide platforms can be applied to ECM content as well.

ECM + EMI + EMR = EHR 2.0

A key focus for healthcare providers today should be to take their EMR to the next level by enabling the entire trove of unstructured and semi-structured medical content to be easily visible and accessible from the EMR system clinical stakeholders use most every day. When done successfully, this effort will result in a comprehensive longitudinal health record that includes all structured, unstructured and semi-structured health data related to a patient. Essentially, it will create the Electronic Health Record 2.0 (EHR 2.0).

Of course, this effort requires identifying where all your valuable unstructured patient data currently resides (e.g., in multiple disparate ECM, PACS, and specialty imaging systems), consolidating it, and then connecting it to the EMR. This is a complex undertaking in a healthcare environment where the system and data interoperability is a challenge. However, it can be done if you tackle the project in small steps and focus on breaking down siloes through standardization. Open, scalable, standards-based and tightly integrated ECM and EMI solutions will be the foundation of this infrastructure.

Achieving ECM and EMI convergence can be achieved in a couple of ways. One is by consolidating all unstructured content and medical images on a combined enterprise platform with a shared storage and presentation layer (i.e., viewer). The other, likely more realistic, the option is to integrate existing systems using a series of Content Services to create a connected enterprise infrastructure for managing unstructured data and linking it to core clinical systems like EMRs.

Coined by Gartner in 2016, Content Services is an alternative strategy to provide a more practical, multi-repository solution to achieve the benefits promised by the original vision of ECM (i.e., to intelligently capture information, disseminate it to the right people, processes, and departments). Some call Content Services ECM in the cloud – but it is more than that. Content Services is principled in integration, bringing together architecture supportive of on-premises and hybrid cloud services, a multi-repository approach to manage content regardless of its source repository, and intelligent functions like enterprise search to create agile, cost-effective solutions.

With a Content Services approach, healthcare providers will want to ensure they partner with vendors that build on their products and support existing and emerging healthcare standards such as HL7, FHIR (Fast Healthcare Interoperability Resources) and XDS (Cross Document Sharing). Furthermore, healthcare organizations should seek out vendors that have invested in interoperability and actually incorporate the specifications and profiles into their existing product management and architectural approaches. A solid practice is to work with vendors whose products have received an IHE (Integrating the Healthcare Enterprise) Conformity Assessment. This statement asserts that a specific product version has gone through a rigorous interoperability certification process. When a vendor has already made the commitment to making its products interoperable, it provides a healthcare organization with tremendous value by lowering the cost of implementations, improving the quality of data workflows, and facilitating the effort to converge ECM and EMI assets with the EMR.

A Foundation for Health Data Interoperability

When you successfully consolidate unstructured clinical content and link it to core enterprise systems, you create a framework that can enable true health data interoperability. The current and future benefits of interoperability to providers and patients are well-documented, and it is worth the time and investment needed to put your organization on this path. The following are just a few reasons to start building a foundation for health data interoperability today while removing traditional barriers to communication.

Data Liquidity

When interoperability is at the core of your health IT infrastructure, vendors can come and go, and the health data itself remains intact. Moreover, access workflows and security profiles can be retained. The need for costly data migrations is eliminated, saving your organization time and money. This is especially attractive in today's healthcare environment where provider mergers and acquisitions are pervasive.

Improved Patient Outcomes

A technology framework based on interoperability facilitates the creation of a comprehensive longitudinal patient record. This health record puts all patient information – structured and unstructured – at the fingertips of a clinician at the point of care, enabling them to make more informed clinical decisions that can improve patient outcomes.

Continuity/Transition of Care

Health data interoperability facilitates the coordination and transition of care across organizational and system boundaries. When existing data can be shared between systems, providers can avoid duplicate testing, medication errors, and other costly oversights. This also helps to ensure patient safety, care quality, and the efficiency with which care is delivered.

Reduced Operational/Administrative Costs

The healthcare industry is rife with waste, and interoperable technology infrastructure can help eliminate much of it. For example, when existing health data can be exchanged electronically, the need to print, mail, and rescan documents, or burn medical images to CD or DVD is eliminated. Furthermore, interoperability makes it easier to centralize data, which reduces the time and effort required by medical staff to locate and access vital patient information.

Enhanced Patient Safety/Cybersecurity

Frost and Sullivan recently produced a report titled '10 Reasons Why You Need Healthcare Content Services.' In it, the firm discusses how a framework that connects structured and unstructured patient information using content services has the potential to yield positive impacts on patient safety and cybersecurity.

For example, Frost and Sullivan believes this type of platform can help improve patient safety by creating a more effective flow and exchange of patient information that can shave off precious minutes in the trauma center, advance patients through emergency protocols more quickly and reduce redundant imaging exams that can unnecessarily expose patients to additional radiation and treatment delays. Similarly, the firm believes a connected framework can help improve cybersecurity by applying security protocols holistically to all unstructured content. Similarly, consolidated and automated ECM workflows can help ensure HIM compliance throughout the enterprise.

Fueling AI, Machine Learning, Data Analytics, and Population Health Initiatives

Finally, an interoperable infrastructure that combines structured and unstructured data is essential when it comes to providing the big data necessary to fuel emerging technologies such as AI, machine learning, data analytics, and population health. This framework enables all information – regardless of originating system – to be included as part of the available data pool for these initiatives. This helps ensure a more comprehensive data set that eliminates potential gaps and ultimately enhances the results of an AI, machine learning, or population health effort.

Case in Point: Yale New Haven Health

Evidence of the impact interoperable ECM and EMI systems can have on pioneering AI and population health efforts are just beginning to emerge. One example learning is a recent research endeavor at Yale New Haven Health. The provider has developed APIs that allow head and spine CT imaging data to be pulled directly from its VNA and run through AI algorithms to determine ways to improve workflow efficiency in the ED. This process allows for large volumes of imaging data to be analyzed rapidly. With the VNA interface, CT scans are randomly sampled, aggregated, and anonymized in an automated fashion. If this step had to be completed manually, it would take a staff member five to six hours to pull and aggregate each study for the AI tool.

The standards-based vendor-neutral nature of EMI solutions also helps support broader population health initiatives by providing a platform that facilitates image sharing among different locations within a health system as well as with other healthcare providers within a region. This capability not only streamlines continuity of care for a patient but also helps to ensure regional population health initiatives are infused with the most comprehensive set of patient imaging data possible, regardless of origin. Breaking down imaging silos enable more robust data sets, and more robust data sets provide more accurate results.

Conclusion

Healthcare IT is shifting as models of consultation, treatment and care change. We must enhance our ability to effectively communicate and eliminate barriers. In the next decade, we will likely see episodic patient care transform into a focus on continuous population management, a reduction in face-to-face consultations and a rise in the number of virtual interactions, and an AI-powered shift toward data being used to provide insight and automated diagnosis and care.

Patient-centric care is about ensuring that this standardized content is viewed in a patient-specific context. The key to unlocking the potential for data is to make it accessible. All patient content – both structured and unstructured – should be classified, controlled, and codified to ensure it is used for its full value – now and in the future.

How Can Health Systems Leverage Technology to Engage Patients, Especially Those Who May Lack Digital Skills, Smartphones, and Robust Internet and Mobile Connectivity?

Amy R. Sheon and Leslie Carroll

At a recent health innovation event, I (ARS) asked a distinguished panel of health system executives: "Patient engagement has been deemed the block-buster drug of the millennium. How should innovators address patient engagement? And what about the patients, such as the 48 percent of low-income Cleveland residents who lack any internet subscription or the 44 percent of all Cleveland residents who lack a mobile data plan?"[1] What about residents who have broadband and mobile data plans but lack the skills needed to use them?"

The answers, such as promoting empathy among providers, were unsatisfyingly health system-centric. With careful thought, health systems may see consumer health technology adoption move faster than the 17-year gap that characterizes adoption of other health innovations.[2,3]

How Will That Unfold?

Health tech firms will widely publicize compelling anecdotes such as a health system that avoided a $12,000 readmission penalty when a patient dashboard alerted Mary's provider that her daily weight measurement – transmitted automatically from her Bluetooth-enabled scale – revealed a sudden weight gain, leading to rapid adjustment of medication for her congestive heart failure. Health systems and insurers will widely promote use – and even subsidize patient purchase of such technology, but be disappointed that the needle does not move on the desired outcome in the subsequent two years. Delving into their analytics, health systems will note very low uptake of patient-focused technology, especially among populations that experience challenges in using digital health technology. A couple of more years of research will reveal other causes of lack of widespread adoption by patients such as biases in who received encouragement from providers to adopt technology; recognition that patients need help in using the technology and in understanding its value; and that some populations face unique challenges with technology use. Examples include patients with low vision being unable to read small screens, or those with limited dexterity having difficulty entering information on small keypads. Health systems will then have nurses, techs and, even physicians instruct patients in how to download apps and operate digital devices. A couple of more years down the road, health systems will find that training will have helped patients who are already adept at using technology with adopting digital health tools but will have left behind the substantial fraction of patients deemed "digitally unready" by Pew Research.[4] Such individuals will still have resisted adopting telemedicine, remote monitoring, or using apps to track their health or report health measures.

Within a decade from now, solid evidence will point to the disastrous impact of the digital divide on the ability of patients to manage not only their health but also to address the factors that make the largest contribution to their health, their social determinants of health – such as education, employment, and housing. Healthcare only accounts for approximately 20 percent of differences in health outcomes, according to models widely accepted by the Institute of Medicine and documented in public health studies.[5–10] The enormous variability in disease and risk factors by zip code, race, and income[11–14] underscores the overall limited impact of healthcare on population health and on the disparities that hold back overall improvement.

So What is a Health Care System to Do?

Patient portals to electronic health records offer obvious benefits in the way of convenience (appointment scheduling, checking test results, requesting prescription renewals, secure messaging). They also serve as a conduit for high-quality health information and can offer the ability to track health conditions and report health outcomes. Portals are ubiquitous and applicable to all health conditions, yet can be personalized to address language and literacy barriers. Instruction in use of a portal could reap a lifetime of dividends insofar as portals could be considered a gateway to other connected health tools including telemedicine, remote monitoring, apps, wearables and more.

Efforts of healthcare systems to address risk factors associated with disease, such as diet, exercise, smoking, and tobacco are growing, with healthcare's use of Screening, Brief Intervention and Referral to Treatment (SBIRT).[15] Innovation can surely help with the difficult task of matching patients to community resources that are convenient and culturally relevant, an approach that we are beginning to call Precision Public Health.[16] To potentiate this approach, however, patients must have ready, secure, and continuous access to private electronic communications. Health systems can be powerful advocates by screening patients for their digital skills and connectivity, referring patients to community organizations that can address gaps, and "prescribing" patient utilization of portals and other such technology.

Local Experience: MetroHealth System, Cleveland, Ohio

We believe there is much to be learned from our own local efforts to promote patient adoption of portals. As Cleveland's only public health care provider, The MetroHealth System had nearly 1.2 million outpatient and 125,000 emergency department visits in 2016. Despite being an early and nationally-recognized[17] leader in the adoption of electronic health records, only 29.1 percent of patients at our local public hospital, MetroHealth System, had initiated patient portal use by 2015, with significant disparities seen by race (23.4 percent for blacks, 23.8 percent for Hispanics versus 34.1 percent for whites), and insurance (17.4 percent adoption for uninsured patients versus 39.3 percent for those with commercial insurance).[18] In multivariate analysis, the strongest predictor of portal use, controlling for patient demographic characteristics, was neighborhood-level access to broadband internet.[18] It may be tempting to assume that lack of internet subscription reflects lack of interest in subscribing. Yet lack of interest accounts for just over one-third (34 percent) among the 11 percent of adults nationwide who do not use the internet. Nearly the same fraction (32 percent) cite difficulty as the main reason for non-use, and 19 percent cited cost as the main barrier.[19]

In conjunction with efforts to obtain federal approval for mergers among large telecommunication companies and cable providers, ISPs in several states began offering, in 2016, discount unlimited high-speed broadband internet to individuals meeting various eligiblity criteria such as receiving SNAP food assistance or Medicaid. (Requirements vary by service provider and by state.) low-income residents.[20,21] Our local community partners, the Ashbury Senior Computer Community Center (ASC3), and Connect Your Community began referring digital skill training clients to these ISPs, but many clients were told they were ineligible for the discount broadband rate *because high-speed broadband was not available in their neighborhoods.* Looking into this seeming catch-22, our partners were startled to discover what appeared to be digital redlining – an ISP that "systematically discriminated against lower-income Cleveland neighborhoods in its deployment of home Internet and video technologies over the past decade."[22] Upgrades to broadband fiber had been made in suburban and middle-income urban Cleveland neighborhoods but the "overwhelming majority" of city blocks with high rates of poverty were left with internet access speeds too slow to allow for signing into portals without timing out. (A similar pattern of digital redlining was found by others for the entire State of California,[23] and by our colleagues in other Midwest cities).[24,25]

Thus, it is important for providers not to withhold portal recommendations based on an assumption that some populations are less likely to use the internet than others, or that non-use reflects lack of patient interest.

> *"Many people still do not have access to a computer, smart phone or internet because of the cost of the equipment"*
>
> *"Health systems interested in leveraging technology to engage patients who lack digital skills and digital resources can employ Digital Community Health Workers to act as a bridge to connect patients to available health system technology and digital resources they may be lacking."*
>
> *"Talking with patients about their portals lets me identify their level of digital literacy and barriers that may exist."*
>
> *"Using portals to communicate digital literacy topics with patients helps to eliminate barriers known as the digital divide."*
>
> *"Most patients are able to activate their portal accounts if they are comfortable with their devices. The patients that need help with activation can come into the Digital CHW office and work together one-on-one to connect to their account. Many patients not using the portal for various reasons such as sight impairment, dexterity impaired, or language barriers are encouraged to designate a "proxy" to access the portal on the patient's behalf."*
>
> Leslie Carroll, CHW

The Cleveland Digital Patient Engagement Model

Confronted with low rates of portal adoption and limited access to internet, we developed a multipronged model system that contains elements that we believe could benefit nearly all health systems. The model consists of the following components:

1. Health systems identify patients not currently using portals, preparing a daily list for the clinic.
2. CHWs screen non-portal users for digital skills and connectivity during a very brief discussion at the end of a patient appointment.
3. CHWs refer patients lacking skills or connectivity to local community organizations for assistance. This referral is more successful when the CHW follows up or even provides some training on the spot.
4. Once they have attained basic digital skills and connectivity, CHWs then directly train patients to use the portals either at the end of the visit or at a later scheduled time.

Development of our program required a number of precursor steps, as summarized in Figure 5.1a. We developed our program in partnership with ASC3, and the local United Way 2-1-1 referral service to identify additional training opportunities such as at libraries, job training centers, and public housing communities.

As is the case in many communities, libraries and "digital inclusion" organizations are experts in assessing digital skills and addressing skill gaps. The National Digital Inclusion Alliance maintains an on-line listing and map of local affiliates around the country (digitalinclusion.org). The United Way 2-1-1 Referral line also geared up to refer patients by phone to the nearest location to obtain digital skill training, free or low cost, refurbished computers and mobile phones, and to enroll in discount internet access programs.

1) Develop list of digital skill training and connectivity support resources.
2) Create referral partnerships with local digital inclusion advocates such as libraries and employment training facilities for basic digital skill training and connectivity support.
3) Recruit and Train CHWs to screen and refer patients to these resources.
4) Train CHWs to use literacy acquisition strategies to teach patients to use portals.
5) Develop reports to track portal use patterns and disparities.

(a)

1) Adopt universal screening of patients for digital skills and connectivity
2) Adopt opt-out policies for portal creation.
3) Work with portal vendors to improve the portal user experience, especially regarding authentication.
4) Generate evidence for digital medicine.

(b)

Figure 5.1 (a) Preparatory steps for digital patient-engagement model implementation. (b) Additional recommended steps to optimize patient portal use and accelerate patient HIT adoption.

Community Health Workers as Key Drivers of Digital Patient Engagement

Community Health Workers (CHWs) are an optimal workforce to help healthcare organizations understand and address patient barriers to technology adoption, and to help patients attain the digital skills and connectivity needed to use health IT.[26] A 1998 study identified optimal CHW qualities and roles[27] that have been widely incorporated into state and national standards and certifications.[28-32] Recommended CHW qualities that support this effort include: being a member of or having intimate familiarity with the lived experience of vulnerable patients, being friendly, non-judgmental, empathetic, a lifelong learner, persistent, resourceful, and committed to community improvement.[27]

Although not adopted in our program, other practices outlined in Figure 5.1b were suggested[33-35] by participants at a recent national gathering of digital literacy experts meeting together with those promoting health portal adoption.[36]

Figure 5.2 shows a crosswalk between CHW roles and tasks needed to promote patient digital engagement.

Modify workflow if needed to ensure provider encouragement of patient portal use. Providers may be reluctant to encourage patients to use portals fearing being overloaded by patient messages. Office personnel should triage these messages which should reduce overall provider burden. *Adopt universal screening of patients for digital skills and connectivity and referral to local digital inclusion advocates to address gaps.* Recognizing that healthcare isn't necessarily the most urgent priority in the lives of many patients, healthcare institutions are increasingly adopting routine screening and referral of patients to address social determinant of health barriers such as lack of housing, domestic violence, or emergency income needs. For example, in the Accountable Health Communities Model, the Centers for Medicare and Medicaid Services is testing such a program in 30 cities across the country including Cleveland where the local United Way 2-1-1 Referral program is working with MetroHealth System. This is a missed opportunity to assess digital skills. Patients lacking skills, equipment, broadband, and/or mobile data plans should be referred to local organizations focused on digital literacy and access. Public libraries and job training organizations address the skill training, but connectivity is an important gap, especially in communities lacking competition to drive down the price of mobile and broadband internet service.[37]

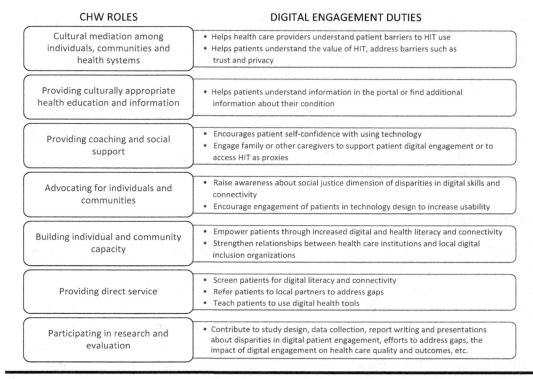

CHW ROLES	DIGITAL ENGAGEMENT DUTIES
Cultural mediation among individuals, communities and health systems	• Helps health care providers understand patient barriers to HIT use • Helps patients understand the value of HIT, address barriers such as trust and privacy
Providing culturally appropriate health education and information	• Helps patients understand information in the portal or find additional information about their condition
Providing coaching and social support	• Encourages patient self-confidence with using technology • Engage family or other caregivers to support patient digital engagement or to access HIT as proxies
Advocating for individuals and communities	• Raise awareness about social justice dimension of disparities in digital skills and connectivity • Encourage engagement of patients in technology design to increase usability
Building individual and community capacity	• Empower patients through increased digital and health literacy and connectivity • Strengthen relationships between health care institutions and local digital inclusion organizations
Providing direct service	• Screen patients for digital literacy and connectivity • Refer patients to local partners to address gaps • Teach patients to use digital health tools
Participating in research and evaluation	• Contribute to study design, data collection, report writing and presentations about disparities in digital patient engagement, efforts to address gaps, the impact of digital engagement on health care quality and outcomes, etc.

Figure 5.2 CHW Roles and Digital Engagement Duties. Source for CHW Roles: Rosenthal et al., 2016.

Adopt Opt-Out Policies for Portal Adoption. Countless studies have shown a large drop off in the number of patients who initiated versus continue to use portals. Many drop off after the initial attempt which may not even lead to a successful login. One system found that going to opt-out policies increased overall adoption and reduced disparities in portal use.[28]

Address Technology Usability. The poor usability of consumer-facing health IT has been widely lamented. Gibbons, et al. found that including individuals who experience technology challenges at the earliest stages of technology development[38] leads to technology that is better adapted to all populations. A local program that trains patients to collaborate in research[39] could train patients to provide technology usability feedback to developers.

Generate Evidence for Digital Medicine. Unlike drugs and devices that require FDA approval, there are no standards or regulations to ensure that digital health technologies are safe and effective. NODE Health, the Network of Digital Evidence for Health is promulgating such standards for digital medicine and creating a registry of technologies to help speed development and adoption of effective technology.[40] In collaboration with other NODE Health leaders, and with funding from Case Western Reserve University's Clinical and Translational Science Collaborative (NIH award UL1TR000439-10), AS has published recommendations for ensuring that digital medicine technologies address populations that have special needs with respect to use of digital health technology.[41] Health systems should participate in studies of digital health technology, paying special attention to the needs of patients who may lack digital skills and robust connectivity.

Conclusion

The $28 billion federal investment in health information technology, plus general advances in technology and cloud computing have created a robust and rapidly growing ecosystem of technology-based tools. Disparities in digital skills and connectivity portent that such technology will accentuate vast and growing health disparities. Health systems can prevent this otherwise predictable result through conscious effort across the full spectrum of the health technology ecosystem. Engage in research on technology development and ensure that diverse populations contribute to all stages of product development. Systematically screen all patients and refer them to local digital inclusion advocates to attain the general digital skills and connectivity needed before they can be encouraged to adopt digital technology. Health systems should engage community health workers to perform this screening and referral, and then train patients, once suitably equipped, to use digital health technology. By adopting such measures, health system executives will have compelling answers to questions about how to support patient engagement.

References

1. US Bureau of the Census. Types of Computers and Internet Subscriptions 2017 American Community Survey 1-Year Estimates, Table S2801. [cited 2018 Dec 6]. Available from: https://factfinder.census.gov/bkmk/table/1.0/en/ACS/17_1YR/S2801/1600000US3916000
2. Balas EA, Boren SA. Managing clinical knowledge for health care improvement. *Yearb Med Inform*. 2000;(1):65–70.

3. Morris ZS, Wooding S, Grant J. The answer is 17 years, what is the question: Understanding time lags in translational research. *J R Soc Med*. 2011 Dec [cited 2018 Apr 18];104(12):510–20. Available from: https://www.ncbi.nlm.nih.gov/p mc/articles/PMC3241518/

4. Horrigan JB. *Digital Readiness Gaps*. Pew Research Center. 2016 Sep [cited 2017 Feb 14]. Available from: http://www.pewinternet.org/2016/09/20/digital-readiness-gaps/

5. Braveman PA, Egerter SA, Mockenhaupt RE. Broadening the Focus: The Need to Address the Social Determinants of Health. *Am J Prev Med*. 2011 Jan;40(1, Supplement 1):S4–18. Available from: http://www.sciencedirect.com/science/art icle/pii/S0749379710005635

6. Commission to Build a Healthier America. *Breaking Through on the Social Determinants of Health and Health Disparities: An approach to message translation*. Robert Wood Johnson Foundation. 2009. Available from: https://www. rwjf.org/en/library/research/2011/05/breaking-through-on-the-social-determinants-of-health-and-health.html

7. Marmot M, Friel S, Bell R, Houweling TA, Taylor S, Commission on Social Determinants of Health. Closing the gap in a generation: Health equity through action on the social determinants of health. *The Lancet*. 2008;372(9650):1661–9. Available from: http://whqlibdoc.who.int/publications/2008/9789241563703_eng. pdf?ua=1

8. Whitehead M, Dahlgren G. What can be done about inequalities in health? *The Lancet*. 1991 Oct [cited 2018 Apr 12];338(8774):1059–63. Available from: http://linkinghub.elsevier.com/retrieve/pii/014067369191911D

9. Williams DR, Costa MV, Odunlami AO, Mohammed SA. Moving Upstream: How Interventions that Address the Social Determinants of Health can Improve Health and Reduce Disparities. *J Public Health Manag Pract JPHMP*. 2008 Nov [cited 2018 Feb 23];14(Suppl):S8–17. Available from: https://www.ncb i.nlm.nih.gov/pmc/articles/PMC3431152/

10. Woolf SH, Braveman P. Where Health disparities begin: The role of social and economic determinants—and why current Policies may make matters worse. *Health Aff (Millwood)*. 2011 Oct 1 [cited 2011 Oct 12];30(10):1852–9. Available from: http://content.healthaffairs.org/content/30/10/1852.abstract

11. Mokdad AH, Ballestros K, Echko M, Glenn S, Olsen HE, Mullany E, et al. The State of US Health, 1990-2016: Burden of Diseases, Injuries, and Risk Factors Among US States. *JAMA*. 2018 Apr 10 [cited 2018 Apr 11];319(14):1444–72. Available from: https://jamanetwork.com/journals/jama/fullarticle/2678018

12. Case Western Reserve University. Cleveland & Cuyahoga Health Data Matters. Cleveland & Cuyahoga Health Data Matters. 2018 [cited 2018 Jan 23]. Available from: https://hdm.livestories.com/

13. Centers for Disease Control and Prevention. 500 Cities Project: Local data for better health. [cited 2017 Jul 14]. Available from: https://www.cdc.gov/500cities/

14. Robert Wood Johnson Foundation and the University of Wisconsin Population Health Institute. County Health Rankings & Roadmaps. 2017 [cited 2013 Nov 12]. Available from: http://www.countyhealthrankings.org/app/ohio/2017/ranki ngs/cuyahoga/county/outcomes/overall/snapshot

15. Agerwala SM, McCance-Katz EF. Integrating screening, brief intervention, and referral to treatment (SBIRT) into clinical practice settings: a brief review. *J Psychoactive Drugs*. 2012 [cited 2018 Apr 13];44(4):307–17. Available from: https ://www.ncbi.nlm.nih.gov/pmc/articles/PMC3801194/

16. Frank S. *Precision Public Health is Why Health Data Matters. Cleveland and Cuyahoga Health Data Matters*. 2016 [cited 2018 Apr 13]. Available from: http: //www.healthdatamatters.org/blog/2016/11/22/precision-public-health-is-why-health-data-matters-blog-by-scott-frank-md-ms-november-2016

17. Kaelber D. *Exploiting Health Information Technology to Improve Health: The MetroHealth 2015 Davies Award Enterprise Application*. Healthcare Information and Management Systems Society (HIMSS). 2015 Aug [cited 2017 Feb 4]. Available from: http://www.himss.org/metrohealth-cleveland-davies-enterprise-award?ItemNumber=46432

18. Perzynski AT, Roach MJ, Shick S, Callahan B, Gunzler D, Cebul R, et al. Patient portals and broadband internet inequality. *J Am Med Inform Assoc*. 2017 Mar 23 [cited 2017 Apr 14]; Available from: https://academic.oup.com/jamia/article/doi/10 .1093/jamia/ocx020/3079333/Patient-portals-and-broadband-internet-inequality

19. Anderson M, Perrin A, Jiang J. 11% of Americans don't use the internet. Who are they?. Pew Research Center. 2018 [cited 2018 Apr 13]. Available from: http:// www.pewresearch.org/fact-tank/2018/03/05/some-americans-dont-use-the-inte rnet-who-are-they/

20. AT&T Low-Cost Internet Program. 2016 [cited 2016 Apr 2]. Available from: http: //connectyourcommunity.org/wp-content/uploads/2016/03/LCBB_SNAP_O nePager_020116.pdf

21. Callahan B. CYC 2.0 calls for digital inclusion investment as price of Comcast-Charter deal|Connect Your Community 2.0. Connect Your Community 2.0. 2014 [cited 2016 Mar 12]. Available from: http://connectyourcommunity.org/cyc -2-0-calls-for-digital-inclusion-investment-as-price-of-comcast-charter-deal/

22. Callahan B.. AT&T's digital redlining of Cleveland. National Digital Inclusion Alliance. 2017 [cited 2017 Apr 16]. Available from: https://digitalinclusion.org/b log/2017/03/10/atts-digital-redlining-of-cleveland/

23. Strain G, Moore E, Gambhir S. *AT&Ts digital divide in California*. Haas Institute, University of California, Berkeley. 2017 Apr [cited 2017 Apr 26]. Available from: http://haasinstitute.berkeley.edu/digitaldividecalifornia

24. Callahan B. Map of Montgomery County, OH Census blocks with AT&T "Fiber To The Node" (VDSL) Internet access at 18 mbps or more. National Digital Inclusion Alliance. 2017 [cited 2017 Apr 16]. Available from: https://digitalinclu sion.org/montgomery-county-att-fttn-available/

25. Callahan B. *More Digital Redlining? AT&T Home Broadband Deployment and Poverty in Detroit and Toledo.* National Digital Inclusion Alliance. 2017 [cited 2018 Apr 13]. Available from: https://www.digitalinclusion.org/blog/2017/09/06/more-digital-redlining-att-deployment-and-poverty-in-detroit-and-toledo/

26. Sheon A. The ROI of digital inclusion for community health and health care [Internet]. National Digital Inclusion Alliance Net Summit 2017. 2017 May 17 [cited 2017 Apr 18]. Available from: https://digitalinclusion.org/wp-content/uploads/2017/04/NDIA-2017-FINAL.pptx

27. Rosenthal EL, Rush CH, Allen CG. *Understanding Scope and Competencies: A Contemporary Look at the United States Community Health Worker Field.* University of Texas—Houston School of Public Health, Institute for Health Policy. 2016 Apr [cited 2018 Apr 20]. Available from: http://www.healthreform.ct.gov/ohri/lib/ohri/work_groups/chw/chw_c3_report.pdf

28. Community Health Workers: Action Guide for CHW Employers. ICER. [cited 2018 Jan 30]. Available from: https://icer-review.org/material/chw-action-guide-employers/

29. Community Health Workers: Action Guide for Workforce. ICER. [cited 2018 Jan 30]. Available from: https://icer-review.org/material/chw-action-guide-workforce/

30. Mejia-Rodriguez C, Spink D. *Training Curriculum for Community Health Workers [Internet].* [cited 2018 June 30]. Washington State Department of Health. Report No.: DOH 140-043. 2015 Aug. Available from: https://www.doh.wa.gov/Portals/1/Documents/Pubs/140-043-CHWT_ParticipantManual.pdf

31. Findley SE, Matos S, Hicks AL, Campbell A, Moore A, Diaz D. Building a Consensus on Community Health Workers' Scope of Practice: Lessons From New York. *Am J Public Health.* 2012 Oct [cited 2017 Aug 4];102(10):1981–7. Available from: http://www.ncbi.nlm.nih.gov/pmc/articles/PMC3490670/

32. Berthold T, ed. *Foundations for Community Health Workers.* 2nd edition. San Francisco, CA: Jossey-Bass; 2016. 736.

33. Ancker JS, Barrón Y, Rockoff ML, Hauser D, Pichardo M, Szerencsy A, et al. Use of an electronic patient portal among disadvantaged populations. *J Gen Intern Med.* 2011;26(10):1117. Available from: https://link.springer.com/article/10.1007/s11606-011-1749-y

34. Peacock S, Reddy A, Leveille SG, Walker J, Payne TH, Oster NV, et al. Patient portals and personal health information online: perception, access, and use by US adults. *J Am Med Inform Assoc [Internet].* 2017 Apr 1 [cited 2017 Mar 21];24(e1):e173–7. Available from: https://academic.oup.com/jamia/article/24/e1/e173/2631484/Patient-portals-and-personal-health-information

35. Ancker JS, Nosal S, Hauser D, Way C, Calman N. Access policy and the digital divide in patient access to medical records. *Health Policy Technol.* 2017 Mar [cited 2017 Apr 25];6(1):3–11. Available from: http://linkinghub.elsevier.com/retrieve/pii/S2211883716300867

36. Harris K, Sheon A, Castek J, Perzynski A, Reeder J, Sieck C. *Workshop: Multidisciplinary Perspectives on Digital Adoption.* 2018 Apr [cited 2018 Apr 14]. Available from: https://netinclusion2018.sched.com/event/DKpF/multidisciplin ary-perspectives-on-digital-inclusion-and-health

37. *Strategies and Recommendations for Promoting Digital Inclusion.* Consumer and Governmental Affairs Bureau, Federal Communications Commission. 2017 Jan. [cited 2018 June 30]. Available from: http://transition.fcc.gov/Daily_Releases /Daily_Business/2017/db0126/DOC-342993A1.pdf

38. Gibbons MC, Lowry SZ, Patterson ES. Applying human factors principles to mitigate usability issues related to embedded assumptions in health information technology design. *JMIR Hum Factors.* 2014 [cited 2017 Apr 29];1(1):e3. Available from: http://humanfactors.jmir.org/2014/1/e3/

39. Theurer J, Pike E, Sehgal AR, Fischer RL, Collins C. The Community Research Scholars Initiative: A Mid-Project Assessment. *Clin Transl Sci.* 2015;8(4):341–6.

40. Atreja A, Bates D, Clancy S, Daniel G, Doerr M, Franklin P, et al. *Mobilizing Mhealth Innovation for Real-World Evidence Generation.* 2018 Jan. Duke University Margolis Center for Health Policy

41. Sheon AR, Van Winkle B, Solad Y, Atreja A. An Algorithm for Digital Medicine Testing: A NODE.Health Perspective Intended to Help Emerging Technology Companies and Healthcare Systems Navigate the Trial and Testing Period prior to Full-Scale Adoption. Digital Biomarkers. 2018 [cited 2018 Dec 7];2:139–54. https://www.karger.com/Article/FullText/494365

Healthcare without Borders: Innovating for Global Impact

Joel Barthelemy

As a former resident of Minnesota, I can testify to its beautiful dichotomies. Weather-wise, it is one of the most extreme places in the country, where 95-degree summers and lush greenery are trampled into submission every year by thermometers reading 30 below zero and enough snow for a lifetime of white Christmases. Maybe I was destined to end up in the Southwest, a land of extremes in precisely the opposite direction. Either way, our surroundings shape us, and seeing the way people adapt and thrive under the most challenging circumstances – and watching myself evolve in the process – has shaped the kind of businessman, innovator, and human being I hope I've become. And the telehealth delivery systems I've helped create which have had an impact around the world.

Minnesota is the backdrop for one reason I founded GlobalMed, a company whose mission is to improve the delivery of healthcare through innovation. My dad was a U.S. Army veteran of both World War II and the

Korean War, to which he lost much of his hearing. His retirement years in St. Cloud included monthly visits to audiology specialists at the Veterans Health Administration (VA) hospital at Fort Snelling near Minneapolis. Dad would wake up at 5:30 a.m., drive to the VA bus stop in St. Cloud and ride two hours to his appointment. He'd wait to see his audiologist. Once seen, he'd wait around the rest of the day for his 85-mile bus ride north. It was usually a 13-hour day.

Mind you, dad lived less than a mile from the most beautiful VA hospital in Minnesota. But it had no audiology specialist. He took an entire day out of his month to fine tune his hearing, so he could communicate with his grandkids. That bothered me.

My company took audiology systems and telehealth systems and merged them into one, creating the ability to do remote audiology literally. Unfortunately, my dad passed before they placed the station in St. Cloud, but until his death, he would bring my case studies to read for anyone who would listen to a proud dad.

But I'm getting ahead of myself.

Diagnosing Machines, Then People

My point here is to trace the way we innovate, from the identification of needs and pain points and common denominators to sparks of imagination and lots of trial and error. Like my dad, I was proud to serve in the military. After leaving the Marine Corps, I went into technology and never looked back. One of my early companies helped dramatically reduce the cost of computer labs in schools by redesigning networking technology for Apple II computers. When the Macintosh replaced the Apple II, we addressed security issues with MacSecure, a program we wrote to give students less opportunity to damage or tamper with their computers. In each instance, and in all of my business endeavors, I identified problems and innovated my way to solutions.

Eventually, I started a company that did quality control on semiconductors for Motorola, Intel and others. Then I bought a camera company and applied camera technology in an exciting way. If one of our semiconductor machines went down, it could mean disaster for our clients and our small company. In those days, complicated issues with machines we'd bought were dealt with by a technician who flew in from headquarters. Not willing to risk the massive downtime that involved, we created a web camera to show the company what was wrong. They could send me the part, my in-house team could fix it, and we would keep our customer commitments.

That is telemedicine.

After the dotcom bubble burst around the year 2001, I needed to reinvent myself once again. I thought about the potential opportunities within medicine, and about my dad trudging halfway across Minnesota for routine care. I also looked at the sad state of our outdated healthcare system and decided I didn't want to be stuck in that same system in 20 years. How could my technology experience help provide affordable, available, reliable healthcare?

Remote Arizona as Inspiration

Living in Arizona, one never feels far from nature. Mountains are often visible on the horizon even in the three largest cities, and hiking among towering Saguaro cacti is a rite of passage.

There's something healing in the quiet isolation of wild places, and yet most of us are mere visitors. Urbanites in America are shocked to learn of the vast numbers of people living in remote or disaster-stricken areas of the world, often without access to quality healthcare. In the remote Native American reservations spread across the state's desolate landscape, the need was clear: people required healthcare no matter where they lived, and technology was the way to bring providers to their patients.

The Havasupai Native American tribe lives at the bottom of a canyon within Grand Canyon National Park here in Arizona, with little or no modern technology or electronic communication with the outside world. The only way in or out of the canyon is by pack mule or helicopter – a big problem when someone needs medical attention. But my company has solved that problem with a portable "clinic in a box" that enables Havasupai patients to be seen via telehealth, either at Flagstaff Medical Center in Flagstaff (FMC) or by a specialist located in Phoenix or Tucson.

This "clinic in a box" is an example of real-world innovation. The Transportable Exam Station™ (TES) can be solar-powered with a battery that lasts for up to a day. TES uses satellite communications to reach remote providers. It can measure vital signs, aid in primary care, ENT, dermatology, urology, cardiology, behavioral consults, and even to help place a PICC line.

Similar to the Havasupai, but a couple of oceans away, the people of Zimbabwe are turning to telemedicine. In many of their villages, like others around the world, healthcare may be limited to a monthly visit from a nurse whose job it is to see as many patients as possible in one day. But what happens when you or a loved one is sick on an off day? The answer is that two of the healthiest people in the village pick you up and carry you to care in the village that has it that day. And we thought my dad had it rough. Luckily, telemedicine, when done right, can carry all of us on its shoulders.

Moving west from Zimbabwe, we turn our attention to Brazil, where GlobalMed's introduction to locals came via oil rigs and our local ties ended up saving lives on the mainland. Petrobras, the world's fourth-largest oil company, partnered with GlobalMed and Albert Einstein Hospital to provide healthcare on oil rigs. Traditionally, patients that couldn't be handled by on-site nurses were airlifted to the mainland for help. Some oil platforms are so far from shore that helicopters have to land on a separate rig and refuel before continuing to their destination. None of this is ideal for injured or sick oil workers, and costs were astronomical. Now telehealth units are installed on rigs, allowing mainland specialists to assess patients via audio, video, and connected instruments. Patients are transported only if the doctor deems it necessary.

Our Petrobras deployments got a lot of attention in Brazil.

Then, in January 2013, small coastal party town Santa Maria hosted students from six nearby colleges. The crowded Kiss nightclub erupted in flames after pyrotechnics were used indoors. The blaze killed 242 people and injured over 600 others. Unable to airlift so many victims to Sao Paolo for care, emergency responders were in dire straits. The Brazilian president, thankfully, was aware of GlobalMed's technology, and our kit was put on a small plane in Sao Paolo and sent to help the victims. Burn experts from around the world were enlisted to help remotely. Local and international doctors collaborated to do the best they could for every victim. They even used our TotalExam camera to match skin that would be flown in for grafts.

GlobalMed employees have not forgotten Brazil. We know our products have meaning outside our four walls.

Disaster Relief

That special meaning was highlighted again, when in September 2017, Hurricane Maria descended on Puerto Rico, becoming the worst natural disaster to hit the tiny island and the third costliest tropical cyclone in history, besides the terrible human cost. The loss of electricity, severe damage to homes and agriculture, the lack of clean drinking water, and a shortage of supplies combined to create a health crisis of severe magnitude. Again, a solution was needed to engage the help of medical providers around the world who couldn't physically get to the island.

With relief slow to come, U.S. Army mobile medics and nurses from Brooke Army Medical Center's (BAMC) Virtual Medical Center and Dwight D. Eisenhower Army Medical Center flew to Puerto Rico and set up camp within the 14th Combat Support Hospital (CSH) from Ft. Benning, GA. The mobile medical team established clinical operations in Humacao, one of the hardest hit regions, and started providing healthcare to the local population.

The team members, who saw over 150 patients a day, used telehealth to provide on-demand, synchronous critical care, and specialty virtual health encounters. Our telemedicine equipment enabled the team to receive remote medical support from providers at BAMC in Fort Sam Houston, TX, Dwight D. Eisenhower Army Medical Center in Fort Gordon, GA, Naval Medical Center San Diego, and the U.S. Naval Ship Comfort. The team has since moved onto other badly damaged parts of Puerto Rico.

To Protect and Serve

Telemedicine does not just benefit people in faraway places. Here at home, the Veterans Health Administration (VA) became an early adopter of telemedicine. Previously, too many veterans lived too far from the specialists they needed, and often missed appointments or didn't seek care. VA facilities were overrun with a patient roster they couldn't handle. By 2016, more than 702,000 veterans annually received care via telehealth. The next year, the VA announced regulatory changes to facilitate the use of telemedicine, as well as the creation of two innovative telemedicine programs. During a live press conference from the White House by the President and the Secretary of the VA, the GlobalMed ClinicalAccess Station and Transportable Exam Station were demonstrated with 187 million views in 25 short hours.

"This is actually the new doctor's bag, the doctor's bag of the future," said the VA secretary.

The demonstration was the result of a decision by the White House Medical Unit (WHMU) to employ telehealth stations to provide high-quality care in a private, secure setting. The WHMU treats the President, the Vice President, their families and visiting international dignitaries, as well as staff members and visitors to the White House.

Telehealth helped saved lives when WHMU staffers were visiting Peru's Andes Mountains. Lt. Col. James Jones, the physician assistant to the President's physician and director of the medical evaluation and treatment unit at the White House, was on a three-day detail hiking in Peru. He used the GlobalMed TES in treating a Secret Service agent and two U.S. students, all of whom suffered from maladies throughout the trip because of the extreme altitude. Lt. Col Jones relied on the telehealth kit to evaluate all three patients and to communicate with doctors back home. Once he stabilized the patients, he coordinated their evacuations and treatments.

The armed forces continue to break ground using telemedicine. Recently, after GlobalMed received an Authority to Operate (ATO) on Department of Defense (DoD) networks, the U.S. Navy began to use GlobalMed technology on its hospital ships. In March 2018, the hospital ship *Mercy* conducted the Navy's first-ever portable telemedicine broadcast from a ship at sea, transmitting vital signs to and enabling ear, nose, throat, head, and neck skin examinations by doctors at Naval Medical Center San Diego. An otolaryngologist in San Diego also guided a corpsman in emergency battlefield medical techniques.

Communication Challenges

Solutions like ours, which lead to stories like these, take years of innovation. The path isn't accessible. While identifying customer pain points and working to develop solutions, we have had to overcome some significant challenges. A couple of years ago, for instance, the White House Medical Unit asked us, "What happens if Air Force One is forced to land somewhere with little or no Internet connectivity?"

Fortunately, we'd already figured that one out years earlier when we developed a store-and-forward system for the VA and ocean-based oil rigs. When a connection goes down, we can hold and encrypt the data on the local station. As soon as connectivity is restored, the stored information is automatically uploaded and synced with the receiving system so that remote specialists can provide synchronous care to the President. The same approach is used when a link goes down during any virtual encounter between a patient and a provider.

We have encountered a different kind of challenge on airplanes that have commercial in-flight connectivity. Since these satellite-based connections provide relatively low bandwidth with sometimes one hundred or more passengers using the limited service, we developed an app that allows the crew on planes to make high-definition medical video calls and maintain the connection even if other users have reduced the available bandwidth.

Similarly, when a hospital ship uses a BGAN portable global satellite transmitter, which has an extremely low bandwidth, their corpsmen can connect and get a virtual medical consult with our equipment. When a team of Navy medical corpsmen goes into a village in an impoverished or disaster-ridden country, they are able to connect our kit with BGAN technology and provide top-quality care.

Correctional Facilities

Even though they are right here, correctional institutions often feel like remote villages or islands, detached from mainstream society. But their residents still get sick, still become injured. The Texas Tech University, Health Sciences Center (TTUHSC) in Lubbock, Texas, has created a program for the Texas Department of Criminal Justice (TDCJ) that provides health services for state prison inmates in 25 locations throughout West Texas. In 2013, TTUHSC began using telehealth systems in prisons to improve access to care, increase public safety, and save money. In 2013, telehealth visits saved the state about $3.2 million.

Telemedicine has also been successful for the California Department of Corrections and Rehabilitation (CDCR), which provides healthcare to nearly 200,000 inmates. Travel time for providers to visit sick inmates and the need for a security detail created additional costs, and in-person encounters increased the risk of escapes. In 2013 alone, telehealth reduced the department's health-related costs by $7.2 million. Five years later, the CDCR is using virtual health to provide chronic and acute care, mental health, and transgender care.

Pride in Helping Care for Kids

Dealing with sick or injured school children has something in common with aiding inmates: Transportation and safety are big problems. Our goal is to alleviate those concerns by enabling on-site nurses. In 2013, Children's Medical Center of Dallas established the largest school-based telemedicine program in the country. The initiative began with two pre-schools in the Dallas area and, with the help of a Medicaid waiver program, expanded to 57 campuses throughout north Texas. A school nurse acts as the patient presenter while the child speaks to a doctor or nurse practitioner at Children's Medical Center using video conferencing software. As a result, children are diagnosed and treated sooner, and parents are spared from having to respond to a sick child call and take their children to doctors' offices or urgent care centers.

Similarly, Ronald McDonald® Children's Hospital/Loyola University Medical Center used telemedicine to solve a major problem with admissions during evening and weekend hours. If an infant was admitted when the attending physician was not in, the resident on duty had to communicate with the attending physician to approve the admission. That typically meant the attending physician would be driving to the hospital and talking on the phone while mentoring the resident and ensuring the patient was adequately cared for.

In 2006, Dr. Kathy Webster, a critical pediatric physician at the hospital, approached GlobalMed and asked whether a pan-zoom-tilt camera that it made could be fitted onto a cart that could be wheeled into a patient room. Using a grant she obtained to buy equipment for the hospital's pediatric and neonatal care clinic, Webster worked with GlobalMed to create the solution. The camera on a cart was used to conduct video conferences with attending physicians and improve response times.

Full Circle

Whether the pain was expensive computer labs in schools, quality control for semiconductors, or saving lives after disaster struck an island nation, the path toward a solution was the same one my mind took after watching my dad board that bus to Minneapolis. Do we just ask why this is the way it is, or can we work to make a change? What knowledge from my past can I apply to the problem at hand? Whom do I know who can help us fix this problem?

As the above innovative examples show, telemedicine has made health-care potentially accessible everywhere. With the right equipment, software, and connectivity for each healthcare setting, care can be delivered to patients in the most difficult-to-reach spots and the most challenging environments.

Innovative healthcare delivery systems can be a great equalizer. Military veterans, Native Americans, isolated tribes, the President of the United States – maybe even you – are all my most important patients.

My own life has changed in ways I never anticipated upon forming GlobalMed. I enjoy meeting providers and patients whose stories of struggle often go untold, and I enjoy leaving their lives healthier, more supported, and more connected. Eliminating barriers and enhancing communication benefits all aspects of society globally.

When Innovation Meets Integration: Developing the Tools for Invisible Healthcare

Drew Schiller

Two hundred forty million Americans own a smartphone,[1] and we spend an average of five hours each day interacting with our devices[2] – nearly one-third of our waking hours. The expansion and mass adoption of these mobile computers over the last decade has implications for how healthcare will function to interact with patients and provide better care in coming years. Perhaps more importantly, the evolution of smartphone technology itself offers a roadmap for how healthcare can integrate novel technology to design an *invisible*, interoperable healthcare system.

The importance of system interoperability is an ever-present, if not prosaic, mantra for many of us in healthcare. Embedded systems must seamlessly exchange information with other technologies inside and outside the clinical walls for both clinicians and patients. Yet, the concept of invisible design, which can be considered *applied interoperability*, is a fairly new construct for healthcare.

Invisible design means something is so well integrated into your routine that you don't notice the mechanics of it, only the outcome. Invisible tools become a natural part of your day-to-day life without consciously thinking about it.

Smartphones, for example, have capitalized on this concept of designing for an invisible experience. With voice-activated assistants, you no longer have to look at your device to access functionality. You can ask Siri, Alexa, or Google to play music, schedule a meeting, or even send a text without opening a single application. You can program your weather or news app to send you a synopsis each morning to prepare you for the day. You can queue your music or maps to play as soon as you enter your car. We no longer have to search or monitor for relevant information. By design, our smartphone pushes it to us.

The concept of invisible design was best summarized by user interface guru Jared Spool, who said: "Good design, when it's done well, becomes invisible. It's only when it's done poorly that we notice it."

And in healthcare, we certainly do notice it. When we talk to patients, providers, and healthcare administrators about the design of the healthcare experience today, we find that challenges and faulty mechanics are painfully obvious to all stakeholders, especially to the patient, a role we all share.

One such patient, Steve, was diagnosed with type 2 diabetes at age 40, like his father, uncle, and grandmothers before him. A decade after his diagnosis, Steve continued to struggle. He struggled to maintain a healthy weight despite working out and leading an active lifestyle. He struggled with his a1c levels despite a managed diet and nutrition program. He struggled with depression and energy levels despite cutting his work hours to part-time. Even with weekly office visits, medication, and an established treatment program, Steve struggled to feel in control of his condition and overall health – and clearly not for a lack of trying.

Steve was tirelessly dedicated to getting better, so much so, that he would routinely fax a copy of his glucose readings – which he kept in an excel file – to his doctor ahead of each visit. But, with no clinical protocol or system in place to manage Steve's data, the endocrinologist would promptly discard Steve's readings and instead continue to manage his condition using only preceding a1c readings. This caused a frustrated Steve to leave his provider and seek treatment with a new kind of program, one that would integrate the data he generated daily to better manage his condition.

Steve found and enrolled in a new program of care, which, unlike any program Steve had been a part of before, leveraged his biometric and observations of daily living (ODLs) data to manage his condition. The program required Steve to take blood glucose readings at least three times a day, usually around meals. Steve's data were collected via his program-issued application, which connected data from his weight scale, a blood glucose meter, an activity tracker, and a blood-pressure monitor (to help monitor the effect of medication on his kidney function).

Steve's continuous data sharing, combined with a programmatic monitoring of his data, revealed an overlooked snacking habit that affected his ability to control his glucose levels. While watching television with his kids each night, Steve would eat a couple of handfuls of chips or popcorn (which Steve thought were "free" because of the relatively few calories he consumed). The late-night snacking sessions caused a consistent spike in Steve's blood sugar each morning. Steve's care manager noticed the trend and informed him on how to amend his diet and actions (corn is high in carbohydrates, and Steve learned that this turns into sugar in his body). As this demonstrates, by employing patient-generated health data (PGHD) in a consistent feedback loop, a previously unidentified and problematic trend was identified, and the patient was able to adjust his lifestyle to achieve his target HbA1c.

Today, Steve is down 50 pounds and has lowered his a1c from 8.9 to 6.5. Additionally, after showing success in consistently managing his weight and condition, Steve's physician amended the number of in-office visits he needed to once every three months. Reviewing his data with a clinician, being accountable for measurements, and building a rapport with a care team helped Steve gain deeper insight into his condition and learn how to better self-manage.

For patients like Steve and the millions more suffering from chronic conditions, the inability to share data with a physician was thwarting better outcomes. His traditional program of care focused solely on his a1c levels, viewed retrospectively every three months. Despite monitoring several aspects of his health multiple times a day, he was not able to leverage this information with his care team to impact his treatment.

So, what did Steve do differently?

In reality, very little. Steve changed almost nothing about his routine. Simply integrating the data he was already generating into the clinical workflow with a defined program of care changed this man's life. The program enabled superior patient-provider discourse by changing the conversation from, "Why isn't this working?," to, "Here's what the data show is not working." To do this, the program did not implement new or groundbreaking technology. The program simply integrated existing information, devices, and clinical systems to yield the improved outcomes.

Oftentimes, true innovation comes from restructuring current technologies in new and interesting ways. Take, for example, the iPhone, released in 2007, and its predecessor, the PalmPilot, released in 1997. The PalmPilot was a bulky smart device with a stylus that offered basically the same functionality as the first-generation iPhone. In fact, there was little innovation in the features offered by Apple's new smart device. Much like the iPhone, the PalmPilot offered phone services, text messaging, a calculator, email, games, a QWERTY keyboard, and a web browser. Apple didn't focus on developing new functionalities for a device; they focused on taking these applications and embedding them within a more seamless, more *invisible* user experience. The focus on invisible design clearly paid off – the phone was an instant hit, and since the launch of the iPhone, Apple has become among the most regarded and valuable companies in the world.

To further enhance the user experience, Apple not only changed the way phones were designed, they also changed the way phones were integrated with carriers. Prior to the iPhone, carriers were white-labeling cell phones and adding their own software. Apple rejected this standard, forming an exclusive launch with AT&T to release the iPhone with Apple's iOS installed and untouched. They wanted to maintain control over all aspects of the iPhone's user experience – because, candidly, consumer electronics companies deeply understand what healthcare has not yet internalized: how important the experience is to engagement.

In 2008, a year after launching the iPhone, Apple released the App Store. It was no longer solely Apple dictating the user experience. Consumers could now personalize their device to the experience *they* wanted.

Now, more than a decade later, smartphones are seemingly sewn to the hands of consumers. With each year, these devices are better designed to integrate directly into our personal experiences – helping us capture, share, and manage our lives.

Similar to 2007 with the launch of the iPhone, healthcare today has the technology – the feature set – to design a better system. However, we have yet to integrate these technologies in such a way that facilitates seamless, personalized user experiences. To move past the current stagnation of the industry, we must apply innovation to the integration of technology to create unobtrusive, invisible healthcare experiences.

In 2017, the Commonwealth Fund conducted an evaluation of the U.S. healthcare system along with 11 similar countries. The group found that the U.S. system performed the worst among the countries, while spending more. Particularly, the U.S. system performed exceedingly poor on most, if not all, measures related to population health, ranking last in affordability, access, and outcomes.[3]

This evaluation elaborates on something many of us know to be true: American patients today are struggling to find available, affordable healthcare that truly helps them achieve their health goals.

"It costs too much."

"It took forever for the doctor to see me."

"I can't access my health record to send to my new physician."

"I have gone to three different doctors and they still don't know what's wrong."

These are common refrains heard from patients like Steve, echoing frustrations with their healthcare experiences. Even as regulatory measures offer guidance, penalties, and incentives to drive the industry toward value-based care, barriers to achieving improved access, affordability, and outcomes remain.

To do this, we need to address two critical shortcomings of the current system's design. First, we need data-driven technology to be integrated into a comprehensive program of care that personalizes the treatment and experience of each patient. Second, we need for this technology to be integrated into the providers' workflows to make the experience of delivering personalized care easy for clinicians.

Data-driven programs, like the one designed for Steve, are the key to a results-driven, invisible healthcare experience. Having a technology-enabled program of care is crucial in allowing care teams, like Steve's, to identify negative progressions and elevate the right data for intervention and engagement. When clinicians are able to see patient-generated data – in real time, in their existing workflow – they are able to more efficiently identify trends that could indicate a looming negative health event. In Steve's case, the care team was able to alert the physician of concerning data, initiating a life-changing conversation. Steve had been tracking these events throughout the management of his condition, but it was not until the data was made available to a care team, actively monitored, and proactively used in care, that changes were able to be made to Steve's lifestyle.

Steve does not have the education of the healthcare professional. He needed a diabetes educator to guide his nutrition and activity, a nurse care manager to monitor his treatment, and an endocrinologist to adjust medication based on a trend of glucose and activity values rather than one a1c reading every three months. And, in return, the care team needed access to Steve's data to provide the right education, monitoring, and treatment to affect his condition. They needed this access provided in the workflow with alerts and triggers to notify when intervention is needed. Both the patient and the provider needed pathways for better communication. For Steve and his care team, data provided an objective, common language for their exchanges. For millions served by the U.S. healthcare system, data can do the same.

Connecting the technology patients are using outside of the healthcare setting, such as fitness trackers and blood glucose meters, to the technology physicians are using in the provision of care, such as electronic health records and care management platforms, is one of the most effective ways to integrate people with their healthcare provider. As patient and provider utilization of this data increases, the healthcare system will be able to serve more patients more efficiently and effectively. And, in 2018, the ability to make care more efficient and effective is critical.

Studies show that over the next twelve years, the healthcare system will be short anywhere from 42,600 to 121,300 physicians.[4] Dissimilarly, both the number of patients in need of care and the complexity of conditions is expected to rise as a result of a growing obesity epidemic in the U.S. By 2030, it is estimated that 42 percent of the U.S. population will be obese, leading to a steep increase in chronic conditions. This substantial rise in obesity indicates there will be nearly 8 million new cases of diabetes a year and 7 million more cases of coronary heart disease and stroke annually.[5]

The numbers make it clear: without the aid of technology, we will simply be unable to support the number of patients needing care in the very near future. The only way to deliver a higher quantity and quality of output – with fewer human resources – is through the deployment of technology. By using technology strategically and by implementing it invisibly, we have an opportunity to augment the care that clinicians and care teams provide to patients today to make it more efficient and more streamlined, in order to successfully manage the health issues patients will be facing.

Rather than reacting solely to patient calls and office visits, we can leverage the information and the data already available to us through existing technologies to more proactively respond to patient needs and intervene to encourage better health behaviors, with the aim of preventing the exacerbation of such conditions.

With effective integration between patients' health apps, wearables, and devices, and providers' EHRs and other clinical systems, clinicians can integrate the information that is already available in disparate sources into the healthcare system. They can seamlessly connect with patients via their device or platform of choice in a way that makes care more efficient. They will have the opportunity to combine remote data with the information collected during visits to garner deeper insights, advance clinical knowledge at the point of care, and make more meaningful, more proactive care decisions. In this way, we can make the technology and experience not only invisible to the patient, we can make the experience invisible for the provider as well.

For years, we, as an industry, have been focused on innovation, on the creation of new tools, new data sources, and new solutions to solve problems and deliver care. The tools we need to reach these goals already exist. Patients are already generating health data that enable care teams to glean valuable insights. Electronic health records are already providing a platform in which providers and patients can access health history and other information.

We must now turn our focus to the integration of these innovative tools. And, we must think more critically about how we bring together technologies and services to design a healthcare system that delivers world-class patient outcomes despite a declining clinical workforce.

There will always be new sensors, new analytics, and new systems that come to market. But, we have the technology today to impact care and improve the quality of life for millions. Progress will remain sluggish until we bring today's technologies together and design for integration. We must design workflows and systems that integrate these tools in a way that is user-friendly, and ultimately, invisible, for all users – both the patient and the provider.

The ultimate healthcare experience will be realized when we can simply live our lives, healthily, and care is invisible.

References

1. "Mobile Fact Sheet." Pew Research Center. *Science & Tech*, 2018 Feb 5. [Cited 2018 June 30]. www.pewinternet.org/fact-sheet/mobile/.
2. Perez, Sarah. "U.S. Consumers Now Spend 5 Hours per Day on Mobile Devices." *TechCrunch*, 3 Mar. 2017. [Cited 2018 June 30]. techcrunch.com/2017/03/03/u-s-consumers-now-spend-5-hours-per-day-on-mobile-devices/.
3. Schneider, Eric C, et al. "Mirror, Mirror 2017: International Comparison Reflects Flaws and Opportunities for Better U.S. Health Care." *The Commonwealth Fund*, 2017. [Cited 2018 June 30]. interactives.commonwealthfund.org/2017/july/mirror-mirror/.
4. Dall, Tim, et al. *2018 Update: The Complexities of Physician Supply and Demand: Projections from 2016 to 2030*. Association of American Medical Colleges, 2018. [Cited 2018 June 30]. aamc-black.global.ssl.fastly.net/production/media/filer_public/bc/a9/bca9725e-3507-4e35-87e3-d71a68717d06/aamc_2018_workforce_projections_update_april_11_2018.pdf.
5. Egley, Sharon. "Fat and Getting Fatter: U.S. Obesity Rates to Soar by 2030." *Reuters*, 18 Sept. 2012. [Cited 2018 June 30]. www.reuters.com/article/us-obesity-us-idUSBRE88H0RA20120918.

Establishing a Culture of Innovation – Eliminating Barriers

Rachael Britt-McGraw

When I came into the healthcare IT field, there were some significant differences between the culture I saw before me and the cultures I had experienced in other industries up until that time. How healthcare defines innovation, from whom it expects innovation, and the acceptance of and valuation of innovation all differed. Whereas in some industries IT is fully expected to constantly innovate and continually improve business processes and profitability, this did not seem to be the case in the healthcare space. In fact, it almost seemed there was a mistrust of IT, and a general mistrust of why IT would put forward new potential ways for operations to accomplish things. I had a lot to learn and determined that I would earn the trust of operational leaders and staff through transparency and dependency as I endeavored to learn and add value. Feeling that the best IT is always in lockstep with operations, regardless of industry, I met with the COO to learn his perspective on how we in IT could serve him. I will never forget his response. He said "You just do the tech," and he turned and walked away. This reaction to an offer of service was completely foreign to me. I had never been so summarily dismissed by my customer, and I knew then that things were culturally quite different than in my previous roles, and I was not going to succeed at all if I "just did the tech."

In my opinion, good IT work is not fully attainable within a tech-only bubble. I had many years of very strong IT experience and education, having built top-shelf IT teams in many different industries and in many geographic locations. But I knew I would first need to learn all about the people, the business, the challenges it faced, and historically how it had overcome barriers before I could bring that experience and skillset to bear. I stood before a group of dedicated, veteran healthcare staff as a complete novice, not even familiar with the acronyms used in the industry. Their IT infrastructure was in dire need of overhaul, the IT team was in shambles and the morale very low, and they were facing installation, implementation, and adoption of an Electronic Health Record system on a necessarily abbreviated timeline with no previous IT guidance or leadership. It seemed an overwhelming and insurmountable task. Looking back, that day was the beginning of establishing a culture of innovation, in that I put forth no pretense – I communicated clearly my ignorance of the industry to which many of them had devoted their lives. I asked them all to help me learn their world, and I began to listen actively. They were surprised by the open communication and genuine desire to learn from them and how much value I placed upon their collective knowledge. And they gave me at least some idea why there was a lack of trust in IT.

Some shared that they had experienced IT staff members in the past who acted superior and talked down to them. They had never had anyone in IT that actually communicated clearly using non-technical terms that people without a lot of technical knowledge could understand and apply to their work environment and needs. They had seen arrogant IT people who were long on promises and short on delivery, and who didn't seem to own those failures but pointed back at them as the problem. I explained that I would build an IT team that was service-oriented, and who would under-promise and over-deliver as central parts of the IT team's culture. They may not have completely believed that would happen that day, but they would certainly support me while I tried. Little did I know, I was removing a barrier even then by simply being vulnerable and communicating openly with these fantastic people. And they responded warmly and soon communicated to the CEO and COO that I was a valuable asset to them. Since this was a trusted group of long-term employees, this endorsement helped remove negative perceptions of IT at the top of the organization chart as well.

We all worked closely together over the next 2 years pulling long hours, correcting infrastructure, and implementing the Electronic Health Record system and Electronic Practice Management. By the end of that time, we had forged genuine and lasting trust, and we had all learned a lot from each other. Every step of the way, I communicated with our physicians and other providers of care, so that everyone in the organization knew what was currently underway, its status, and if we were hitting or missing targeted deadlines and budgetary guidelines. The result of openly communicating deadline misses and failures and then eating humble pie while getting those projects teed back up again until they were successful was fertile ground upon which to turn out innovative ideas. The trust forged allowed operational management to feel comfortable that IT had their best interests at heart, and would be honest. Thus they were able to view potential innovations with an open mind and add in their ideas and suggestions freely. We implemented a patient portal, and then an electronic means to exchange health records and new clinical communications systems. The sky became the limit.

After that our next innovation was to leverage technology in the exam rooms to give those doctors who wished to use it more ready access to images, studies, and medical records when speaking with their patients privately in the exam rooms. This had been widely opposed before. From there, we have pushed deeper into innovative ideas, introducing proximity cards and strict security protocols. Today, we are continuing to constantly innovate and reshape the practice through partnering with a local, innovative entrepreneur who is developing new systems for patient intake, verification of insurance, and payment collection. We have other potential partnerships in the wings, and the excitement of innovation is a part of our environment now. I feel a great sense of accomplishment now as IT has a seat at the strategy table, and is now expected to suggest innovations and keep the practice out front from a technology perspective.

In my experience, IT can be seen by the business in one of three ways: as a utility, an advisor, or a partner. As a utility, the business sees IT like the power company – flip the switch and the lights need to come on. These businesses see IT as only an "expensive overhead." If seen as an advisor, the business will reach out to IT for potential ideas when it faces a particular challenge or finds itself in a bind. These businesses see IT as a "one-off solution provider." But the real value of IT in business today is unleashed when the business sees IT as a partner. These businesses include IT concerns and potentials in business and growth strategy, and weave in technology and the ability to continue to innovate and progress within its routine decisions. We've moved through these roles, and what allowed us to do so was open communication to remove existing barriers, and produce trust.

Security as a Driver of Innovation

Mitchell Parker

Innovation is about empowering who you surround yourself with around a noble mission. A mission where the environment is constantly changing and over which you have no control. Where your focus must continuously change and strategies adapt. Where, despite the barrage of change, your motivation remains precise on excellence and quality. Innovation is forged from such circumstances.

It's not about trying to relate to frameworks or emulating people who are on the cover of magazines. It's about people. It's about a message of teamwork and continually supporting who you surround yourself with to change for the better and to challenge themselves to do better not only as a team member, but as a parent, family member, community member, and citizen. As a leader, it means that you have to continually set the example and put others before yourself.

The final product is one small miniscule piece, and in the end, the product doesn't make a difference. It's the results of how you affect those you surround yourself with that matter. No one is going to remember you for a project you did. They will remember you for who you are and what you did (or didn't do) to improve those around you.

This essay is about making innovation real and practical. We're going to get there. Information security is the last item people think of when you think of innovation. Especially in healthcare, where organizations are known for glacial change and a lack of it. Combine that with the fear, uncertainty, and doubt caused by misunderstandings of HIPAA and cybersecurity, siloed corporate structures, and fierce competition that stifles cross-organizational cooperation, and you have a situation that many people do not want to deal with.

We make it real and practical by consistently communicating our mission and values to our fellow team members. We are not about scaring people into conformance or being the HIPAA Police. We genuinely want our team members to do better every day and improve as participants in the shared mission of improving the health of our patients and community. You don't do that by focusing on the technology alone or being of the mindset that some product or service is going to improve statistics and make you look better in front of a C-suite or board that judges you like Damocles.

You do it by putting yourself out there every day and focusing on what your team members need to be able to improve not only the health of their patients and community but also themselves. These are the techniques we use to do so.

The first one is customer service. We emphasize empathy, listening to our customers, and working with them to guide them through complex processes and methods they do not understand. We look at everyone as if they were our parents, friends, or family. We take the time to explain what we do. The news media scares people about information security. We combat that fear with understanding, calm, and support. We deal with people at genuinely bad times in their lives, and we understand that. We want them to feel better after calling us, and that they've contributed to improving a situation, not making it worse. Bad customer service earns you a reputation and does none of that. It makes people less likely to call you or avoid you when something does happen.

We have two sayings we live by. The first is that "we are nothing without our customers." The second is that "we want people to trust us enough to call us when they see something." If we do not value our customers, then we are not trusted enough to work as part of the team.

Second is understanding. We approach resolving issues by continually looking at how we can address the real issues, instead of putting a bandage over a gaping wound. We take the time to speak with our customers and understand their concerns and issues and focus on what the real issues are. We want to solve the business problem, not claim that some new "innovative" technology is going to fix it. I would rather have my team or a vendor take longer to understand an issue, architect a solution, and get a practical date to implement it than attempt to put something together that looks good on paper that will probably fail given unreasonable constraints.

The major issue we see with cybersecurity that we have to deal with is that products are continually marketed as being innovative and able to solve issues. From 15 years of being in this field, 10 as a CISO across two organizations, I have learned that is not the case. We have observed that products by themselves ultimately do nothing without people or processes they can follow. The major challenge is that every day the CEO on downward are presented with solutions or products presented as innovations, and that oftentimes we are asked to vet solutions or take phone calls because someone targeted our C-suite as a way to get to either information security or infrastructure. These people don't understand our business or our real risks and many think they can use fear to scare our executives into acting.

When we interview people for risk assessments or risk management plans, we do so with a mindset of being able to understand what the risks are, how to reasonably and appropriately address them, and how to demonstrate that on a continual basis. Technology is a minor piece of this. A major focus of what we do is to develop that understanding across the entire team, not just a targeted few.

We let people know that we care about them and their success, and that we want to address these risks because they will help the organization better fulfill its mission. We don't want to have people drop everything and act out of fear because you can only do that for so long before alarm fatigue sets in and people ignore you. We want to do this on reasonable and yet aggressive timeframes. No one is going to give you the time of day if you don't understand them, their needs, or their concerns. They're not going to be empowered to change if you don't show confidence in them or the mission. If you don't approach security as a team, you will lose.

If you cannot demonstrate a change so that others understand that it will improve the ability of the team to deliver on the mission, then it's not worth doing.

The third is continuity and continually putting yourself out there. You're not always going to succeed. You will have vulnerabilities. You will have data breaches, malware, or successful attacks. You will fail. The day of the project is over. There is no longer a beginning, middle, or end. There is only a cycle of assessing, planning, addressing, and repeating that ad infinitum. You will not be perfect. However, you will always be there for the customers.

You need to communicate that message continually. We deliver messaging on a regular basis to the world, leadership, the team, and to our own team members in IS and InfoSec. People know us and remember us from the messaging more than the team members. We write articles, present at conferences, attend conferences, and speak to our internal and external customers regularly because we have to deliver the message that we need to think about lifecycles, not just about a beginning, middle, and end.

We need to think about the impact any change has on the organization, on its people, and on its processes, and make sure that we communicate them out. The best example we can give is when we rolled out our anti-phishing training, part of which involves sending fake phishing emails to our users. We held off on this until we had a communication plan that involved upper management, the service desk, the email team, and the infrastructure team because we wanted to meet the objectives of good customer service, having people reach out to us, and preventing the issue of having people complain to senior leadership and being pressured to stop the campaign. We worked with our public relations team to not only craft the phishing messages, but also a one-page document that was sent to senior leadership which emphasized the connection to the mission of the organization, reducing risk, and preparing to address real phishing emails.

What has happened since is that our senior leadership team has become some of the most enthusiastic supporters of the program, and regularly send in the phishing messages we send out. We have received very few complaints this time. Most important is that we involved leadership through good communication, which was a force multiplier.

We regularly prepare internal presentations for our team. Every month we prepare one for our Privacy and Security committee and IS teams that specifically focuses on security events and breaches that occur outside the environment in a non-technical manner. As part of these monthly presentations, we do mini risk analyses on the events and what we've found. We focus on two key items, which are takeaways for our audience and internal changes we make based on the findings.

No matter how hard it is, or how much you don't want to, you have to put yourself out there every day with consistent messaging. It's not easy to deliver a message consistently and make sure that every communication articulates like an accounting statement. However, the message is remembered longer than the person who delivers it, and part of that message is that changes and innovation are continual. As a leader, you need to set that example. Your team will follow what you do, whether it is conscious or not. Innovation comes from setting the example and following it yourself.

The fourth is self-review. You are not perfect. You never will be. The more you attempt to present that picture that you are right 100 percent of the time, the more you will ignore the opportunities and chances presented to improve, innovate, and create real change that matters.

The purpose of a risk assessment is not to check a box for the Office for Civil Rights (OCR). It is an opportunity to objectively look at your organization and where you can change for the better. It's not a scoring exercise to see how good you can do and hopefully look good for OCR. It's about reviewing what works and what can change.

If you are not honest with yourself about what the risks are and where they are, you will not know where the real opportunities to innovate lie.

What we do to further reinforce this are two quantitative risk exercises. The first is the bi-annual risk assessment we complete for the Risk and Insurance team. This involves gathering and scoring risks from across the IS department that involve people, processes, and technologies. These risks also cover business and environmental factors. We use a scoring system designed by our Risk team to measure them and submit the combined list to them twice a year.

The other exercise is the HIPAA Information Security Risk Assessment that we complete yearly. We made the conscious decision to use the same risk scoring system for both exercises. This allows us to score and prioritize our risks so that we know what top ones to address, and more importantly why. It also gives consistent messaging to our leadership as to how we view it. When you have a limited amount of time to present, consistency is key to getting the message across quickly.

The fifth is change through innovation. According to *Webster's Dictionary*, innovation is the introduction of something new. There are two issues with innovation that can cause it to get stifled in favor of old familiar ways.

The first is not planning for it. The risk management plan, a traditional information security tool, uses the risk assessment to determine the path and plan forward for addressing risks in the organization. We use this as an opportunity, more so than the risk assessment, for interviewing our team and determining the best ways to address identified high risks. From our experience, we understand that most information security risks have their root causes in business process issues, not just technology. Part of what we do is to take more time to develop plans to address risks along a longer timeframe. We do this because we understand that a change for our customers' needs to be effective, well-communicated, long-lasting, and well-documented. We are asking people to change their processes to address a risk that they may not see as applicable.

We use risk management plans as an opportunity to connect with the rest of the organization and get their input and views on what we are doing and why. We want everyone to own the plan and work with us to implement it. Security cannot operate in a silo, and neither can our customers. True innovation happens through getting multiple parties working together on a measurable plan to address risks as an organization. We make sure to put it in writing, define metrics for success, and most importantly, a communication plan with four targets, which are the board, executive leadership/ upper management, line management, and everyone. We want people to know what we are doing, why we are working together on this, and how we define and measure success. We also want people to know that we are collaborating for the benefit of the organization, and that measurable and successful solutions take time and effort, and don't happen overnight.

The second is through innovating in silos. In many graduate programs, including the ones I attended, they teach that innovation is normally isolated to separate organizations still operating in the corporate structure, much like the initial internationalization attempts that companies undergo. While we don't expect companies to end up as a fully matrixed organization like Nestle overnight, we need to set two expectations in our organizations.

We need to encourage collaboration across departments, divisions, entities, and even competing organizations. In the world of information security, we are all facing common threats and challenges. With the limited resources we have due to low profit margins and the complexity of our environments, duplication of resources and lack of collaboration puts all of our organizations at risk. We openly collaborate with other institutions and use our memberships in HIMSS, Scottsdale Institute, and numerous other organizations as vehicles for working with our peers. If there isn't an event that addresses what we need, we will host it ourselves or bring people in to discuss it at one of several forums we use. We will present on what we do at conferences because we want to collaborate, innovate, and franchise our processes so that we set expectations with our peers and vendors. We also want to educate the security professionals coming up through the ranks now.

We put ourselves out there internally and externally with all team members, especially our medical staff, IS department, collaborative groups, and leadership. We want to work with everyone and volunteer to do so in the hope that others will follow. We make sure our messaging is on point with the audience and speak to their issues so that we can get everyone understanding and working together as a team to address our risks.

A major component of collaboration and innovation that often gets forgotten is that you need a good open-door policy. While this lately has gotten press due to its apparent use by a certain business icon to flag people "breaking rank," we have found that this use is not an isolated practice. If you're going to change for the better, you need to solicit input and listen to everyone, and if you use this policy to flag people, stop right now. This means that you have to make sure your organization respects and listens to their fellow team members.

One of the best groups of people for soliciting security changes has been desktop support. Traditionally in a lot of organizations that I have worked in, they have been treated as "grunt work," i.e., easily replaceable and just "techs." We consider those words dehumanizing and disrespectful. They have found more issues and reported them to us than most other teams within the IS department and innovate every day out of need. There are only so many support team members, and a torrent of tickets. They figure out more ways to be efficient and complete their job well. We recognize that and have several former desktop support specialists working in information security because of it. We want people with that mindset helping reduce risk in our organization.

We have also seen multiple teams in IS departments ignore them because they are "just techs" that do what they are told. This is as far from the truth as you can get.

Finally, you need to be constantly reinforcing the benefits of change and innovation. To truly support change in your organization, you have to show measured success. Innovation is good, but you need to have facts and statistics to show that the organization is improving. You have to consistently communicate with everyone, and you have to follow up. Part of evolving a team to innovate as part of its DNA is to make sure that it replicates and persists. The NIST Risk Management Framework specifies that you need to constantly follow up. Innovation cannot come in dribs and drabs. Change is constant. You have a choice to make, which is whether or not to harness it.

Innovation doesn't come from products, EMRs, or tools you buy. It comes from within, and it can take many forms. You have to empower the organization on multiple levels to be successful. It's easy to say that you do it in areas, but to really innovate, you need to focus around a mission and continually reinforce it.

Cultural Considerations for Innovation in Technology

Rosie Sanchez

Over the past 14 years, I have had the opportunity to work in various roles at a large community healthcare organization, on the Méxican border, primarily targeted to an unserved patient population. These included roles such as: a clinic front desk support staff, administrative assistant in the business office, support staff in the medical education department, and as an entry-level analyst in various IT department roles; ultimately leading me to my current role as the Senior Director of IT/clinical information systems. Through my experience I have found that my passion lies in healthcare information technology. I learned that many of the manual processes I used in the early years of my career were leading to human errors that could have been improved with the use of technology. I also learned how process changes and workflow modifications (even those thought to be an improvement for the end uses), through the adoption of technology, could ultimately have drawbacks for both the frontline staff and patients. As a Hispanic female, mother, and daughter of elderly parents, who are patients in this healthcare organization, I can directly relate to our patients' needs. I believe that innovative technology, when considering the needs of the population served, along with the people serving them, can open doors that will ultimately help organizations better support our socially and culturally diverse communities.

In order to be able to successfully implement a new technology, it's important to consider the approach used and the audience that will engage with the technology. Failing to do this can result in a project that either fails or has long-term growing pains or adoption issues. There is also the risk of ongoing issues related to the project, which can take a lot of time and resources away from both the implementation team and the clinics expected to use it. Understanding your audience/target group is extremely important. Too often, those at the top making high-level decisions cannot accurately gauge the impact their decisions can have on clinical staff and patients. To be successful, it's my opinion that the best approach is to shadow the clinical staff and their interactions with the patient population, if you do not already understand the details of their workflow and how they interact with patients. Speaking with the staff, observing them, and understanding how the patients use healthcare and interact with any existing technology is vital. I strongly recommend this approach to any healthcare IT leader. Immerse yourself in their world, and you will be able to find ways to successfully implement innovative technologies in even the most seemingly difficult populations.

In our healthcare organization, as mentioned before, we have greater than 80 percent of the population as Hispanic. This is comprised of people that have lived on the border their whole lives, the majority of which speak Spanish primarily at home, are ESL, speak no English at all, or are first generation. This applies to both the patients and the frontline staff. A population like this has very different cultural needs and considerations. Many also may be older or unfamiliar with technology. As a result, historically, we have had very low adoption rates of technology in the past. To overcome this, we have had to identify potential areas of strength in this population of people, as well as come up with work-around solutions for weaknesses.

Our last big implementation was of an automated patient intake platform. This was supposed to reduce clerical/human errors at the front desk and improve the speed at which patients were registered/checked in for appointments. Many thought that due to the use of technology, patients would reject or decline to use the platform. This could have been an obstacle that prevented successful adoption. However, even though the patients themselves may have been a largely older and Spanish-speaking group, in Hispanic cultures it is common for adult children and grandchildren to accompany aging parents/grandparents to doctor's appointments. Knowing this, we decided a better way to target the patients was to use this to our advantage and target the family members. Our patients trust their family members and rely upon them so much, that getting the family member to accept the technology (when many of them are younger and heavy users of technology outside of the healthcare setting), was a very successful approach in getting the patient to accept it as well. Even our organization's leadership was surprised at the quick and successful adoption of the patient intake platform.

We also used this same approach to improve our enrollment/usage of patient portal. Since many of our patients do not have email addresses themselves or would have access to a computer, we took the alternative approach to having the front desk target the family members to enroll on their patients' behalf. By explaining to the patient/the caregiver the benefits of having an electronic location to store pertinent health data that could be accessed by their family member for current information, or possibly shared with other healthcare providers in the community, we were able to almost double our percentage of enrolled patients from one year to the next. The front desk staff saw the benefits of enrollment and were able to sell the patients and their family members on enrolling in and using the portal with much more success.

Those were just two examples. Putting this concept into action in any organization is feasible. You have to first consider the needs of your patients or staff. Look at the unique characteristics of the cultures and values of the population you employ or serve. It's important to try to view the differences or what appears to be a problem as an obstacle that needs to be overcome. If you yourself do not personally have experience with the population you're assisting, it's important to consult with people that do. They can provide personal insight into the potential issues that may be preventing you from success. We took a problem of non-English speaking patients who typically do not even own their own smartphones, and found a way to have unique aspects of their situation benefit them: their propensity to have younger, technologically proficient family members heavily involved in all aspects of their lives, especially healthcare. I personally have experience in this area and could really relate to the patients and how they accessed care, but many of the other team members that worked alongside, or leadership that approved the projects or created the plans, did not. My input (along with others) helped to convince them that successful implementation of innovative technology was possible here, with the right approach.

Another way we were able to get personal feedback from our diverse group of patients to determine their attitudes toward a potential new technology venture (telemedicine) was to conduct a survey. The Neurology Clinic was considering the possibility of bringing in telemedicine for patients with epilepsy that, historically, had high rates of cancellations due to transportation issues, families not being able to accompany them to appointments, etc. Many stakeholders and leadership members doubted that our patients would be interested in using this technology, based on their backgrounds, speaking primarily Spanish, their ages, or assuming they had limited technology access. To really find out what the patients' views were, we decided to create a simple paper survey, with English on one side, Spanish on the other, and have the front desk staff in the clinic hand it out to all patients while they were waiting. Due to the fact that it was given on paper, it was easy to administer and required very little use of resources and no new technology. Also, because both languages were presented, no one had to spend time asking patients which language they preferred to be asked the questions in. From the survey, we discovered our patients were really interested in the new technology, even those without access personally to technology said they would be able to access through family members. Another surprising result of surveying the patients was that their interest wasn't correlated to their preferred language. Additionally, many were very enthusiastic and wrote comments requesting to bring the technology soon.

When having meetings with internal employees regarding new implementations or potential tools, be sure to involve the front staff, or create committees/groups which allow them to feel part of the process as well as voice any concerns they may have. These are the staff that have to really believe in the tools you are trying to introduce and understand how to use them effectively so they can also help assist patients. We did this when creating the telemedicine survey for our Neurology clinic and the staff really was dedicated to passing the survey out to each patient. You will have a much more successful implementation if staff concerns and needs are addressed beforehand. The frontline staff are a key component to this since they interact with the patient first. So it's also important that they are on board and really understand how any new tool will improve the patient experience or make their jobs easier.

The importance of knowing the culture you are supporting is paramount to success in innovation. We have a unique opportunity in my border region to serve a special population of underserved patients. In the future, given the way that healthcare is moving, and many initiatives by CMS and other government-related agencies, it appears that engaging patients with innovative technology tools will only increase in importance. This is just one aspect of healthcare, but it's important because patient engagement with technology affects things on so many different levels. Even meeting requirements of programs such as Meaningful Use, MIPS, or implementing technology to streamline copayment processes, or enrolling patients into an HIE, requires the organization to successfully convince their patients to be engaged with the tools. As technology continues to evolve, so does the need to understand the culture and environment of your unique healthcare organization.

Chapter 6

Stress Simplicity

Do not overcomplicate a solution to a problem; keep the following principle in mind: "When you have two competing theories that make exactly the same predictions, the simpler one" is better to implement.

It seems counterintuitive, but the majority of innovations are rather simple. The temptation to take a problem and create a complex solution exists in most of us. We tend to overthink an opportunity and therefore overengineer a fix. Innovation is often as basic as developing an elegant yet simple solution to a complex issue or opportunity, not the opposite way around. If the innovation can't be easily explained, start again.

Advancing Innovation

Daniel Barchi

Simply begin. Most innovation fails not in its execution but at its inception. Health systems are built and tended by bright people with innovative ideas, yet many of their ideas are never put into action. If perfect is the enemy of good, over-planning is the enemy of starting. When facing a monumental project, the planning is almost always easier than doing the work, and more planning can feel safer than starting a project and facing the risk of failure. Yet time spent creating plans and budgets that foresee every contingency is time that is not spent learning lessons by putting ideas into play. General Colin Powell famously said, "Once you have information in the 40–70 percent range, go with your gut." I wanted to create an environment where our team felt loyalty to the project, not the plan.

This "learn-as-we-go" approach has far-reaching benefits. I find that it offers a subtle change in mindset. Instead of focusing on a plan, our eyes are open to solutions. By simply beginning, we are freed of the need to defend a plan, and we are better positioned to receive input from our users who are normally the people on the front line of medicine. All too often, the IT team are viewed as the reason why nurses cannot log in or pharmacy labels do not print, or worse, as remote people who push new systems upon an already pressed staff. When we simply begin, we are automatically part of the same team, and anyone in healthcare knows teamwork is an essential part of delivering the best patient care.

As our IT team prepared to implement a refrigerator temperature monitoring system, I thought of Powell's sentiment and my own experiences. Years ago, the responsibilities of a hospital IT team were generally limited to supporting mainframe and desktop computing. As technology has developed, even hospital beds are connected to the network. Biomedical Engineering has aligned with IT, and we are now responsible not only for computers, printers, and televisions, but IV pumps, MRIs, and refrigerators that store vaccines, breast milk, and medicines.

To ensure that these critical medical supplies are kept between 1 and 3 degrees Celsius, nurses on hospital floors used to manually check the temperatures twice a day and log the results on a piece of paper attached to each refrigerator. Although such monitoring seems a simple task, nurses are busy, and hospital safety inspections routinely identify fluctuating refrigerator temperatures as a major problem. With the goals of freeing nurses of this responsibility and achieving reliable daily monitoring, our team installed temperature probes in each refrigerator and networked them back to a central monitoring station. No one we knew had done this before, so our team struggled with the technology, clinical workflow, and the process for addressing temperatures that fell out of the parameters for safe storage. I met with the team twice in January of 2016 as they bounced back and forth between hospitals, the data center, clinical meetings, and planning sessions. They wanted to get everything perfect for an April 1 "go-live" across six hospitals, but I was skeptical that we knew enough to count on a single, flawless launch. "Just turn it on now in January for one nursing unit and see what you get", I told them. They were reluctant because they had not yet resolved problems with network communications and nurses' notification. They were also concerned that refrigerators would alarm at the central station every time the door opened for a nurse to retrieve a vaccine. "Let's just start", I insisted, "and see what we get".

So, we simply began and turned on remote monitoring for four refrigerators. One day later, we were glad we did. We learned very quickly that when a nurse checks the temperature at the same time every day, we got the temperature we expected:

When we used IT to remotely monitor and sample the temperature every five minutes, however, we found that the temperature fluctuates wildly in between readings:

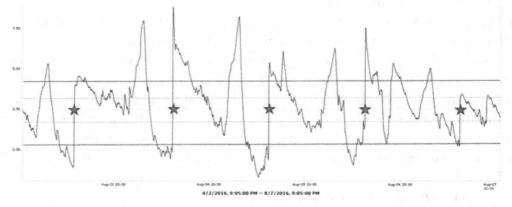

In the midst of trying to perfect the system, we did not consider the variable at the heart of this innovation – the temperature of the refrigerators themselves. Our eyes were opened. As it turns out, the refrigerators we had in place were not meeting our temperature specifications even when the refrigerator doors remained closed. Our computer-based monitoring revealed that each time the compressor started or stopped, the temperature dropped precipitously or spiked above the threshold.

When we began the project, our focus was reducing the time nurses spent on equipment monitoring so they could spend more time with patients. By starting our work rapidly, we gained key insights early and recognized that we needed to solve a different problem entirely. Of the 1,350 refrigerators humming throughout our six hospital campuses, 780 had this issue and needed to be replaced with upgraded refrigerators at a cost of $3,000 each. A little more than $2 million later, we solved the temperature fluctuation problem and resumed our focus on centralized monitoring.

By April 2016, we set up a desk in one of our former data centers and staffed it 24/7 with an analyst who monitored refrigerator temperatures across our enterprise. The formerly local and manual temperature recording process was now automated, and any time a temperature moved out of the specified range an alert prompted the analyst to contact the appropriate nursing unit to identify the problem and follow up with an engineer as required.

While this was clearly a step forward, we realized that centralizing alarms and data feeds presented additional opportunities. Now it was time to get creative. We took advantage of the space and the 24/7 staffing inspired by 1,350 refrigerators to create a second team dedicated to remotely monitoring the vital signs of patients in the emergency department of one of our largest academic medical centers.

It seems counterintuitive that even when a patient's vital signs are being monitored in the emergency department, there are times when no one is directly looking at the screens or listening for the alarms above the noise of the environment. More importantly, even when the nurse or physician is looking at the monitor, it is often challenging to identify a patient whose condition deteriorates slowly and unremarkably over time. Sometimes the recognition of a patient's frail condition comes too late. By having a clinician sit at an offsite location and monitor 50+ patients at once without the distraction of being in the emergency department, we added a layer of safety. Instead of adding to the demands of an already busy environment, we now had an experienced clinician whose only responsibility was monitoring the data of each patient. When the remote clinician identified a significant change in the condition of a patient, the patient's assigned nurse was immediately alerted to the situation. Within the first few weeks of remote monitoring, we had more than six of what we called "great catches" in which the patient's deterioration was identified early and in time.

Instead of building an entirely new remote patient monitoring center, we had taken the former data center, added minimal equipment and staffing, and created what we called our Clinical Operations Center or CLOC.

Other innovations followed – we found that in our health system, new ideas sometimes would not be put into practice because of a lack of space or resources to make them happen. So, we began to expand our capabilities at the CLOC.

We next moved operators from four of our hospitals into the CLOC and sought ways to maximize their productivity. Formerly, they had simply answered phones and transferred calls. When a patient called for a prescription refill, our operators queried the patient for data, completed a form, then faxed it to the appropriate physician's office. We saw that these talented people were underutilized and could help us improve and streamline the process. We taught them to use our electronic medical record, trained them to coordinate telemedicine video calls, then promoted all of them from the role of Call Center Agents to Account Representatives with an average 13 percent increase in pay. In their new roles, they became active participants in the clinical care process, increased first-call resolution by solving issues themselves, and even reduced the time patients waited for prescription refills from an average of eight hours to only five minutes. Patient care improved, and our staff advanced their training. Our innovation in this case was simply to take the people and resources we had and make them more efficient by focusing on their training and their workflow. IT teamed up with patient experience, and we were all better for it.

We took this simple approach to innovation to new heights in the summer of 2016 when our Chair of Emergency Medicine said he would like to try telemedicine visits within the busy emergency department of one of our hospitals. While urgent care visits by video are nothing new, he thought we could make physical visits to the ED more efficient by offering patients with less serious conditions the option of a virtual visit with a physician. Like the CLOC, we decided to simply begin.

Within two weeks, we installed video equipment in an existing room in our Emergency Department (ED), added a camera to an existing physician office 200 yards away and started seeing patients in what we call NYP OnDemand ED Telehealth Express Care. Patients are greeted at the front door and triaged by a nurse. Those whose injuries or illness are mild are presented the option of a traditional visit (about 2.5 hours) or a video visit (about 30 minutes). The patients who opt for a virtual visit enter a private room and immediately begin a one-on-one consultation with a physician by video. At the end of the visit, the remote physician sends discharge instructions to a printer in the patient room and can send prescriptions electronically to the pharmacy of the patient's choice, when necessary.

We simply began by leveraging people, space, and technology we already had on hand. By starting rapidly, we learned what worked and what needed improvement within two weeks of our initial idea. Patients of all ages loved the service – when a 21 year old patient and an 89 year old patient were seen back-to-back, it was hard to tell whose comments ("This was the coolest," and "I am going to tell all of my friends.") were whose. We started with 10 patients, rapidly tweaked the process, saw 50 more patients, evaluated the process, then opened it up broadly. We have now seen more than 10,000 patients through the service and reduced ED wait times and revisits.

Net Promoter Score (NPS) is a way to gauge the satisfaction and engagement of customers. Ikea has an NPS of -9, Lego an NPS of 6, and Apple an NPS of 72. Our ED Telehealth Express Care Service is well-liked by our patients and has an NPS in the mid-90s.

This service is one of 10 different telemedicine modalities we now offer patients. In each case, the offering was not the result of years or even months of planning, but a rapid response to an identified need. When we realized that nursing homes would send patients to our ED in the middle of the night "to be safe", we created a TeleNursing Home service that allows nursing home staff to connect with our ED physicians 24/7 to determine if a patient really needs to be transferred. When we realized that patients in our EDs sometimes waited up to 24 hours to be seen by a psychiatrist or transferred to a facility with psychiatry coverage, we used existing equipment and our own fellows to create a TelePsych service which shortened that wait to within two hours.

Innovation is not consistent with multi-year plans. Rapid implementation and real-world testing quickly demonstrate what innovation has value. While clinical interventions that have a direct impact on patients can and should undergo rigorous clinical trials and testing, operational process improvements can be put into place rapidly and refined using real-world feedback. The mantra to fail fast can only be followed once work has started with a process in place that can succeed or fail. By simply beginning, we create an environment which is free from the stigma of mistakes. As hospitals strive to identify risk and prevent mistakes, it is important for IT to follow physician leadership and do the same. With loyalty to project before plan, a willingness to embrace rapid change can significantly improve not just operational efficiency but patient and employee experiences as well.

Stress Simplicity

Marc Probst

Consider gauze. Consider that loosely woven, cotton fabric in ways that no one does these days. Then consider how healthcare takes gauze for granted – how it's a staple in care provision but rarely marked for its importance. Now, consider that once in history gauze was innovative, but outrageously simple.

Simplicity in innovation doesn't translate to simple ideas. Instead, simple innovation solves problems for people. Yes, there is much to be said about the glory of volcanic and disruptive innovations, but such innovations are few and far between and often unearth a bevy of new problems to be solved. Simplicity in innovation is almost harder to achieve; overcomplicating ideas is easy. Reinventing the wheel, as they say, is most often a delay in progress and dreaming, as opposed to doing, isn't innovation.

We don't have to go back to ancient Palestine and the invention of gauze to see how simple innovations can have lasting impacts on people and their lives. We need only go back 15 to 20 years and enumerate the slew of simple innovations that have shaped – and continue to shape – healthcare, like new medication delivery systems, electronic health records, and automation. Innovations that improve care the most quickly are usually about the application and use of existing tools in new ways, just like when someone discovered that gauze doesn't adhere to wounds and tissues like denser fabrics do.

If you want a culture of innovation in your organization, I suggest simplicity. In my organization, Intermountain Healthcare, we've established a framework of innovation that touches every employee. We also make sure that all 37,000 of our caregivers are invited to the innovation party. No one is exempt from idea creation, and sometimes some roles are expected to generate a given number of ideas each year. No idea is too small even if the market would snub its non-complexity. We are rewarded through every contribution no matter how seemingly small or mundane. No idea is too simple to be explored as a potential innovation or innovative use of a tool.

I urge you to keep Peter Drucker in mind as you move through this essay:

> An innovation, to be effective, has to be simple and it has to be focused. It should do only one thing, otherwise it confuses. If it is

not simple, it won't work. Everything new runs into trouble; if complicated, it cannot be repaired or fixed. All effective innovations
are breathtakingly simple. Indeed, the greatest praise an innovation
can receive is for people to say: 'This is obvious. Why didn't I think
of it?'

Here's how I unpack Intermountain's success at simple innovation:

We Seek to Solve Problems for People

At the root of all innovation is need. That's why focusing innovation efforts
on solving problems that affect people has a high return on investment (ROI).
At Intermountain, we take multiple approaches to doing just that. Here are
just a couple:

One initiative at Intermountain, something we call *Design for People*,
seeks to observe people in the context of their daily work while looking for
ways to make the work more efficient, safe, and complimentary to the goals
of healthcare. We've found that developing innovations that make a difference starts with a deep understanding of the work our physicians, clinicians,
staff, and patients are doing. By understanding the context, we are best able
to find simple innovations that improve the way the work is done.

Case in point, our *Design for People* team went to two of our hospitals
to observe the work in the endoscopy labs. During those visits, the team
noticed that the stationary position of sinks the Endo Techs used in cleaning and preparing scopes was of concern because of the various heights of
Endo Techs. To remedy the situation, the team recommended the installation
of variable height sinks, which resulted in less back strain for the techs and
more efficient use of the sinks.

Such small changes can have big impacts, so we encourage all our caregivers to look around their work areas for ways to improve processes. We
empower caregivers to take the responsibility to observe and share ideas for
improvement, then we collect those ideas, assess them, and implement those
that we can.

Collecting ideas is at the heart of innovation. As leaders we often think
that we have all the information we need to address issues efficiently and
effectively, but the truth is the information we have is usually lagging or
outdated by the time we have it. When an issue is discovered in post-
problem reports, it can be too late to institute a change that can really affect
outcomes.

That's why Intermountain has invested time and resources into creating a series of tiered escalation huddles that begin on the very frontlines and ensure items that need executive level influence reach executives in a timely fashion.

Intermountain learned early on that it's insufficient for ideas to simply go from the frontline to manager, ideas sometimes need to be escalated even further up the chain of command. Our escalation huddles make that possible each morning as caregivers meet in Tier One huddles to discuss problems and ideas for improvement that, when warranted, reach the executive, Tier Six huddle by 10:30 am.

We also make it simple for caregivers to submit ideas through an electronic tracking tool. Some caregivers are expected to submit a quota of ideas per year, and that quota is tied to performance evaluations and goal completion. Simple innovation, however, doesn't stop with caregivers today, with the rise in healthcare consumerism, we recognize that innovation must also embrace and take the burgeoning trend of healthcare consumerism into account.

Here's my note on consumerism: Smartphones and other smart devices are enabling consumers – patients – to monitor everything from blood glucose to heart rhythms. Sensors are becoming ever cheaper and being integrated into these devices. The tech is simply exploding, and gamified incentives, like badges, encourage consumers to use these tools. This unprecedented self-gathered data gives patients insight into their own health that, when leveraged correctly, will significantly change how consumers access, use, and select healthcare options. Simple innovation must embrace this trend and begin looking at how these consumer-facing tools can create efficiencies the like of which healthcare hasn't seen. But, the smart phone in healthcare won't stand the test of time if we don't start innovating around its footprint. Electronic medical records need to fit that mold and become as streamlined as apps like Uber's.

We've Built A Platform for Innovation

Beyond our *Design for People* initiative and escalation huddles, Intermountain has also created a program to take ideas that offer market potential – and the people who come up with them – to the marketplace.

The Intermountain Foundry, part of our business development area, provides structured support and resources to advance caregiver innovation. The Foundry uses a proprietary, market-tested curriculum to help internal inventors, innovators, and entrepreneurs determine the commercial viability of their concepts and scale them throughout our organization and the broader healthcare industry.

Through a structured eight week course, innovators refine their concepts, validate market opportunity, identify methods of product development, and create a plan for growth, including strategies for taking a product to market and funding options.

Each year, Intermountain selects – from a competitive applicant pool – the four most promising innovators to present their innovations to the Intermountain Innovation Fund Steering Committee and make funding requests. The Foundry gives perspective to the meaningful impact that new innovation can have on healthcare delivery.

Healthcare delivery is the center of our Kem C. Gardner Healthcare Transformation Center, available to a worldwide audience of healthcare leaders and innovators – such as those in our Clinical Programs – who seek to improve healthcare through innovation. The center will house two of Intermountain's nationally and internationally recognized institutes – the Healthcare Delivery Institute and the Healthcare Leadership Institute.

We Collaborate with Others for Success

The collaboration that comes from training the best leaders in healthcare delivery and leadership is one way Intermountain partners with others to share the fruits of innovation. But, sometimes a problem is too big for one individual or organization to solve. That's why it's important in today's healthcare industry for like-minded organizations to band together to solve problems.

Intermountain has partnered this way in several areas, but most recently we've teamed up with other organizations to help patients by addressing shortages and high prices of life-saving medications. So far, 120 health organizations that represent about one-third of the nation, have expressed interest in joining Civica Rx, a not-for-profit organization.

Civica Rx seeks to stabilize the supply of essential generic medications administered in hospitals, many of which have fallen into chronic shortage that places patients at risk.

Such partnerships make solving big problems more manageable and create a community within the healthcare industry that solidifies the aims and goals of medicine – to encourage, maintain, and restore health.

We Share Results for Posterity and the Greater Good

It's been said that innovation is a team sport. That's why Intermountain often shares its extensive clinical experience, the results of years of improvement data, and our commitment to transforming the healthcare industry. One way we do this is through our Clinical Programs and the critical research and development they participate in.

Since the late 1990s, Intermountain's Clinical Programs have been working to set clinical improvement goals and leading system efforts to accomplish those goals. However, we find that it's not enough to just develop those goals just within the system, so we share the findings we reach with others to improve care nationally and internationally.

Today, our clinical programs identify, develop, and deploy best practice protocols and guide Intermountain in a multitude of processes and decisions including: improvement goals, clinical staffing models, regulatory standards, purchasing, medical necessity requirements, pay-for-performance metrics, education, and documentation standards.

By sharing the results of this work – and the methods for conducting such work – Intermountain helps others to innovate, truly honoring the idea that innovation and healthcare are a team sport.

So, I urge you: Think simply, but create a culture of innovation in your organization. You can do this based on four simple areas: solve problems for people, build an easy-access platform for idea generation and innovative thought, collaborate with others, and collaborate with others. Healthcare needs every idea and innovation it can get right now. We're facing such tremendous change and stressors – like quality, diminishing resources, and clinician burnout – and we must syphon and harvest every idea if we want to continue helping people. Innovation will only prosper if we keep it simple and seek to make our solutions as common as gauze.

Innovation, Simplicity, and Mindfulness

Richard Gannotta

Innovation is frequently characterized as an end product of an ever-evolving set of complex interactions leading to a new, more efficient, effective, and value added product or outcome.

Although this notion holds true in many cases, deeper analysis reveals that effective system design usually is at its core "simple."

In biological systems the notion of "emergence" where individual (simple) components of a large system work together to establish complex supporting behaviors (think an ant colony or flock of birds) is a well-established example. The "survival" and advancement of the "whole" is predicated on this collective behavior.

In some ways the same can be said for the pursuit of applications and new approaches not yet fully developed that are intended to solve or remedy some problem or challenge.

Starting at the base level, the most deconstructed aspects of any approach can create a path forward where efficient and efficacious development can occur without the friction and drag that may be associated with a complicated calculus.

A key example from healthcare can be found in instances where human factors have been identified as a significant issue in safety events. The interaction between an individual and a set of complex variables (technology, biology, psychology) can lead to an overwhelming and sometimes cascading set of events which can lead to a significant adverse outcome.

Is there a relatively simple yet highly innovative solution which can focus an individual's attention in those situations where high-reliability performance is required and reveal an emerging set of options and alternatives which can lead to better outcomes?

One such solution is the application of a "mindful" approach, which can serve to focus and frame a significant task at hand while objectively recognizing ones past experience or bias in a way which does not unduly influence the performance of the task or interaction but instead enhances and highlights areas where hidden patterns or variables can (not unlike the biological process previously described) emerge and be identified and untoward situations avoided.

We know this practice has "high utility" in complex areas such as medication administration, surgery and other healthcare areas, but also air traffic control, nuclear power, and aviation. All examples where small negative variances in performance can have catastrophic impacts.

In the realm of technology the same holds true and the need for a mindful approach when inputting data, performing successive or rapid keystrokes and analyzing information given the potential impact faulty conclusions can have on system outcomes is essential.

A quick approach to applied mindfulness as it relates to interacting with technology starts with:

1. Mindfully "check in" anchoring yourself in the present moment through breathing awareness and subject focus then engaging the task at hand
2. Prior to entering data
3. When interpreting information displayed in complex formats
4. If display fatigue may be possible
5. In any instance where interfaces between technology and biological processes yield actionable data

So how do we adopt a mindful approach to unlock the simple side of innovation allowing for a more efficient and value added approach to "emerge"?

Organizations should consider adopting a culture of high-reliability powered by a formal mindfulness program.

The end product could not only produce a safer more reliable environment but also empower individuals to identify and deploy corrective measures in areas of vulnerability, experience-enhanced team work, and be more present in the moment, allowing for new innovative approaches to solving complex processes emerge.

Innovation in Healthcare Information Technology: Stressing Simplicity

Adam Buckley, MD

Innovation. Revolution! Upheaval! Radical, industry rattling change! The word itself denotes such an inexorable alteration of the landscape, it is hard not to get swept up in the possibilities of creating that next great disruptor. In 2017 we undertook a complete redesign of IT services at our parent academic medical center. As part of that work I envisioned a research and development team that would be wholly within the "innovation space" and create nothing but new and exciting ways to deliver care. The fact that I planned to monetize their work via patents and licensing also created a great deal of excitement within the halls of finance. So with my vision in front of me I recruited and put together a crackerjack team. My next move was to talk with people I knew who had lived in the innovation space. I have some friends who have made crazy money in Healthcare IT (HIT) and had real-world experience in exactly what we planned on doing. So I put together my pitch deck and my elevator speech about all the work done to date ready to hear their secret to success. Imagine my surprise when it came down to just four words. Solve a real problem. That's it I thought? They had made untold millions on that? My next thought was why did I go to medical school if it is that simple to improve the lives of patients? With my renewed calling to focus on solving real problems for our patients and providers, my team and I refocused our efforts.

The team I created had individually created real value for the organization over a number of years by producing niche applications that various parts of the organization had asked for. Most of these existed in gaps between what vendors offered in the commercial space and the need providers and operations had doing their day-to-day work. Many of these were also solutions that could be homemade as opposed to spending vast sums to acquire. One of the more successful creations was a mobile application that gives patients' families the chance to see where their loved ones are in the process of having a procedure performed in our largest facility. Is the patient in holding? In the operating room? In recovery? This was necessary since the facility had three IT systems to perform the work of supporting admitting, the operating room, and the postoperative and in patient stay. Patients have grown to love this application. It solved a simple communication issue for the staff and yet gave patient's families vital information. Simple. The team also developed an emergency desktop notifier that popped up whenever there was an issue that required mass notification. When this was developed over ten years ago, there was nothing on the market to help. It was built not at the request of IT, but from facilities. They wanted to know how to communicate broadly to all employees about widespread issues. The organization uses it today for a variety of simulations (active shooter, baby abductions etc.) as well as facilities issues and IT issues. It has become one of the many ways that we contact staff in an emergency. Simple.

With the past successes as a starting point we decided to move ahead. That began with securing a lawyer with expertise in intellectual property. With their input we developed a process whereby the team could document while they developed in a way that lent itself to a patent application should their work bear fruit. We also began a process to perform suitable due diligence to receive provisional patent protection as the work continued through alpha and beta development. This is a vital step. Receiving full patent protection is a long, painful process that requires a significant commitment of time, money, and resources. It also requires very specific documentation that calls out the novel and new way that you are approaching an existing problem. Provisional protection at least offers an opportunity to develop and not worry about someone else stealing the idea. One can then determine if a full patent application is worth it after the application is fully developed and the concept behind it fully realized. We have actually received such protection on a few applications that we believe may eventually be licensable.

Our next step was to integrate our existing internship program with the new development team. We require our intern teams to produce an application by the end of their internship. One team produced an application that calls up maps of our various facilities and helps facilitate patients finding their way through the myriad of 100 year old buildings that we have on our campus. Historically, the organization produces an oversized novelty map that is impossible to read at great expense annually. The map project, while not patentable, produced an application that has the potential to save money for the group. Again, simple.

The most recent step has been to integrate the new development team with our newly formed clinical innovation lab. The innovation lab is charged with looking for opportunities to map out new methods of delivering care in a "value" -based reimbursement model. This lab is focused currently on filling the gaps in care that our health network has with referring providers. We are in a rural region and many referrals come from out of state or great distance and there are no existing means to exchange information easily. Many health systems such as ours have experienced the disappointment that despite leveraging eHealth Exchange and other methods of exchanging clinical information, there is a still a significant gap in what is provided via the exchanges and what providers and patients need. This effort is currently ramping up as a pilot and we have a provisional patent, so the excitement over the work is building. However, it is also trying to solve a simple problem: helping providers and patents communication about their care.

We have much to learn as we continue in the world of development and innovation in healthcare. There have been failures as well as successes. That being said, my belief is if we stick to the simple premise of finding solutions to real problems we will succeed in the long run.

Methodist Le Bonheur Healthcare

Cynthia Davis

Stress Simplicity in Innovation

As a nurse, technologist, leader, and a caregiver, I am most excited about the ongoing transformation of the delivery of health. Throughout my career, my focus has been on identifying opportunities to improve the quality and outcomes of patient care delivery with a strong foundation of effective cost management, process, and systems of care. We are at the first ten mile marker of a journey of 10,000 steps which will take curiosity, collaboration, and innovation to support provider/clinician and consumer transformation.

Here is an overview on how my organization stresses simplicity in innovation in every day practices of care.

Methodist LeBonheur Healthcare (MLH) is a six-hospital integrated delivery health system serving the Mid-South region. We are celebrating our hundred year anniversary serving our community. We do $1.92 billion in revenue, and see 405,000 ED visits, nearly 64,000 hospital admissions, and 1.4 million ambulatory and home care visits per year. Our promise is to improve every life we touch through our organization's values. What that means for us is that we are a learning organization and embrace new ways to get better results. This includes the following guiding behaviors:

- I am personally willing to change.
- I am curious and openly seek new approaches, processes, technologies, and practices to improve outcomes.
- I collaborate with patients, families, and my team to implement new ways of improving the healthcare experience.

Like many other healthcare delivery organizations, MLH invested early in health IT and enhanced those capabilities in part through funding from HITECH. Those EHRs now contain quantitative data (e.g., laboratory values), qualitative data (e.g., text-based documents and demographics), and transactional data (e.g., a record of medication delivery). The big benefit with the EMR is the aggregation of patient data over the long term.

With the foundation in place, this phase of care innovations enabled by technology now allows for a transformation of care by delivering information directly to patients and empowering them to play a more active role in their care. We're now exchanging data — not just for Meaningful Use, but to improve patient health. We're connecting with Methodist partners and physicians in the community (including providers who serve both underinsured and self-pay patients) through mobile applications and text messaging programs that provide disease-specific education and reminders.

We also have cutting-edge initiatives underway, including joint projects with Cerner, Big Data work with the University of Tennessee, and precision medicine and population health programs – all of which are aimed at serving a unique underserved patient population.

And in fact, it was that culture of innovation that led to the development of a simple life-saving alert system based on Cerner tools. With 90 percent of doctors using iPhones, iPads, or Apple Watches, the IT shop created an algorithm that sits on top of its EHR platform to continuously monitor changes and alert clinicians accordingly.

This algorithm has already saved thousands of lives by shrinking the time it takes to notify a physician when a patient is diagnosed with severe sepsis from six hours to fewer than five minutes. It also alerts physicians when a patient is at risk of fall or readmission; users can hover over the alert for clinical decision intelligence that explains the steps that can be taken to avoid readmission.

Our EHR vendor, in turn, has added that algorithm for other hospitals to use. It's been amazing to see an innovation like this take hold.

Here are some key takeaways to enable patient-centered roadmaps of innovation:

1. **Maintain organizational leadership and develop blue chip-focused support structures.** At present, many organizations are trying to manage enormous numbers of requests for IT changes. If these are not actively addressed, value is not likely to be achieved, with the consequence that "sharp-end" providers may become discouraged. The systems that vendors offer tend to be "bare-bones," and the implicit assumption being made is that organizations will use the system tools offered to make care improvements. But achieving this requires organizations to continuously develop local human resource and governance structures, and focus on key blue chips and priorities for patients and families.

2. **Look for look hanging fruit and focus on small simple improvements.** Innovation in so many ways can be the simplest of things. We just need to be doing it more successfully and efficient than anyone else, working the most effectively with what we have. The simple act of chewing an aspirin has shown to improve clinical outcomes from an acute heart attack.

3. **Improve the basic care and business process first.** Before taking on new initiatives, focus on improving today's business or clinical problems. Success breeds success. Agreement in relation to goals is important to ensure that optimization efforts of stakeholders are aligned. Look for small simple improvements and continue to improve.

4. **Promote transparency as a cultural norm.** If we don't promote transparency of results outside regulators or payers will do so, and not very gently. We have the data in our EMRs. Those leaders who promote this will find that the benefits outweigh the risk. The more the data are used, the better it will get.

5. **Create a top-down vision and stimulate bottom-up innovation.** Actively managing the process of change is essential because all organizations have difficulty in navigating major organizational change. Effective organizational transformations require long periods of time and constant effort.

6. **Set a specific benefits-driven approach.** Start with a benefits-driven method. Our approach begins with the identification of a specific aim (e.g., 5 percent reduction in hospital readmissions within 12 months), followed by an assessment of current and future states. After these important preliminary steps, relevant data items are identified and specified, which allows monitoring of progress toward this goal.

We're seeing small and simple innovation take hold and produce results. Advancing health outcomes and ensuring that healthcare fits seamlessly with an individual's lifestyle is our key focus.

Chapter 7

Recognize and Reward

> Recognize or reward the efforts of stakeholders to innovate even at the smallest levels.

To maximize innovation potential, we must not forget the power of motivation in human behavior. People will largely do what they are primarily rewarded and recognized for. For innovation to thrive, consider launching multiple reward and recognition programs to reinforce culture, enhance engagement, and encourage collaboration. Programs should not only reward those who generate ideas, but all the support teams enabling the success. That which is rewarded and recognized is repeated. Innovation will multiply commensurate with affirmation given.

Sustaining a Culture of Innovation

Edward Marx

We tend to repeat those things we are rewarded for. I have served with several progressive and innovative organizations. The key from a leadership perspective was sustaining our culture of innovation. There are plenty of forces at work that want to push back the boundaries and return to the status quo. If you are not purposeful in holding ground that you have captured, you will lose it to cultural inertia. It took us a while, but in each case, we realized that it was imperative to reinforce the new culture through reward and recognition. In fact, reward and recognition became the catalyst for sustaining our innovation culture at every organization.

We learned to enhance the probability of success, reward and recognition were equally important to apply when we failed. Counterintuitive for sure, but one of my colleagues argued that celebrating failure was more powerful than celebrating success. So we did. Most individuals are at least modestly influenced by fear and failure. As a result, over time we become increasingly risk-averse. Aversion to risk is one of the primary enemies of innovation. Embracing failure casts out fear.

Perhaps my biggest innovation failure was investing resources in a product originally called Surface. The year was 2010 and there was nothing on the market like it. We built an interactive application that would enhance the clinician–patient experience. Less than one year later Apple came out with the iPad and the rest was history. Instead of licking our wounds, we decided to use Surface as a coffee table in our office. It was a daily reminder that sometimes we fail but we are unashamed. As it turns out, that experience was a catalyst for us to develop an application on the iPad that would help diagnose Alzheimer's.

As a result of us rewarding and recognizing both success and failure, our innovation culture ran deep. When we had success, we certainly highlighted the person, team, and product. In one organization we were able to set up a shared incentive program. An individual developed a unique application that took a feed from the electronic health record and combined with other medical markers, displayed the output through a wall mounted display device. As a result, patient falls were reduced by 35%. The vendor who enabled that application inside of the hardware device resold the technology to other organizations. Royalties were collected with each sale. There are many ways to set up success-sharing opportunities, with financial rewards being a strong draw.

Simple recognition is also effective. Most of us have an innate need to feel appreciated and valued. When we delight a customer or develop some sort of breakthrough, it feels good when someone notices and acknowledges the effort. In fact, I believe this is a more powerful motivator than the financial incentive method. At one organization we would have the person or team who developed something innovative stand before their peers at a monthly town hall and showcase their creation. They would beam in delight. Some might be embarrassed to be recognized in person so I would send out a firm-wide email highlighting their innovation.

Yet another way to reward and recognize innovation is to hold a contest on a regular basis. We conducted a pitch day where anyone could sign-up and showcase their invention. There were a couple of screening rounds but ultimately three finalists were selected by our executive team. The opportunity for someone to be able to present before executives is a powerful draw. We saw many proposals that were very impressive. Once the executives selected the finalists, we had each of them do a final pitch before our TEDx audience. We then selected the winner by vote of the TEDx audience. That individual's invention was then funded for full development. One year, we actually hired the person who won to lead our innovation efforts.

At a different organization, we stood up an internal site for innovation. Individuals could submit their invention on the site completing an online submission form. Once the site was closed to submissions, employees throughout the company were invited to vote. All of this was conducted online asynchronously which made it very convenient. Contributors were recognized and again the leading vote gatherers were rewarded through modest gifts. Through this process, a couple of the submissions were given the resources required to completely build out, in this case, mobile applications.

We can never discount the human factor in all we do, especially in regards to innovation and the culture required to maximize the opportunities. People want to know that what they do matters for something. When we recognize and reward individuals, it is food for their soul. There are so many different ways to recognize and reward and the examples I have shared are just ideas that can easily be adopted anyplace. If we are so bold as to ask people to go above and beyond and to innovate, the least we can do is to reciprocate in some way. Your culture will determine what kind of reward and recognition is appropriate and you can lever up and down as needed. But you must do something. Especially if the innovation fails.

Recognizing and Rewarding Innovation

Michael Fey

Overview

Innovation in every industry is as challenging as it is elusive, part science, part art and part magic. As the world's leading cyber security company, innovation is core to Symantec's mission, and in our experience, the best way to spark innovation is to create a culture where it is a fundamental part of everyone's day-to-day work. We never want our employees saying to themselves: "Today, I need to spend the next six hours on my assigned tasks, and then I'm going to spend two hours on innovation." Rather, innovation should simply be built into the fabric of each employee's daily activities. This is, of course, easier said than done and requires ongoing encouragement, recognition and rewards for developing breakthrough ideas. Below are a variety of programs and approaches we've implemented in our company that highlight to employees the premium we place on innovating across every aspect of our business.

Innovation Days

We've had a lot of success running regular "Innovation Days" in our organization. These events occur at different sites, where employees (typically engineers, in the case of our company), organize into teams of two to four people with the goal of building a quick prototype of a new idea over the course of one to two days. Each team then presents their prototype/demo to the entire group and the "winners" are chosen by various mechanisms (e.g., a vote of all participants, a panel of judges, etc.). In our experience, the ideas generated at these events are often innovations that offer great benefit to customers and can be commercialized relatively quickly. In fact, at our initial Innovation Day events, we would often find ourselves asking engineers, "Why didn't you propose your great idea as part of your regular day-to-day job, why did you wait until this innovation event to propose your idea?" The response was often, "I assumed that I needed to do my assigned tasks before proposing some new idea, and my assigned tasks take up all my time. From these early experiences, we've revised our product development processes to help ensure engineers get the encouragement and the opportunity to propose innovations as part of their everyday jobs.

Based on their feedback, these changes have made our engineers feel more appreciated and have helped create a steady stream of innovations. And our Innovation Days continue to be a fun and popular way for our engineers to prototype their innovative ideas, helping to create a strong pipeline of potential new products and technologies.

Test Drives

We have also found that a great way to inspire innovation and energize our engineers is to give them exposure to work occurring in other teams that may spark new ideas. To help drive cross-pollination, we have instituted a series of "Test Drive" events. At each Test Drive session, experts from one specific area of our business (e.g., software developers working on a particular technology) run a training/deep dive so that other employees can learn more about the area. The primary goals of these sessions are to cross-fertilize ideas between teams, to expose engineers to other areas of the company that may be of career interest to them in the future, and to give the "trainers" a chance to highlight the interesting innovations and new capabilities they've implemented in their areas of focus. At the end of the training, the "students" are given a series of technical problems to work on and to reinforce what they've learned. We also keep an online leaderboard that's a fun way of showing the progress of everyone working on these exercises. We've found that these sessions often lead to teams thinking about problems in new ways and finding new collaborators, leading to new ideas that would have been much less likely to occur without cross-team collaboration.

Patent Program

Protecting intellectual property is an important part of commercializing innovation. An effective patent program not only encourages employees to protect the IP developed by their novel ideas, it can also help spur breakthrough innovation. Our patent program includes several components that have proven to be very effective.

First, at our company, any employee can submit a relatively simple invention disclosure to our internal Patent Committee, outlining the details of their innovation. Once a disclosure is accepted by our Committee, a patent attorney is assigned to work with the employee to formally file a patent application with the US Patent Office – the attorney does the bulk of the work in this process and takes minimal time on the employee's part. Employees receive awards once their initial disclosures are accepted by the internal Patent Committee and are given additional awards once their patents have been filed and/or granted. In the past, these awards have included monetary rewards, patent jackets, plaques, or other recognitions. These awards serve as incentives for employees to protect intellectual property, and also provide recognition and encouragement to pursue breakthrough ideas.

To ensure the success of a patent program, it is very important to provide appropriate training for employees. This training should cover how employees can identify that a specific portion of their work is potentially patentable, and how to easily and quickly communicate the essence of the breakthrough idea in their initial disclosure to the internal Patent Committee. Ideally, the process required for employees to protect the IP generated by their innovations through patenting should require very little additional effort beyond conceiving the innovations and sharing the relevant details with a patent attorney.

Recognition Awards and Events

We have implemented a variety of different mechanisms to recognize innovators in our organization. These approaches have a broad range of costs and occur at different frequencies, giving us a diverse set of opportunities to drive our culture of innovation. These recognition awards and events are listed in order roughly from lowest to highest cost:

1. **Thank You Notes from Senior Executives**

   We have found great benefit in having senior executives send thank you notes (typically via email) to specific employees expressing appreciation for contributions to the success of our business, including for new innovations. These notes provide employees with very personal recognition of their work and we've found that the recipients are very pleased to receive them directly from senior executives.

2. **Recognition at All Hands**

   Several of our executives have recognition programs for their own organizations, allowing them to highlight and acknowledge great work from specific employees at all-hands meetings. This gives each executive the chance to highlight innovation or other contributions in front of a large audience, and we have seen the employees being recognized take great pride in receiving congratulations in front of their peers/

co-workers. These awards can also be accompanied by monetary bonuses (as permitted by local law) – we've found that even relatively small monetary bonuses are much valued by the recipients as these add some weight to the public recognition.

3. **Employee-Nominated Awards**

   Internal programs in which any employee can reward any other employee for their work in delivering new innovations or making other successful contributions to the company are also effective. These awards can also have a cash bonus component. We've found that our employees greatly appreciate being empowered to directly reward the great work and innovation of their colleagues.

4. **Innovation of the Year Awards**

   Each year senior members of our company's Patent Committee propose a short list of those patents filed in the prior year that were found to be the most innovative and valuable to the company. Our CEO then chooses from this final list to recognize the Innovation of the Year, which entitles the named inventor(s) to special recognition and monetary awards above and beyond those which are offered for other patents filed under the patent program. In addition to receiving special recognition from the CEO, the inventor(s), and their winning inventions are highlighted in a special article on the company's intranet.

5. **Recognition Events**

   Another effective program to consider is holding regular (ideally annual) innovation recognition/award events. In our company, we've used such events to recognize employees who have been successful at filing patents, as well as highlighting specific innovations/innovators that have made a significant impact to the business (e.g., "Innovation of the Year"). Another example is to recognize the best innovation from a more junior employee (e.g., an employee who has only been at the company for a limited period of time, or who is below a certain level of seniority). By recognizing innovations from more junior employees, as well as the most important innovations from all employees, we help inspire a new generation of talented people at the company to innovate. It has been our experience that these events play as important a role in recognizing and encouraging innovation as the direct financial benefits that employees receive for patents that we file. If holding a central event for all innovators is prohibitive from a cost perspective, we recommend doing smaller regional events, attended by senior executives, and/or recognizing top innovations on the internal company website.

Innovation Newsletters

Regular innovation newsletters have proven to be very effective at our company for keeping innovation top-of-mind as well as highlighting exciting new products/technologies that have recently shipped; cool prototypes and early-stage research that we're developing in our labs; upcoming events (e.g., Innovation Days, patent training, etc.); interesting curated online information around innovation, etc. These newsletters serve to highlight the innovators and their work across the company, reinforcing the importance and culture of innovation that we seek to drive throughout our organization.

Fellow and Distinguished Engineer Program

We have two engineering titles reserved for our top innovators at the company, Fellow and Distinguished Engineer (both relatively common designations in the industry). These titles specifically recognize engineers who have made breakthrough innovations of importance to our products, our company and the industry. We also have more traditional engineering titles (e.g., architect) intended to recognize engineers who have designed and provided technical leadership and implementation on very successful products in the market. We have found that the Fellow and Distinguished Engineer roles have provided a great career path and meaningful recognition for our top innovators.

Learning from Failure – Black Box Thinking

One of the most powerful ways that we've found to recognize and inspire innovation comes from a very unlikely source – failure. All too often, when something goes wrong inside a company, the response is to try to isolate the explicit cause of the failure, fix it quickly and move on (or worse, try to cover it up so nobody notices). By contrast, we've embraced the idea of "Black Box Thinking," a name coined by Matthew Syed and taken from the airline industry. Commercial airlines have steadily improved safety over time by objectively analyzing data from their on-board black box after any accident, and then implementing steps to address any discovered issues. In our organization, we examine failures by looking at the entire end-to-end process that failed – we don't simply isolate our investigations to the point of failure; rather, we try to discover systemic improvements we can make to the entire system. Numerous innovations and improvements have come from such black box analyses among our teams, and this approach has helped create a culture where continuous innovation and improvement are recognized and rewarded.

Summary

These are a few of many possible mechanisms to encourage and inspire innovation in your organization. Every time you run such an event or activity, it provides another opportunity to highlight that innovation is not an activity done by a separate group or overseen by a special department. Rather, innovation is the job of every single employee, every single day.

Recognize & Reward

Pamela Arora

In my experience across numerous industries, I have consistently found that innovation is born of a desire to grow and make a difference. Of course, this desire can make up the fabric of an organization's culture; however, that very fabric cannot be possible without a team of individuals who believe in a common goal or mission. Our organization's mission is to make life better for children. With such a compelling mission, we are fortunate to attract team members who are drawn to this sacred mission.

But a mission alone isn't enough. In order to innovate, you need to establish a culture that seeks to grow, and this includes promoting the growth of your team members. As a leader in such an organization, I have a firm belief in the importance of recognition and rewards, not only for individuals but also for the organization as a whole.

Internal Recognition in Day-to-Day Activities

We operate in a high-performing, fast-paced organization, and it can be easy to get lost in the day-to-day operation of delivering care to patients and families – and in the technology realm, we can get lost in supporting those noble efforts. That's why it's critical that we look for ways to recognize internal customer service and teamwork, exemplary service to other groups/departments, collaboration/teamwork across departments, and (most recently) recognition for team member efforts to promote the security of our organization and patients' data. Whether it's a handwritten note, an email, a kind word, a challenge coin, or – in pediatrics – a toy, these small tokens of recognition demonstrate to team members that they have truly made a difference.

Internal Customer Service – Bendy Award: For team members within the Information Services group at Children's Health, when a team member is recognized by a fellow colleague for going above and beyond or for exemplary customer service, the recipient is given a "bendy." A bendy is a small toy (like Gumby) that demonstrates an ability to be flexible – this token of appreciation may seem small, but many times it's the fact that a team member took time to recognize a colleague that makes a big difference in a team member's day and/or feeling of value to the team. The value of this type of gesture cannot be overstated.

External Customer Service – Duck Award: For team members who are recognized by someone outside of the IT department, we have the "duck" toy. Similar to a bendy, the duck is a reward for recognition received from someone outside of our IT group.

External Partner Recognition – Partner Car Award: Everyone likes to get a new car! The partner car program is designed so that IT team members and leader can recognize those outside of the IT department for their partnership with our team. Recipients are given a small toy car and a card thanking them for their partnership.

Security Awareness – Tin Star Award: We established our Tin Star award to recognize Children's Health team members across the organization anytime they report a suspicious cyber event, such as a phishing or social engineering attempt. Whenever an employee proactively recognizes the phishing attempt and forward it to our Cyber team, they receive a Tin Star award. This program recognizes and rewards good security behavior.

Vendor partner recognition – for vendor partners who have truly made a difference in helping Children's Health, we take time to write letters of commendation to those organizations and their team members. In some cases, we also work with our partners for industry awards and recognition so that the partner representative(s), their own organization, and others in the industry will know that they are making a difference.

With these programs, we keep track of all recipients throughout the year. Quarterly, the names are entered in drawings for gift cards, and we use a "Name Ninja" application to randomly pick the "winners" during our quarterly department meetings, and the winners get to randomly pick a gift card. At the end of the year, the team members with the most bendies, partner cars, tin stars, and ducks each receive a large trophy, which is presented to them at our holiday IT team meeting. It's quite a fun celebration! Pictures of each year's recipients are taken and posted on the wall of our facility – in fact, we have pictures dating back a decade where some individuals have since retired; but we, *and they,* know they will forever remain a part of our history of success.

External Benchmarking

Children's Health is continually seeking to improve its processes and procedures. To that end, we place a high value on benchmarking both within our own industry and across the industry. We appreciate our HIMSS membership, as this helps us learn more from our colleagues in the healthcare industry, as well as contribute to the success of other organizations who see the benefit in our own experiences. Children's Health sought and earned the HIMSS EMR Adoption Model Level 7 certification (and recently recertified) because we believe in the importance of comparing ourselves to the best in the industry and then being ranked according to the highest criteria and best practices – it's an honor for us to be counted among health systems who have demonstrated their commitment to excellence through the HIMSS EMRAM Level 7 certification process. We are also deeply grateful to have been recognized with a HIMSS Davies Award of Excellence for our deployment and use of healthcare IT across our organization.

In addition to HIMSS benchmarking, Children's Health has obtained recognition via the *InformationWeek* 500, *InformationWeek* Elite 100 and Most Wired (now led by CHIME). Our organization works with Gartner for cross-industry comparison and best practices, as well as the American Hospital Association (AHA) and College of Healthcare Information Management Executives (CHIME) for benchmarking within the industry.

The bottom line is that we believe in the importance of working with others in the industry (and those outside of healthcare) to make ourselves better and to promote a culture of innovation and growth.

Recognize the Individual Contributions of Team Members

Of course, recognition in a financial sense is a motivator for some team members. However, I believe a stronger motivator is recognizing contributions and singling out individuals for growth opportunities. That's why I often ask my team to take on new responsibilities in areas where they aren't as familiar because gaining a breadth of knowledge benefits our organization by infusing new perspectives into established groups. This also helps team members expand their horizons, which adds value to the organization and to their individual careers.

When it comes to staff gaining confidence in roles beyond their core, the key is to have leadership and peers provide frequent feedback and encouragement. Once the team member gains comfort with the new responsibilities, they also tend to be more sympathetic when one of their peers is placed in a similar position of stretching their capabilities – and they then help serve as an ally to support their colleague.

If a leader views this type of talent development as a potential drain on productivity, I'd challenge them to flip their thinking. Productivity can be unfavorably affected by someone who isn't able to think outside of their own area because they may be unable to consider a bigger picture perspective. Certainly, there can be legitimate productivity issues when you place a team member in a new area – this is the learning curve. But in the end, the expanded knowledge and perspective the team member gains provide a much higher benefit to the organization.

Recognition and Reward: An All-Important Part of Sustaining Innovation in Your Company

Jonathan Scholl

With apologies to Hamlet and Shakespeare, if we are speaking about innovation in today's world, "to be or not to be" is not the question.

The question is "how?"

How do you keep the flame of innovation alive at all levels and in many different locations inside a big organization – knowing that to do so is critical to the enduring success of the enterprise?

Or, to look at the same question from another angle, how do you maximize innovation – without sacrificing the discipline needed to take care of business and satisfy the customer in the here and now of today?

Managing innovation is a difficult, but by no means impossible, balancing act. At Google, they say, "Take Friday and invent something." At Leidos, we may be a bit more structured in our approach to innovation. To inject the necessary level of practicality into our thinking, we define innovation as "the implementation of new ideas with business impact." We look for new and valuable ways to solve difficult problems for our customers. In our contract R&D work for a variety of governmental and commercial customers, we aim to develop products or systems that they will be eager to purchase in expectation of getting an excellent, or even an exceptional, return on their investment.

Probably everyone who is reading this book would agree: innovation isn't hierarchical; good ideas can come from anywhere. However, to be successful in promoting a culture of innovation, your organization has to have the optics to see it. There should also be an assortment of public mechanisms for celebrating and rewarding innovation.

With that in mind, I will begin with a short self-introduction, as Leidos is not exactly a household name (and, to answer the first, most frequently asked question, the company name is a creative shortening of the word *kaleidoscope*, which itself comes from the Greek *kalos*, beautiful; *eidos*, forms; and *skopien*, to see).

Establishing a Culture of Innovation Attracts Employees Whose Reward Is the Work Itself

I've long said that culture is the only sustainable competitive advantage that a company can create. Products and service offerings, financial positions, and market positions can be replicated with some effort. But replicating a culture is tougher. Look only to the automotive industry, where Detroit's capabilities in quality management took decades to replicate its foreign competition. I recall a story about a factory worker in Japan leaving the plant after their shift and, as they were walking out, straightening windshield wiper blades so they were "just so" on the new cars. Culture drives meaning, purpose and a willingness to invest beyond the norm.

So I offer a brief review of the culture of Leidos, best illustrated by a brief history, so that you might understand the length of time and leadership attention needed in establishing a culture where innovation thrives and is its own reward.

Leidos at Nearly 50 Years – A Short History of Who We Are and How We Got to Where We Are Today (A Solidly Profitable Company with 31,000 Employees and $10 Billion in Annual Revenues)

It's no guarantee of future success, but it certainly helps if the founders of the well-established company you work for imbued their creation with some of the best aspects of their own DNA – as seen today not just in the technical smarts of the people, but also in the retention of a good deal of the original character and purpose of the company. At Leidos, we think we have been very fortunate in both regards. The lesson for innovators? It starts with culture. Leaders have to live – and reward and advance – innovation as part of their own ethos.

J. Robert Beyster, the founder, was both a brilliant scientist and an unselfish (I could also say *enlightened*) manager. Born in 1924 to parents of modest means living in Detroit, Michigan, Beyster grew up during the Great Depression. Shortly after Pearl Harbor, at the age of 18, he enlisted in the U.S. Navy and served on a destroyer. Following the war, he went to college and on from there to earn a PhD in nuclear physics at the University of Michigan. That was in 1950, when he was 26.

Bear in mind: This was the golden age of physics – and of nuclear physics most especially. The biggest names in science at this time were Albert Einstein, Otto Hahn, Enrico Fermi, William Teller, and other luminaries in nuclear physics. They bestrode the scientific world like the greatest of giants.

In the 1950s and first part of the 1960s, Dr. Beyster worked for a company called General Atomics. This was a hot time for startups and stocks related to nuclear energy – similar to, if not so numerous as we have seen in more recent time with the booms in dot.com and biotech startups. Our founder worried that too many of these young companies were dedicated to the personal enrichment and glorification of small numbers of people. He wanted to create a different sort of company – one in which *all* of the people working for the company would do more than just share in the financial rewards of ownership; they would see themselves as stakeholders and principals in an exciting business. In a handwritten organizational plan for a new company, he called for employee ownership as a hallmark of the company.

In 1969, at the age of 45, with a wife and three kids to support, Dr. Beyster used the family home as collateral to secure a bank loan and invested $50,000 to fulfill his dream – launching a company first known as Science Applications Incorporated (SAI), later to become Leidos. SAI earned a grand total of $20,000 in 1969. Dr. Beyster rubbed his eyes in disbelief when he did the accounting. "After a year, a surprising thing happened," he exclaimed. "We made a profit!"

If you look at our company timeline over the next several decades, you see a growing involvement in big and important events, all of them opportunities captured by a workforce driven to bring science into applied use in serving our customers. Among other things, there were these achievements:

■ SAI played a key role in orchestrating the clean-up operation after the partial meltdown of a reactor at the Three-Mile Island nuclear station in Pennsylvania in 1979.

■ In 1983, President Ronald Reagan announced the Strategic Defense Initiative (SDI), a missile defense program to defend the country form a Soviet nuclear attack. Two years later, the Pentagon awarded SAI a $5 million contract to research how SDI's anti-missile system should be designed. DoD chose us as a key integrator in the program that was dubbed "Star Wars."

■ In 1986, SAIC (as SAI became known after the name was altered to Science Applications International Corporation) collaborated in the design and building of an unmanned aerial vehicle that prefigured later generations of drone aircraft.

Even so, SAIC remained almost completely under the radar screen in terms of public recognition until 1987 – when we won our first 15 minutes of fame for what was purely a fun and patriotic exercise in innovation. SAIC co-engineered *Stars and Stripes*, the America's Cup winner in that year. In defeating the Australian defender *Kookaburra* four races to nil, she brought the cup back to the USA in high style. With our help, *Stars and Stripes* set a new standard in hydrodynamic design.

After 34 years as CEO, Dr. Beyster retired in 2003, at the age of 79. Two years later, the Board of Directors voted to take the employee-owned company public. Was this a sudden reversal in the original character and purpose of the company?

Not at all.

Culture is persistent: the company has not lost the spirit of being a place where people can continue to think and act as owners – or as self-propelled entrepreneurs in a high-tech, high-stakes business.

Innovation Continues…

■ Thirty years ago, Leidos built the first electronic health record for the DoD. That's something we are replacing today. Over all that time, we have managed the health records of all of active-duty and retired military personnel and their dependents. The current number of beneficiaries in this database is close to 10 million people. We also have more than 70 health clinics around the country serving veterans and providing access to a network of more than 12,000 physicians and caregivers.

■ We also developed a highly sophisticated platform (called LEAF for Leidos Enterprise Application Framework) that we leveraged to develop solutions that the U.S. Air Force uses at its operational centers around the world. Right now we are making a big effort to extend LEAF's reach through similar interoperable platforms to serve hospitals and other providers of healthcare.

Our goal is to eliminate waste, reduce costs and help optimize the delivery of care for millions of people.

■ Finally, we are doing pioneering and exciting work in the field of bio-medicine. At Leidos, we created the first Zika antiviral vaccine based on the human genome. With the scientists at Leidos Biomedical Research (which manages the NCI), we have helped advance curative therapies for certain cancers – specifically, a certain type of neuroblastoma – using big-data analytics combined with cutting-edge advances in using the human body's immune system to destroy invading cancer cells.

Gabe Gutierrez, one of a prestigious group of Technical Fellows at Leidos, leads a small unit that has been working closely with the NIH and DoD. As a Leidos employee since 2007, he was pleasantly surprised to find that there is far more teamwork and camaraderie at Leidos than there was in the academic world that he left behind. Still more, he found it was easier to think big – in assembling the resources to focus on major problems.

When Gabe, who has a PhD in genetics, speaks about the now-gathering immunotherapy revolution, it is impossible not to share his sense of wonderment and excitement.

We may be coming to the end of an era in medicine when it was common practice to inject poison into people's bodies in the hope that it would kill the cancer before it killed the victims of the disease. Now we are learning how to create and deploy new molecules that alert the body's immune system to the presence of invading cancer cells and enable it to destroy them and save the patient.

Leidos Health – Reaching from Lab Bench to Bedside through Innovation

The health business within Leidos has the highest concentration of PhDs in the company. So we have a lot of very talented people. But how do we motivate them? How do we recognize their contributions to the enterprise? And how do we reward them?

As I see it, there are four key elements. We give them

1. Opportunities to do interesting work,
2. Time and resources, for the many and not just the few, to pursue their passion,
3. Recognition and accolades woven into the social fabric of the business and

4. Rewards, incentives, and career progression that works for creative individuals who prefer product innovation to management or sales.

Let me address each of those points.

First, there is no greater gift that you can give to inventors and other creative people than plenty of opportunity to do interesting work. You can start with the worst problem your customer is having in some area (one example: doing what Gabe does trying to stop the spread of certain cancers) and turn it over to your most innovative and creative people to come up with a solution. They will love the challenge. That's what they live for.

We are lucky at Leidos to have hundreds of assignments every year with our customers – thousands over the span of years – and therefore, we have the ability to rotate people and give them variety of work and opportunities to work in areas around their passion. To accomplish this, we have deliberate structures that help our people manage their careers, see the new work that is emerging and voice their preference in work assignments – preference that cannot always be fulfilled, but often can.

Second, and this is like the Google culture mentioned previously, we don't want to have too narrow a focus on the top guns. We also want to capture the creativity of many other people across the enterprise. We encourage our employees, particularly the scientists and engineers, to propose innovation projects every year. Their submissions are reviewed by senior panels of respected innovators and leaders. Every year, we make a number of awards – with projects receiving $50,000 in funding to pay for their time and materials in pursuit of their ideas. A year later, senior executives review the results and express their personal gratitude to individuals who have done an outstanding job of exceeding customer expectations and enhancing the company's reputation for innovation and technical excellence. The selection, and the recognition for the work, reaches the highest levels of our organization. Our Executive Leadership Team and Board of Directors often review and see the work that our people do, reinforcing the culture.

Third, many companies do a great job at finding ways to motivate high-potential people (or "high pots," as they are sometimes called) in sales, finance, and executive management, but very few give equal attention to inventors and talent in technical positions. That is a bad mistake. We believe that recognition and accolades for innovation should be every bit as common and command the same recognition and respect as "manager of the year" or "salesperson of the year." The high-potential employees with technical expertise and talent should be singled-out and put up on something of a pedestal for their achievements in innovation, no less than the up-and-coming stars in other important company functions. Without going into all the details here, we have done that at Leidos in showing our appreciation of and respect for two levels of achievement: one for "technical fellows" (fewer than .05% of Leidos technical staff) and another for "senior architects," mostly reserved for a few holistic thinkers with the multi-dimensional gift of seeing things through in complex programs from initial design through development and the resolution of problems that crop up in early implementation or production. We celebrate the dedication and achievements of these same people in a multitude of other ways as well, including them in big annual events that we call "technical showcases," celebrating their achievements in internal publications and encouraging them to attend speaking engagements and international forums at the company's expense.

Finally, make sure you have a career path that does not lead to a "Dead End" sign for the technically-minded people who love invention and innovation. Do not force them to go into management. Pay them well and allow them to continue to flourish by staying in the laboratory and continuing to be creative. At Leidos, we have a technical career track that lifts the most senior, accomplished innovators to a pay rank commensurate with their contributions to the firm, and our best innovators and scientists are paid like management.

It's not really about the money. I've found that the best innovators make their contributions for the love of the work that they are doing. But employees – even the inventors and innovators – don't like to be ignored or taken for granted when they know that they are making a great contribution to the well-being of the company or organization. There has to be a base-level expectation for your technically-minded employees that they are being recognized and treated as the integral part of the company that they are.

In short, celebrate the success of some of your smartest people and make sure they know you're passionate about them – almost as passionate as they are about the work they're doing!

Chapter 8

Co-Create Solutions

Appreciate the complexity of attention that innovation requires and expose the organization to demands from all stakeholders.

Innovation does not happen by innovators alone. We must be careful not to fall into a belief that innovation is reserved for one person or a special team whose primary function is to develop solutions to problems or invention to opportunities. Innovation is primarily cultural and thrives in team-based organizations. Avoid the trap that innovation is for a select few and all others are discounted. Innovation happens best when it becomes the culture of the entire organization and everyone has the opportunity to engage.

The Structure and Processes of Software Co-Creation at the Johns Hopkins Medicine Technology Innovation Center

Paul Nagy, Jasmine McNeil, Dwight Raum,
Emily Marx, Amy Hushen and Stephanie Reel

The Johns Hopkins Technology Innovation Center (TIC) partners with care providers and clinical researchers to improve patient care through medical software. The TIC works with these change leaders to co-create novel Health IT solutions and help scale those solutions to market. Launched in 2014, the TIC is a professional design and software development team serving as a central resource for the Johns Hopkins Medicine enterprise health system, including Johns Hopkins Hospital, home care, community and academic hospitals, as well as our insurance and accountable care organizations. In four years, the TIC has conducted development projects with 42 clinical leaders representing 35 clinical departments and organizations across our health system. Located on the main Johns Hopkins medical campus in Baltimore, the TIC is home to 29 developers, designers, project managers, and data architects. Through technical guidance and clinical partnerships, the TIC has helped launch nine companies scaling impact beyond Johns Hopkins Medicine into 69 other health systems.

Core Strengths

An internal, professional engineering team built inside a health system reduces the degrees of separation between developers that build solutions and the care providers who use them. The TIC's on-site co-creation development process has advantages over traditional external software development when the solutions require intimate clinical domain knowledge, high usability, dynamic clinical workflow, and changes in care providers' roles. The TIC has expertise integrating clinical devices and information systems in the development of clinical decision support tools and digital health patient engagement applications. Clinical decision support tools aggregate health records and generate predictive algorithms to help care providers diagnose and treat patients with complex health conditions. Patient engagement tools employ smartphones, and wearables to enable convenient remote patient monitoring and proactive care management.

The center embraces core principles of teamwork, respect, opportunity, and audacity, with a pledge to stoke innovation in all corners of our institution. Nine values (Figure 8.1) define how the center curates and executes its work. A few of those values are essential to defining the TIC's co-creation culture when carrying out innovation.

Co-development: the TIC will only provide design and development support to projects – whether they come from clinical staff or Johns Hopkins leadership – if there is a clinical champion who agrees to co-develop the software with the TIC project team. This means that the clinical champion must become part of the project team throughout design and development sprints. The project team relies on the champion to provide expertise and communicate needs based on their daily workflows. In turn, the technical team uses the collaborative time to expose the clinical partner to the inner workings of software development. Consequently, time to completion for software projects is significantly lowered, feedback loops are faster, and the clinical champion knows the details about how the project is progressing.

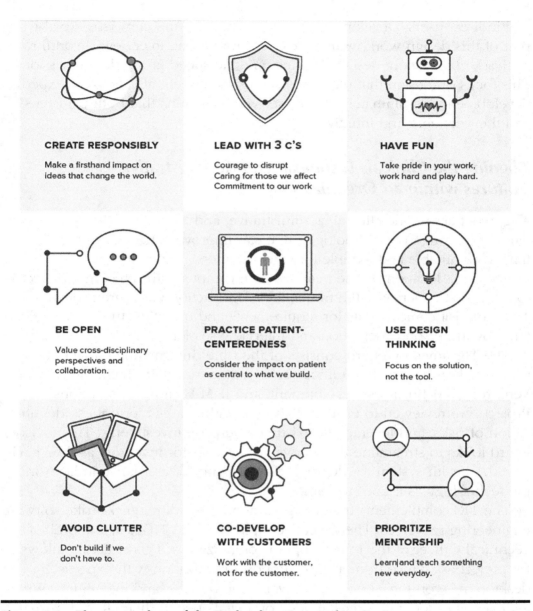

Figure 8.1   The core values of the Technology Innovation Center.

Patient-centered design: Other software development teams might use designers at the end of a software project to work on the user interface. The TIC practices patient-centered design throughout the design and development phases by leveraging its proximity to the hospital, clinicians, and their patients. An integrated design team works throughout a project to identify features and create a user experience based on the real needs of the direct and indirect users. Developers, product managers, and clinicians are also part of this design work, which includes one-on-one interviews, workflow analysis, observation, design research, and facilitated group design sessions. This focus on design that ultimately serves the patient also helps to expedite development and ultimately creates software solutions that both clinicians and their patients find intuitive.

Aligning the Clinical, Technical, and Administrative Cultures within an Organization

Alignment across the clinical, administrative, and technical cultures is essential to exploring new technologies that can improve patient care in a way that is sustainable and feasible for care providers.

The TIC's location on the main medical campus with direct indoor access to the hospital increases the frequency of interaction with care providers. TIC staff visit clinical areas for requirements and usability studies that facilitated by in-person observation and interview sessions.

The TIC advisory board consists of the Chief Information Officer, the Chief Medical Information Officer, and leaders from JHU Technology Ventures, JHM Business Development, and JHM Healthcare Solutions. Projects are reviewed to ensure alignment with strategic priorities, identification of risks, and leverage to existing enterprise investments. The advisory board looks to streamline the innovation process for inventors as they navigate the health system for deploying a pilot and for assistance in licensing the technology as it goes to market.

The TIC complements the IT organization, providing quick-strike software engineering resources. The executive director of the TIC is also the Chief Technical Officer of the Johns Hopkins organization. This structure allows for project assistance from a large support organization with expertise in desktop, networking, server, security, mobile devices, and integration. When a clinical partner contributes an idea or a challenge to their clinical care, the TIC team consults with their IT colleagues to see if parts of the problem can best be solved within the electronic medical record or other existing information systems. This also helps the institution avoid overlapping or competing services.

Financially, the TIC is not funded through operational dollars and functions as a profit and loss center with its own budget accountability. The TIC is run with a lean startup mentality which is self-sustaining through internal projects and grant awards in partnership with faculty.

Convening a Hub for Inventors across Johns Hopkins

The TIC acts as a hub connecting internal inventors with resources across Johns Hopkins. To promote an entrepreneurial culture, the TIC hosts a collaborative community for inventors to socialize their ideas with access to diverse areas of knowledge. The center does this by leveraging the Johns Hopkins academic mission and by building active relationships with schools such as the Johns Hopkins Carey Business School, the Johns Hopkins Whiting School of Engineering, the Johns Hopkins Bloomberg School of Public Health, as well as the Maryland Institute College for Art. TIC staff regularly speak in these settings to recruit students, graduates, and enlist faculty to advise our teams. Beyond the academic community, the TIC draws upon the local business community to provide mentorship. The TIC uses its physical space as a natural base of operations for researchers, business, and industry partners to interact with clinical staff and Johns Hopkins engineering teams. The center's offices are built in a 10,000 square foot open concept with abundant whiteboard walls and swing spaces for offsite partners to work and collaborate. The environment promotes impromptu design sessions, side-by-side developer/clinician collaboration, and introductions of cross-disciplinary subject-matter experts. The TIC connects future entrepreneurial team members in this hub space with clinical partners to understand a new project's scope.

TIC staff also host events and training programs across campus to bring the Johns Hopkins entrepreneurial community together. The largest annual event for the TIC is the annual Digital Health Day, which attracts clinical innovators from across Johns Hopkins to learn about and share innovation in digital health. In 2017, the TIC and its organization partners hosted 340 faculty and students along with 26 groups that research aspects of digital health and are piloting experiments in our clinical setting. Groups presented their work and shared experiences on digital health as a promising new opportunity for faculty career development, education, research, and improving patient care.

Building and Training Teams in Leadership

Hexcite is a 16-week adaptive leadership program that partners TIC clinicians with multidisciplinary teams to develop new ideas. Hexcite participants spend four months ideating and team building, with the following six months focused on building and deploying their pilot within the health system. The goal of this internal accelerator program is to enable rapid experimentation from ideation to deployment and evaluation within one year. Clinical leaders who apply must pay tuition and commit 20% of their time to join the program. Clinical participants split that time between cohort training sessions, team collaboration sessions, and interviews with potential customers. To enter the program, clinical leaders pitch a problem to a group of Johns Hopkins/local entrepreneurs and are evaluated on their leadership potential, idea, novelty, impact, feasibility, and organizational support. Participants are recruited from:

■ Business students from the Johns Hopkins Carey Business School
■ Engineering students from Johns Hopkins Whiting School of Engineering
■ Design students from the Maryland Institute College of Art
■ Design students from the Johns Hopkins Medicine Arts as Applied to Medicine program
■ Other Johns Hopkins researchers and administrators

Teams participate in a series of workshops designed to develop early-stage startup ideas into prototypes. The Technology Innovation Center uses its expertise in software design and development to help teams design a software product. Local startups and seasoned entrepreneurs serve as business teachers and mentors. Those entrepreneurs help teams to design their business using the evidence-based business model canvas.

By the end of the program, the teams have a practiced proposal for potential investors, mock-ups of their application, technical requirements (including architecture and data integration plans), an evaluation plan for testing their prototypes in a clinical space, a plan for obtaining seed funding (most often from translational grants), and a cohesive team ready to launch an independent startup company. Hexcite primes teams to co-develop with the Technology Innovation Center once the 16 weeks are finished; the initial design and requirements planning allows the technical team to dive into development with fewer resources than a typical software development project.

What makes Hexcite unique among early-stage accelerators?

■ It breaks down the barriers to co-creation that often inhibit innovation in large institutions.

- The TIC helps teams to navigate institutional security standards, Institutional Review Boards, data access and integration, marketing, technology transfer, and more.
- The program also seeks to build teams from the depth of expertise the institution offers instead of requiring that clinical leaders find resources on their own.
- Perhaps the most valuable element of the program is that the Technology Innovation Center staff train Hexcite teams in the IT principles of the institution so that they can easily integrate their technology and pilot it using an *internal* clinical founder.

The TIC continues to support the startup teams that come out of Hexcite by providing technical mentorship, assisting with funding through grants support, connecting teams with other startup resources at the institution, and ultimately providing the technology team to build out the software solution.

The TIC identifies five key roles care providers bring to successfully co-creating solutions:

1. Inventor. They bring ideas and insights on how to fix broken healthcare systems.
2. Learner. A learner's mindset that aids the adoption of systems and design thinking to explore the potential solutions fully.
3. Partner. A peer partnership with the technical, design, and business team members to execute as a high-performance team.
4. Scientist. A scientific mindset to question their hypotheses and fully evaluate pilot solutions for learning what indeed improves patient outcomes.
5. Leader. They offer leadership in deploying new solutions and getting their peers to adopt new roles and technology.

Hexcite started in 2015 with yearly cohorts, and now after three cohorts the TIC has helped teams gain over $500,000 in startup funding, trained 56 faculty/staff/students through the program, and helped 13 teams assess a combined 474 hypotheses about their technology and business. The training of technology and business leaders has led to intuitional gains beyond the startup space. Participants reported the following learning improvements during the 2016 cohort:

- Understood how to lead a technical project 36% -> 84%
- Communicating the value of their clinical solutions 42% -> 89%
- Effectively evaluating the competitive landscape 26% -> 89%

Decision Support Case Study: ReHAP

The process of co-creation that Hexcite brings to Johns Hopkins can best be understood by following one startup team who participated in the first cohort of the program in 2015: ReHAP.

Dr. Krishnaj Gourab, a clinical partner and former chief of physical medicine and rehabilitation at a Johns Hopkins community hospital was working to improve rehabilitation services to make sure patients who needed therapy the most weren't missed. Prior to Gourab's effort, therapists had no way to communicate which patients to prioritize between the multiple floors they needed to cover and often lost information about patient's therapy needs with shift changes.

With some mentorship from the Technology Innovation Center, Gourab built a low-fi prototype using MATLAB software to centralize the prioritization of patients and therapy caseload management. The software improved the therapy caseload management process for his team, and he quickly recognized a commercial opportunity as he interacted with rehabilitation groups from around the nation.

Gourab joined the Hexcite program to drive his commercial opportunity forward. He was paired with Johns Hopkins Home Care innovator John Adamovich, who brought financial and business expertise to the team. The two worked to complete the business model canvas through over 40 interviews with potential customers. They also began to explore the data access and integration through workshops held with Johns Hopkins IT. Additionally, they learned about translational funding opportunities available to them, ultimately applying to and winning three separate grants to rebuild the technology as a secure application using the Johns Hopkins technology infrastructure.

According to Gourab, "The TIC helps us negotiate potential roadblocks when looking at the deployment so that ReHAP can work on the data."

Gourab and Adamovich were also able to refine their pitch through the program to gain further funding and leadership support for their project. They took these skills back to their roles at Johns Hopkins.

"This fellowship is unlike any other training I have had in my clinical career," said Gourab. "Apart from the training to create a healthcare technology startup, it has exposed me to completely new ways of thinking while designing solutions in the healthcare arena. One of the most valuable parts of this fellowship is the focus on doing customer interviews and then to use the insights gained from the customer interviews to develop our products/ideas."

The first prototype deployment of the application at the Johns Hopkins community hospital saved therapists an average of 20 minutes per day, freeing up more time for them to care for patients. Revenue increased after bed utilization in the acute inpatient rehabilitation unit when up from 36% to 72.5%.

Through the interviews that Gourab and Adamovich completed, they were able to secure five pilots at rehabilitation centers around the country. ReHAP is currently supporting those pilots and continuing to build its business.

Hexcite was developed to support and validate ideas like ReHAP through co-creation with business, technical, clinical, and design components.

Digital Health Case Study: EpiWatch

The success of co-creation around wearables and digital health is seen through a research study turned startup working to alert patients with epilepsy and their caregivers before a seizure occurs.

EpiWatch, a research study and the first ResearchKit app built for Apple Watch, is the result of the collaboration between Dr. Gregory Krauss and Dr. Nathan Crone, both professors of neurology at Johns Hopkins Medicine. In 2015, Drs. Crone and Krauss began building the app from a research study into a seizure prediction tool to serve all epilepsy patients.

The app helps patients and caregivers manage epilepsy by tracking seizures, possible triggers, medications, and their side effects. Drs. Crone and Krauss were able to collect enough data through seizure tracking (with over 1,000 study participants) to define a preliminary algorithm for seizure detection and alerts.

In order to make that data secure and accessible to researchers for algorithm development at Johns Hopkins, Drs. Crone and Krauss began working with the Technology Innovation Center in 2016. Backed by existing IT infrastructure at Johns Hopkins, the TIC developed a cloud-based architecture, allowing researchers to use a one-stop-shop for data collection, manipulation, and analysis with the ability to scale increasingly large data volumes from device sensors without requiring architectural modifications. The development team placed these tools in the hands of researchers to enable real-time comprehension and analysis of data. When a seizure event happens, the integrated system allows the researchers to immediately access, interpret, and export wearable data from that event. Leveraging this infrastructure has enabled refinement of the parameters that control the algorithm to help identify and reduce the number of inaccurate readings. The TIC also deployed design resources to interview patients and streamline app workflows (Figure 8.2).

According to Dr. Crone: "It is really been a great experience working with the TIC because of the proximity and availability... It is more of a collaborative relationship with people who have the right expertise for the project."

Here, the TIC's alignment with the institution's technical resources and its ability to pair that with the goals of two clinical change leaders in epilepsy research led to the first algorithm for seizure detection.

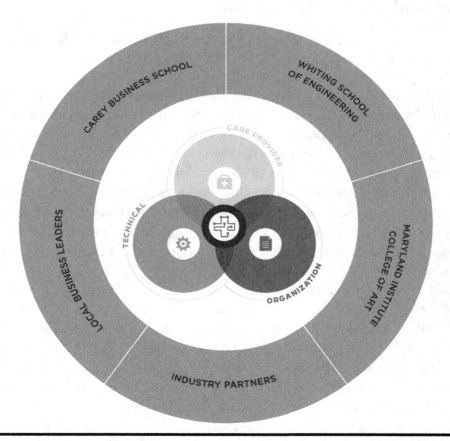

Figure 8.2 Aligning with the clinical, technical, and administrative cultures within an organization and connecting to resources outside the health system.

Innovation, Simplicity, and Interdisciplinary Science: How the Intersection of Healthcare and Engineering is Enhancing the Lives of Florida Seniors

David Rice

Driving through the 32 square miles of The Villages in Central Florida might include spotting a few souped-up golf carts and some decent early bird specials once you've navigated one of the popular town squares.

From the roadside, this appears to be a typical senior living community. But step inside the doors of its villas, ranches, and cottages, and you'll find a scientific endeavor that could transform how the nation cares for its burgeoning ranks of seniors in the years to come.

In the hallways, bathrooms, kitchens, and bedrooms of this planned community, two University of South Florida (USF) researchers, armed with a student workforce, have devised a low-cost way to connect seniors with their caregivers and loved ones like never before. HomeSense, a project spearheaded by Dr. Carla Vandeweerd and Dr. Ali Yalcin of the Tampa-based University, is a remote patient monitoring system that uses an array of commercially available wireless sensors to detect the daily activities and movements of seniors within their homes.

Vandeweerd, PhD, a specialist in aging, dementia, and elder mistreatment, is also Director of Research for The Villages Health Unit and has seen firsthand the evolution of this booming community. Named the nation's fastest-growing metropolitan area each of the past four years by the U.S. Census Bureau, The Villages is now home to more than 124,000 residents, a population projected to continue rising rapidly.

That growth mirrors the larger graying of America. Every day between now and the end of the next decade, about 10,000 baby boomers will turn 65, the Pew Research Center reports. At the same time, the healthcare industry is grappling with a nursing shortage and challenges finding enough home health workers.

The work of Vandeweerd and Yalcin holds promise in bridging this gap between demand for aging-related healthcare services and the supply of caregivers.

Over the past 27 months, the USF team has installed 15 HomeSense systems in The Villages to monitor research participants' sleep patterns, personal hygiene habits, and sedentary time, along with their use of appliances such as refrigerators, microwaves, and coffee makers. It is a digital window into the seniors' daily routines – from how much television they watch, to how many times they use the bathroom during the night to how often they leave their home.

The broad range of activities monitored can act as determinants of a senior's health – key indicators that, when analyzed as data points, can pinpoint behavioral changes that otherwise wouldn't be revealed without a live-in caregiver.

"For healthcare practitioners, this type of project offers the opportunity to connect data to real health outcomes and observe that good quality data combined with the appropriate analytics can positively influence health and quality of life," Yalcin says.

Designing and Co-Creating a Solution

Five principles form the foundation of the HomeSense system:

- Functionality – the practicality of setup across environments
- Flexibility – ability to adjust for an individual's special circumstances or living arrangement
- Simplicity – end users can easily glean actionable information
- Affordability – ensures higher rates of adoption
- Modularity – seamless incorporation of technology such as wearables and physiological monitors

For all the glamour surrounding the dawn of artificial intelligence, or AI, the HomeSense system could be considered part of a parallel revolution in science and technology – ambient intelligence, or AmI.

"If we know your next medication time is at 8 p.m. and you're sensed in the kitchen – where your medications are stored – at 7:55 p.m., ambient intelligence is us prompting you to take your medication while you are in there," says Yalcin, who has a PhD in Industrial and Systems Engineering. "That is the next step in the intelligent part, the system thinking ahead.

"Intelligence is a combination of sense, reason, and action," he says. "Right now, we are focused on sense and reason, which is monitoring and understanding the situation."

Although similar research is being conducted around the world with different approaches and technology, the USF team found existing commercial systems lacked critical components.

So, with Yalcin bringing the technical know-how to the drawing board and Vandeweerd the healthcare expertise, the pair set about designing a system capable of capturing and cleaning data before ultimately sharing it with patient care decision-makers.

Working with students, Vandeweerd identified conditions that commonly affect older adults, including typical symptoms and likely spots where emergencies could arise.

"The health side of the team came up with a laundry list of things they wanted to be able to detect," Yalcin said. "A person's cleaning habits, toileting habits, shower habits, activities of daily living basically. We took that and came up with metrics we can measure using the sensors, things that would indicate what we need to know about the lives of these individuals.

"That is where we decided the specifics in terms of where to put the sensors in the house. We were looking at what to sense in the house and what is going to keep costs manageable, but also provide us with sufficient information to make informed decisions."

To safeguard participants' privacy, Yalcin and Vandeweerd recognized the research project could not involve the intrusion of cameras or microphones into the homes. Additionally, a noninvasive system that required no active-participation by the seniors would yield better results.

To start, the researchers needed readily available sensors that could be tested in various environments and integrated with a gateway the team would design and program. Part of the solution came in the form of a tiny computer with a little price tag.

The Raspberry Pi costs $35 and originally was designed to provide internet access to people in developing countries. Slightly bigger than an Apple TV or Roku streaming box, the Pi is a relatively inconspicuous presence in a research participant's home. But it packs enough punch to allow for the collection and transmission of HomeSense data via the residential internet network.

The mini-computer's ability to tap into the communication protocols of wireless sensors makes it possible to receive and store data in real-time on two servers at USF that the team has named Mango and Noni. From there, the data can be used to create web pages where participants, analysts, and caregivers can see data visualizations of activity the sensors monitor.

Connecting to Caregivers

With a system design in place, the next phase was deployment. Vandeweerd and Yalcin began examining the reliability and robustness of the data storage capabilities. Was all data being captured? Did the system always respond? Could it recover connectivity after power and internet outages?

For fine-tuning the system and testing the sensors, Bay Care's John Knox Village, a continuing care retirement community just blocks from USF's Tampa campus, offered the use of a senior living apartment to serve as a "living lab."

Vandeweerd and Yalcin then gave their research assistants a simple task: try to break the system. The research team tested the sensors for everything from battery life to optimal placement until they were ready for real-life deployment.

Today, more than two years later, HomeSense is "in a place where it is fairly mature," Yalcin says. "We can deploy the technology consistently. Every house is different, but you find a workaround."

Once in the field, the USF team began designing notifications and evolving the system. For example, a framework now is in place to alert the loved ones of a person who wanders from home at night.

Able to measure motion, pressure, luminance, temperature, and contact, HomeSense can indicate how a person is moving throughout their home, whether they are alone, what time they shut their lights off, and whether typical behavior patterns have deviated drastically. That is vital information for monitoring patients with conditions such as dementia or depression or who are dealing with new medication side effects.

Yalcin and Vandeweerd continue exploring new uses for the data, as long as it supports their core principles, particularly functionality.

"For us, the most important thing is not to do what we think is useful as scientists in a lab," Vandeweerd says. "What we want is a system that has high utility. So, what do end users, caregivers, and health providers feel will make the technology most functional?"

By modifying sensors, she says, they were able to "separate signal from noise in a way that is effective."

"Anyone can throw some sensors on the wall and say they have a system," says Vandeweerd. "But how do you design a system that is measuring behaviors that will help identify potentially adverse situations or things that make people more resilient so that we have data that are useful and meaningful, and that providers, case managers, daughters, and sons can all interpret?

"Being able to mine our data for the activities that signal a need for intervention, that is the part that has been a challenge. But now we are able to do that effectively in a way that will lend itself to other populations as well."

With a project cost of $400 to $700 to outfit a two- or three-bedroom home with HomeSense, the USF professors met their affordability goal.

"We designed this thinking that, at some point, this could go nation-wide," says Yalcin. "You look at other research in this area; there are excellent results in specific things like being able to monitor sleep quality for example. But these are using sensors that can cost hundreds or thousands of dollars. You're not going nationwide with expensive technology looking at one attribute that is part of bigger, broader wellness indicators."

Although they developed HomeSense with older adults in mind, the USF researchers wonder about its potential appeal beyond senior caregiving. That could come from companies marketing products to parents of latchkey kids or pharmaceutical firms monitoring behavior in clinical trials.

"Really what we are doing is human behavior datafication," Yalcin says. "Taking human behavior and turning it into data. Cause once it is data, we can analyze it."

The Collaborative Community

Securing approval for academic field research presents no shortage of hoops to jump through: convince a College of Medicine and College of Engineering of the project's necessity, and meet the standards of an Internal Review Board. For Yalcin and Vandeweerd, however, the process was relatively smooth courtesy of the USF community's support.

"Because we have a Community-Based Participatory Research approach, we have been able to identify the important issues, and how we meet the needs of providers and users," Vandeweerd says. "Since we oriented our research questions in that way – so it is not about bench science and doing what we think – we have gotten a lot of great support from across the university. We are now working with faculty from Public Health, Pharmacy, and Nursing, and we have had great support in the field."

Seventy-five miles north of the USF Tampa campus, The Villages Health System, with more than 40,000 patients and 120 providers, is expanding HomeSense to more of the community's residences. The pilot project will allow healthcare professionals to respond to system-generated notifications when data shows significant behavioral changes or an adverse event requiring intervention.

The researchers have biweekly phone calls with the participating Villages residents, who report how they are feeling and provide feedback on the collected data and the functionality of the HomeSense dashboards.

"Your participants are not paying for the service, but they are," Yalcin says. "They are paying with their time and by sharing their lives with you."

To ensure they were targeting the right audience, the USF team partici-pated in a National Science Foundation I-Corps program to examine the system's commercial potential and provide customer review. One interested market segment was senior home care service providers. By the end of the exercise, Yalcin and Vandeweerd were more convinced than ever that the platform is ideal for that audience.

"When you talk to them about their pain points, they are things this tech-nology would address," says Yalcin. "For example, are the people they send to these homes actually providing the services they are there to provide? We can tell you if they actually bathed the person; we can tell you if they stayed the full amount of billed time.

"From a quality assurance perspective for that company, but also for the customer who is paying for these services, it ensures they are getting their money's worth."

Building Innovation into Curriculum

The HomeSense project also is impacting the education of USF students. Yalcin recently authored Healthcare Data Mining and Predictive Analytics, a required course for students pursuing an MSHI Healthcare Analytics degree. He envisions incorporating de-identified HomeSense data into the course-work and, eventually, the broader curriculum.

Students from disciplines including health sciences, engineering, and even anthropology are now involved in HomeSense, and the lessons for them extend beyond the classroom.

"They are installing sensor systems, collecting information and interacting with older adults," says Vandeweerd. "They are thinking about the location of devices, and they have a much better perspective on it than if they were just interpreting data on a screen. That data now has real meaning – it is a real person, a person's life."

HomeSense also bridges a chasm that can exist between the ideas of engineers and the reality of the problems they want to address.

"For engineering students, the project offers an opportunity to see how data should be managed from creation until decision-making," Yalcin says. "It is rare to have the chance to present students with such a complete data analytics experience.

"You cannot design something in the confines of a lab and expect it to work perfectly. It is not going to happen," he says. "To design a solution that is effective and functional, you have to understand the problem and see the problem in action."

Yalcin and Vandeweerd's view of the student has evolved over the course of the project as well. They relish the challenge of finding, training, and retaining students from diverse backgrounds to become as invested in the project as they are.

"First thing in the morning, I'm checking on the project, and that is what I hope our students also do," says Yalcin. "Dedication is not something you can see on a transcript. I started out looking at only A students. Now I find value in things that make somebody dedicated, caring, and invested, in addition to academic aptitude.

"Qualities that I did not give much thought to before this project are now high on my list, as high as academic success."

The Silver Tsunami and the Power of Data

Healthcare thought leaders speak extensively about the challenge that lies ahead courtesy of the oncoming Silver Tsunami. Over the coming 40 years, the number of Americans 65 and older will surpass 98 million, representing nearly a quarter of the nation's population. Nearly 20 million will be at least 85 years old, the Census Bureau projects.

Providers must innovate in their use of data and technology to deliver affordable care to patients who are living longer and with more chronic disease. Care, as HIMSS CEO Hal Wolf III puts it, "has to extend beyond the walls of the clinic or hospital."

A system such as HomeSense allows providers to do more with less and optimize effectiveness. By flagging conditions such as cognition loss earlier, physicians can better counter degenerative effects, and patients can spend more time living independently or with loved ones.

For Vandeweerd, HomeSense aligns with a vision where care no longer stops at the door of the physician's office. She hopes the USF research initiative will demonstrate an ability to improve outcomes, save money, and arm physicians with information to ensure patients are engaged participants in their care plans.

"We have piles of data everywhere, but people are not harnessing that data for good utility," says Vandeweerd. "We are separating good strong data mining that is practical and intervention-based from fluff that isn't actionable.

"Old age does not have to be a period of decline where you just give up on all the things you once enjoyed," she says. "In a perfect world, you would live strong and healthy until the end of your life when you have a period of acute stress."

Scrappy Innovation in a Safety Net Hospital

Daniel Clark & Kyle Frantz

It takes evolution and innovation to thrive as a public hospital, especially in a city with a wealth of outstanding healthcare systems.

On May 6, 1837, Cleveland City Council designated an infirmary as City Hospital, a forerunner of The MetroHealth System. The initial charge was to care for the chronically ill, aged, mentally impaired, and poor – and 181 years later we are still doing that. Essentially, we have been practicing population health for decades before it was a buzzword. Our commitment to Cuyahoga County has remained the same. What has changed are MetroHealth's advanced and advancing technologies and the number of dedicated experts tied to our mission. All this has led to our Transformation – clinically, operationally, and physically, under the leadership of our president and CEO, Akram Boutros, MD, FACHE, and his executive team.

The physical transformation is needed to support our continually improving clinical and operational functions and our increased emphasis on a value-based delivery system of care. Long ago, we had a hospital with 1,600 beds. Our current hospital has more than 700 licensed beds, and we are building a new 10-story hospital with 270 single rooms. This downsizing reflects MetroHealth's innovative strategies to get our community healthier, resulting in a decreased need for acute care. In addition to the smaller state-of-the-art hospital, there will be a new outpatient plaza, central utility plant, parking garages, and walkways/connectors. It also includes creating green space in almost half of the 52-acre campus. Expected completion is the end of 2022. With Cuyahoga County supplying less than 3% of MetroHealth's total operating revenue, funding was boldly secured through the May 2017 sale of hospital-revenue bonds.

While MetroHealth proudly serves as a county hospital, our leadership rejects the broad stereotypes that sometimes accompany safety net hospitals. The senior leadership of the organization comes from a variety of backgrounds – public and private hospitals, consulting, technology leadership, private equity and venture capital, clinical and operational leadership, and academia among others. Our senior team and many of their direct reports have firsthand experience in organizations that are not structured like a public not-for-profit. We draw on that collective experience in everything we do. When cohort data is available, we are more likely to compare ourselves to our integrated delivery network or even for-profit counterparts than other public hospitals.

In a sea of health system consolidation, MetroHealth has remained unaffiliated. The growth has been steady over the decades and accelerated in recent years as clinical centers of excellence and nationally-recognized physicians have joined our ranks. Our size – 700+ beds at our primary academic medical center and $1 billion+ in operating revenue – works to our advantage when it comes to innovation. With 1.4 million patients a year, we have a meaningful cohort to implement new approaches to better health. At the same time, we are a size that allows for a strategy to quickly be understood and scaled across multiple facilities within what may be competing cultures and leaders.

In the last several years, we have begun to create an internal organization that is designed to support innovation. The Department of Integration and Transformation (DoIT) is the umbrella organization broadly charged with the transformation responsibility. The Center for DARE (Disruptive and Radical Experimentation) is a component of DoIT. DARE has a mission to "have a safe space to experiment with ideas" and challenge and "disrupt the status quo that is not working." DARE also acknowledges that everyone who works for the organization has an "individual passion" to advance how we provide care and treat patients, whether they are in a direct caregiver role or have a non-clinical focus.

The tenets of DARE are:

- We are scouts and scanners of our system paying attention to emotional climate, morale, and commitment
- We work on culture, helping all of us have a voice in creating the culture that will help MetroHealth thrive
- We also help "ideators" in the organization develop their ideas for change
- We "curate" information and resources about new ideas, best practices in innovation and leadership and approaches to change

Change management is also a critical component to making this culture change both initially and permanently. As we implement new technology and workflows, our leadership team believes that changing established processes are incrementally more difficult than technology alone. We often use the word "calcify" to describe how good processes corrupt easily and how those bad processes harden and take root. The goal is to break up the hardened calcium deposits so something new can emerge.

DARE also includes a focus on helping the organization change:

- We share best practices for employee involvement, working with resistance to change and communication approaches
- We facilitate change and conversations
- We convene a group to focus on critical issues
- We bust silos and get people working in multidisciplinary groups to leverage a variety of perspectives and skills.

Like other organizations, project management and the Project Management Office serve more than the IT department. Recently, the PMO has been centralized outside IT and reports to a vice president who is responsible for both project management and analytics. These two functions serve the business needs of the organization, not just the reporting needs of IT. This separation of the reporting structure ensures that the data and information coming from our systems are the intellectual property and responsibility of the entire organization, not just the IT department. The co-creating enabled DARE structure has also helped give others in the organization a broader understanding of how projects are managed. Staff come to appreciate how complicated it is to manage a project – that it requires technical knowledge, attention to detail, political savvy, and an understanding of human behavior and motivation. In some instances, non-project managers have managed projects while being mentored by more experienced project managers. However, we also recognize the role of the professional project manager and believe having dedicated staff to work on critical initiatives – both big and small in the budget – contribute to the likelihood of a project being successful.

We embrace technology and were an early adopter of electronic health records. MetroHealth is Epic client #15 and first went live with computerized provider order entry in 1999. Over the decades, we have expanded our footprint considerably and now have one of the most well-integrated systems in the country. Our IS staff, approximately 140 team members, support a wide range of applications for the clinical and business organization. Operating at staff ratios well below national benchmarks and those recommended by our strategic technology suppliers, we manage a meaningful use that earns us national recognition.

Population health is a necessity when you serve a largely urban population. Early population health efforts were impressively successful. Through novel approaches, our Medicaid Waiver Demonstration Project generated claims that were nearly 30% lower than expected when compared with the CMS actuarial budget for the same patient population. To further manage this group, MetroHealth is a frontrunner for new models of Accountable Care Organizations (ACOs) and has been chosen as 1 of 16 sites nationally to participate in a "Track 3" ACO model, which brings both upside and downside risk for the population attributed to MetroHealth.

All of this requires a combination of unique problem solving and analytics to support it. Dashboard solutions and pushing real-time comorbidity information to the electronic health record (EHR) is a combination of clinical care and technology that helps paint a more accurate picture of how sick our patients are. Moreover, recognizing social determinants of health makes evident the need for risk-adjusted reimbursement.

Outside of IS and the DoIT/DARE project management, a separate innovation structure keeps the organization attuned to new and developing technologies. Members of the team are encouraged to identify new technology that could be important to how we manage patients and organize the business. They then report to a senior vice president of Innovation and Strategy who is part of the CEO's cabinet. The innovation department follows by working with dedicated business development resources, IS, and DoIT/DARE to scope the opportunity, identify a budget and implementation plan and take it through the governance process. We look for opportunities to identify and maximize alternative revenue streams inside and outside the health system while maximizing and leveraging our existing resources. We are seeking new technologies and partners as we drive healthcare innovation.

We see innovation as the key to everything we do and integral to fulfilling our mission and vision as the safety net, the county hospital in Northeast Ohio. We believe it so much that we include being "renowned for our innovation" as part of our organization's Vision Statement.

Mission

Leading the way to a healthier you and a healthier community through service, teaching, discovery, and teamwork.

Vision

MetroHealth will be the most admired public health system in the nation, renowned for our innovation, outcomes, service, and financial strength

MetroHealth has used limited resources as a catalyst for innovation and community partnership throughout its history. MetroHealth, like most health systems, faces a constant challenge as to how to continually evolve the fundamental care delivery process and infrastructure (inclusive of technology and programmatic roles) to adequately care for our population in growing unmet social and clinical needs. This challenge is made more difficult by the pressure to deliver high-tech, high-touch, and highly effective chronic care management to both the general population and the attributable populations MetroHealth sees in the Cleveland area. Pursuant to these bold objectives, MetroHealth has launched more than 100 programs and initiatives designed to target various aspects of care for these patients with clinical and social determinants of health needs.

As a national pioneer for accepting new models of risk, the focus on finding value from the social determinants of health for MetroHealth could not be more pressing. Experts have found through repeated research that 50-80% of outcomes and costs are directly impacted by the Institute of Medicine (IOM) categories of social determinants of health, inclusive of health literacy. The IOM made strong recommendations to HHS in 2016 to include social risk factor scoring for Medicare and Medicaid patients care strategies. Fundamentally, EHRs lack access to social determinants of health (SDOH) data and to the community resource inventories, while care plans and Clinical Decision Support (CDS) predominately use clinical and claims data and are not firing based on social need and thus CDS potential is not being realized. The continued shift from fee-for-service to value-based contracting is forcing providers/networks to become broadly responsible and accountable for patient outcomes. The data clearly demonstrates the link between the SDOH, care outcomes, and the overall cost of care. The cost of care is significantly higher for those patients who have ongoing unmet social needs.

MetroHealth has an almost exclusively employed provider population that is incentivized to collaborate. Combining this with the commitment to its community and willingness to assume the risk for patient outcomes, MetroHealth is an ideal early partner for Socially Determined – a Washington, D.C., based company that is creating the science of the social determinants of health. Together, our two groups are striving to quantify social risk and match it with targeted social interventions, while tracking the outcomes with traditional health system quality and outcome measures, thus forging the path for making social interventions an integrated and sustainable way of delivering care.

During the initial phase of the partnership, Socially Determined is developing a *SocialScape* for Cleveland and Cuyahoga County which quantifies social risk for the community at a census block level. Patterned after how an HCC score captures clinical complexity, the *SocialScape* captures the social complexity for economic well-being, housing, food insecurity, transportation, health literacy, social isolation, and crime and violence displayed geospatially, and each individual is assigned a risk score based on clinical and social factors. In parallel with this technical work, both entities are evaluating health system and community benefit programs that may best be leveraged for social interventions. Socially Determined is then using advanced analytics and machine learning to determine selected cohorts of patients who share similar social and medical traits which will benefit from selected interventions while outcomes are aligned with value-based contract incentives and tracked for efficacy. Once these findings are presented to MetroHealth leadership, a second phase of the partnership will begin with the execution and iteration of these interventions on other patient cohorts and will be funded by shared savings on value-based incentives and improved clinical outcomes. It is a partnership that both parties hope to share for the next 3 to 5 years, and while doing so provide a roadmap for the future of U. S. healthcare while enhancing MetroHealth's role as a leader in innovation.

This relationship is one example of finding partners that are the right fit and targeting areas where we can make the most impact. The concept of non-clinical factors impacting health is not new to most in healthcare and is not new to MetroHealth. Collaborating with experts from outside allows us to leverage our assets, look at things differently, and gives us the ability to develop a replicable solution that can impact more lives than we can physically touch today. Our care teams and employees have a tremendous amount of knowledge that when supported by technology and innovation can change the world of healthcare.

Targeting efforts that make our community stronger while helping other organizations get the most out of their limited resources is laying the foundation to implement future innovations. The willingness to adapt how and where we impact patients' lives is essential and fosters innovation. Limited resources helped make that adaptive excellence a part of who MetroHealth is. It has taught us not just to survive, but lead.

Innovations in Interventional Informatics

Dr. Christopher Longhurst and Marissa J. Ventura

As a practicing physician and the Chief Information Officer at UC San Diego Health, driving and supporting innovation in health IT across my team, organization, and beyond, is a key part of what motivates me to do my part to improve the delivery of healthcare.

I have taken to heart the concept of The Triple Aim[1] to optimize health system performance – and have embraced its expansion to The Quadruple Aim.[2] This approach encourages healthcare institutions to pursue improvements in:

- ■ Population Health,
- ■ Patient Experience,
- ■ High-Value Care,
- ■ Moreover, now, Provider Experience.

With this four-pronged approach in mind, I encourage my leadership team and my peers on the executive team to design health IT solutions that align with these goals – and meeting all four is the Holy Grail! To do that, co-creating solutions to the critical issues we face in our own organization, across our hospital and practice affiliates, and in the healthcare industry as a whole is a key facet of the work we do today and the work we have ahead of us.

In my own experience, bringing the right people together to collaborate on new ideas in health IT could not have been more important in most of the projects I've been involved with in my career.

Integrating Home Monitoring in the EHR at Stanford Children's Health

During my time as chief medical information officer at Stanford Children's Health, I helped lead strategic efforts to improve children's health and provider workflow using health IT. One way we did this was to innovate a way to integrate continuous glucose monitoring (CGM) data in the electronic health record (EHR) using widely available and reliable consumer technology.[3]

Working in both pediatrics and clinical informatics, my colleagues and I recognized that Type 1 diabetes is one of the most common chronic diseases of childhood. Ensuring the appropriate level of insulin therapy could mean the difference between needing to manage hyperglycemia (high blood glucose) with aggressive therapy and inadvertently putting a young patient at risk for hypoglycemia (low blood glucose).

For years, we had recognized a need for a more straightforward way to collect and analyze home glucose data through what has become the center of our workflows: the EHR. While some cloud-based, self-monitoring diabetes applications exist, their use has been limited given the plethora of applications and EHR platforms.

A yet-to-be-tested solution to this problem began to take shape in 2014: Apple announced that it would update its operating system with HealthKit,[4] a now well-known app that enables health data interoperability. Two additional announcements followed: Our EHR vendor (Epic Systems Corp., Madison, WI) and a major CGM device company (Dexcom, San Diego, CA) both announced they would leverage HealthKit for their patient-facing applications – the Epic MyChart app (patient portal) and Dexcom Share app, respectively.

By partnering with Dr. Rajiv Kumar, a pediatric endocrinologist at Lucile Packard Children's Hospital and junior faculty member at Stanford University, we brought together the technology platforms from these diverse industries: a medical device company, a mobile device company, and an EHR software provider. Getting these three platforms to "talk" to each other, we thought, could enable providers to better triage care between clinic visits and improve our workflow – features that would ultimately lead to more effective and efficient patient care.

While blending these platforms would help us determine the feasibility of integrating automated data into an EHR, we were also keenly aware that the process would be most useful in healthcare settings if the workflow could be replicated without the need for institutional-level customization or specific technology platforms. Moreover, to increase the likelihood of adoption among providers, we realized that there needed to be an easy way to visualize patients' glucose values over time. To overcome this potential barrier, my colleagues and I developed a model day visualization with a custom web-service embedded in the EHR. This clinical decision support tool is publicly available at https://gluvue.stanfordchildrens.org. It is agnostic to EHR vendor, and the workflow requires no institutional-level customization.

Our pilot demonstrated two things, quoting from our published findings in the *Journal of the American Medical Informatics Association*: "First, continuous information delivery is feasible through the use of commonly owned mobile devices. Second, passive EHR-based data delivery, coupled with automated triage and intuitive visualization, facilities more efficient provider workflow for reviewing data and improved communications with our patients. In our pilot, this was associated with better care between scheduled clinic visits."[3]

Fitting the pieces of the puzzle together enhanced the patient experience through improved care, and improved the provider experience with a more streamlined workflow for the diabetes care team. It also supported improved population health with an EHR-integrated, risk-prioritized dashboard of all diabetes patients using CGM monitoring.

Bedside Tablets at UC San Diego Health

When I moved to UC San Diego Health as CIO, the 2016 opening of Jacobs Medical Center provided the opportunity for my new team to introduce what has become an often-cited, local patient satisfier: connected iPads in every inpatient room.[5]

Our tablets allow patients to be in charge of many aspects of their own inpatient experience with a simple swipe or tap. They have secure access to their own medical records, through an app provided by our EHR vendor. Through this app, they can view their test results, photographs and biographies of their healthcare team, a schedule of medications or upcoming procedures, and educational materials prescribed by physicians.

Using Jamf for mobile device management, we are able to protect the patient's privacy upon discharge, as well. Each tablet is automatically wiped of a patient's data immediately following discharge, leaving no trace of the user's history. It is then ready for use by the next patient. Moreover, the software communicates with our Epic EHR system to coordinate iPad management with patient records.

The tablets also leverage a Crestron application to give patients control over their environment, including the blinds, room temperature (+/–3 degrees), and lighting. Entertainment apps are available with streaming to the 70" television in every patient room. Patients can also download some of their favorite apps. Our preliminary data suggest that this room automation is an attraction that is correlated with an increased likelihood of patients accessing their medical record.

The partnership with Apple was a nice carryover from my days at Stanford Children's Health. Our collaboration has helped us improve the patient experience at UC San Diego Health. Sometimes it is the simplest of amenities that help patients feel more in control and at home with their healthcare. The first week I saw patients in the Jacobs Medical Center, one new mother told me that, after her repeat Cesarean section, her husband had gone home to care for their first child, and having the tablet in the room helped her feel more in control.

A Hackathon at UC San Diego Health

When my team got involved with the hackathon at UC San Diego Health in 2017, little did we know the caliber of disruptive ideas that would come from bringing a multidisciplinary group of people together for a brief period to co-create solutions that address some of the critical issues in healthcare today?

Our first-place winner is a prime example: "Realty Art Therapy: Incentivizing Patient Mobility through Augmented Reality" was developed to help motivate patients to get out of bed and socialize with other patients, as they search for art around Jacobs Medical Center. The app leveraged the iPads provided to patients during their hospital stay and took them on a hunt through the hospital's 150-piece therapeutic art collection. Each patient room includes an art piece, and the remaining pieces are scattered throughout the hallways and lobbies. The app is designed to promote patient mobility, diminish social isolation, and improve mental wellness through expressive arts therapy.[6,7]

With these potential health benefits, my team and I are helping the group of students who dreamed up the idea to develop the app further. One day it could become another tool in our arsenal to improve patients' experience and their well-being at our own hospitals.

Yet, what excites me about this project is the collaboration and partnership behind it. Our event, dubbed UC Health Hack, brought together technology professionals, engineers, clinicians, and undergraduate and graduate students to fulfill the ambitious goal of "closing healthcare gaps from the acute-care setting to precision medicine at home, empowering patients and their providers."

Nearly 200 students from institutions across California participated in the event. They were joined by more than 70 academic and industry experts, who served as mentors, judges, or volunteers to help provide guidance and steer ideas into reality. Additionally, the event drew in notable partners, including UC Irvine Health, Rady Children's Hospital-San Diego, the UC San Diego student-led chapter of Engineering World Health, as well as some corporate sponsors, including Optimum, Amazon Web Services, Epic, Jamf, and West Health.

Partnering with Our UC Health Sisters

Collaboration and co-creation are at the heart of an important innovation for UC Health, the moniker for the University of California's five academic medical centers (AMCs) and 18 health professional schools. In a first-of-its-kind technology collaboration within UC Health, UC Irvine Health and UC San Diego Health began sharing the same instance of our EHR platform. This also marked the first time that our EHR platform had been extended from one AMC to another in the U.S.

By sharing a platform with UC San Diego Health, UC Health cut the cost of implementation by an estimated 30%! This collaboration advances UC Health's strategic goal to share health services and generate efficiencies across campuses through the shared implementation and maintenance of technology platforms. It also promises to enable better management of medical information, help align clinical pathways and practices that leverage the best of both organizations, as well as better support joint research efforts.

Full implementation of the shared EHR platform with UC Irvine Health began in November 2017. UC San Diego Health also shares its EHR platform with the clinics at UC Riverside Health and community practice affiliates; this has been a cost-saving arrangement that has improved coordination of care among physicians.[8,9]

Again, the puzzle pieces came together in a way that has enabled us to address cost considerations, patient experience, and population health across a couple of our sister UC institutions in Southern California. When I cared for a newborn born to a surrogate mother at UC San Diego Health, the parents, who lived in Orange County, began asking how to best able to share the medical records with their pediatrician in that area. I was pleased to be able to share that my colleagues could easily access his child's medical records at UC Irvine Health because of our shared EHR platform.

Leveraging Apple's Health App – Again

Bringing us full circle, another collaboration with Apple is still in its infancy. In January 2018, Apple announced that the iOS 11.3 update would include a new feature to its Heath app: Patients would be able to view their medical records on their iPhones.[10] Among the dozen healthcare institutions invited as a pilot partner, the only state-run health system is UC San Diego Health.[11]

This allows patients who have received care at UC San Diego Health or one of our affiliates, who are a part of Apple's beta program, and have access to the iOS 11.3 (beta) release, to securely store their medical information from various institutions on their mobile phones. The data is encrypted and protected with the user's iPhone passcode.

The evolution of this new feature empowers patients with access to their own health records, consolidated in a secure place. Moreover, it has the potential to improve provider workflows, as patients can share accurate information about their own health from a device in the palm of their hand. Will this make a difference to patients? Only time will tell, but we are committed to collaborating with patients, providers, and industry partners to continuously innovate.

Lessons Learned

As I review these projects, I noted that collaboration and partnership play a key role in helping to bring disruptive innovation forward. I also see common themes of The Quadruple Aim that we can pursue to drive and support innovation across health IT:

- How are you ensuring technology enhances the patient experience?
- How can health IT be expanded to improve the health of your community? Could the automation of glucose data in the EHR be used to analyze trends across young patients with diabetes? What lessons can we bring to our communities based on the data we aggregate in the EHR?
- How are you addressing the need to reduce the per capita cost of healthcare?
- What about healthcare providers? Let's develop health IT that allows healthcare providers to focus on what they do best – provide quality care.

One last thought: When you think of innovation are you also thinking about The Quadruple Aim?

References

1. Berwick DM, Nolan TW, Whittington J. The triple aim: care, health, and cost. *Health Aff.* 2008;27(3):759–769.
2. Bodenheimer T, Sinsky C. From triple to quadruple aim: care of the patient requires care of the provider. *Ann Fam Med.* 2014;12:573–576.
3. Kumar RB, Goren ND, Stark DE, Wall DP, Longhurst CA. Automated integration of continuous glucose monitor data in the electronic health record using consumer technology. *J Am Med inform Assoc.* 2016:3:23:532–537.
4. Apple. *Apple Announces iOS8 Available September 17: Introduces new Messages & Photos features, QuickType Keyboard, Extensibility, iCloud Drive & new Health app.* Cupertino, CA: Apple, 2014. https://www.apple.com/new sroom/2014/09/09Apple-Announces-iOS-8-Available-September-17/. Accessed for verification: March 2018.
5. UC San Diego Health. *UC San Diego Health Prioritizes Patient Experience with iPad and Apple TV: New Hospital Gives Patients Control of Their Environment.* San Diego, CA: UC San Diego Health, 2016. https://health.ucsd.edu/news/r eleases/Pages/2016-12-06-uc-san-diego-prioritizes-patient-experience-with-i pads-and-apple-tv.aspx. Accessed for verification: March 2018.
6. UC San Diego Health. *Students Propose Solutions to Critical Health Issues at Annual Hackathon.* San Diego, CA: UC San Diego Health, 2017. https://health. ucsd.edu/news/releases/pages/2017-03-23-uc-health-hackathon-solutions-to-he alth-issues.aspx. Accessed for verification: March 2018.
7. University of California. 2017 *Sautter Award Winners Announced.* Oakland, CA: University of California, 2017. https://cio.ucop.edu/2017-sautter-award-winners-announced/. Accessed for verification: March 2018.
8. UC San Diego Health. *Epic Sharing with UC Health.* San Diego, CA: UC San Diego Health, 2017. https://health.ucsd.edu/news/releases/pages/2017-11-14-epic-sharing-within-uc-health.aspx#sts=Campus collaborations allow for shared services, greater efficiencies. Accessed for verification: March 2018.
9. French R. Rollout of new electronic medical record partnership is an "Epic" achievement: Partnership between UCR and UCSD is first of its kind among UC Health organizations. *Inside UCR:* June 8, 2017. https://ucrtoday.ucr. edu/47454. Accessed for verification: March 2018.
10. Apple. *Apple Announces Effortless Solution Bringing Health Records to iPhone: Health Records Brings Together Hospitals, Clinics and the Existing Health App to Give a Fuller Snapshot of Health.* Cupertino, CA: Apple, 2018. https://www.apple.com/newsroom/2018/01/apple-announces-effortless-solu tion-bringing-health-records-to-iPhone/. Accessed for verification: March 2018.
11. Sisson P. UCSD among 12 nationwide to pilot Apple Inc. new medical records system. *The San Diego Union-Tribune:* January 24, 2018. http://www.sandiegou niontribune.com/news/health/sd-no-apple-medicalrecords-20180124-story.html. Accessed for verification: March 2018.

Clinical Collaboration with Application Development

Laurie Eccleston, MPA, RN, CPHMS and
Suzanne Richardson, MSN-HCSM, RN

As clinicians, specifically nurses, we typically are not trained on "innovation" or project management skills. Rather like most clinicians, we tend to develop unique skillsets by the problems we identify and through the use of work arounds as quick fixes for a solution. We see the needs of the patient through the lens of our nursing education and experiences.

With the advent of the EMR and digital health, the ability to be involved as subject matter experts (SME's) on design teams, provide the opportunity to be involved as valuable members of a cross-functional team for input into decision making. Our years of expertise in our own clinical domain and work experience, allows us to brainstorm and innovate in seeing potential solutions that not only provide clinical efficiency but improve the quality of patient care, satisfaction, enhanced functionality.

Our innovation journey began with a simple sketch on the back of an envelope. We realized we had an opportunity to put the patient at the forefront, by identifying a specific population at-risk that would benefit from remote patient monitoring.

From an innovative project standpoint, we approached our idea very similar to how we as clinicians practice in delivering patient care, through critical thinking and problem solving skills. In comparison to an IT project, we tailored the typical project management steps into what made sense to us in relation to patient care initiatives. We assessed, diagnosed, planned, implemented and evaluated the problem, or in this case the "innovative idea". We were trying to achieve and deliver, through an iterative process, the best solution to affordable quality of care and positive patient outcomes.

As with any large-scale integrated custom built application project, it takes a village to deliver a well planned and executed meaningful solution. Understanding the bricks to build the program and how it's all held together with the required elements, are essential for a successful program launch.

We knew that one of the critical measures of success for this project was clinical collaboration....designing for clinicians by clinicians...through the use of a cross-functional team. Collaboration and communication between interdisciplinary teams, recognizes that clinical needs drive technology solutions and translates how technology functions to transform program needs.

It allows for a common language with clinical and technical translators, who understand workflows, EMR functionality, and how the delivered services will support and integrate the proposed technology. It also provides a collective suite of recommendations for enhanced outcomes that infuses evidence-based practices for those who will use the technology.

Incorporating varied skill sets brings a wealth of knowledge and perspectives on how to create value. Pooling our talents together, exchanging different perspective, knowledge, and innovation helps to achieve a common solution.

We believed that utilizing a "rights" concept could provide a best practice framework when developing and implementing a multidisciplinary innovative program such as this. Getting the "right" information to those who need it, at the "right" time, for the "right" patient, at the "right" place, with the "right" access, and the "right" results would help to yield informed decision making for improved outcomes while harnessing the use of technology. In other words…get it right the first time…on time…all the time!

Our innovative journey was not the yellow-brick road to say the least. It was fraught with variances throughout the course of our project. We realized early on that as "innovators" we needed to embrace some fundamentals of our own, to succeed and incorporate them as the foundation for the next scalable project. Some of our nuts and bolts were:

■ Dream big
■ Put the patient front and center
■ Present and market your ideas to anyone who will listen… internally and externally
■ Have thick skin
■ Be a risk taker
■ Don't settle on "no" as the final answer or "that's the way it is"
■ Have the "right" individuals and decision-makers at the table from the beginning
■ If the solution can't be the way you thought or intended it to be, look for alternative ways to achieve the same solution or outcome
■ Don't let adversity get in the way of success
■ Always ask and keep asking "why"
■ Have clear defined roles and responsibilities and hold team members accountable for tasks and timelines

- Build, test, show, validate often...don't wait until the end for buy-in
- If you don't succeed today pick yourself up and start again because tomorrow will bring a new day of challenges and victories
- Be determined and relentless
- Learn from your mistakes early on including those detected with a pilot
- Take corrective action in the present and incorporate
- Communicate, communicate, communicate

Open communication, clinical collaboration, and strong project management skills ensure various disciplines are clear on roles, responsibilities, timelines, and scope.

Always look to the future for scalability and sustainability. Interprofessional innovative projects involving custom built clinical applications are complex, labor-intensive, but highly rewarding.

Finally, be the champion and "voice of the innovator." Advocate for the delivery of patient care, through the use and infusion of evidence-based practices into technology solutions, which contribute to quality outcomes and end-user satisfaction.

Innovate or Evaporate: The Value-Driven PMO

Dr. Greg Skulmoski, Gareth Sherlock & Craig Langston, PhD

Introduction

Project Management Offices (PMOs) are commonplace in today's technology-driven healthcare organizations. This case study is about a Middle Eastern PMO that was instrumental in opening a greenfield hospital and optimizing the services provided by the technology department. The Hospital opened in 2015 by delivering simple clinical services (e.g., ophthalmology exams). However, to provide just this single service, a comprehensive suite of integrated applications needed to be in place (e.g., ERP, Nurse Scheduling, Electronic Patient Record, RIS/PACS, Laboratory systems, Learning Management Systems, firewall security systems, call center systems, etc.) in addition to Eye Institute specific applications like Zeiss FORUM. This first service offered the opportunity to stabilize, learn and optimize systems, processes and the tasks caregivers complete to deliver exceptional care. More complex services followed such as additional ambulatory clinics (e.g., allergy and immunology), opening acute care, intensive care, and emergency services. The team planned and managed the purposeful stabilization, optimization, and learning for each progressive systems and service deployment. The purpose of this paper is to explain the maturity of the Hospital's IT PMO where principles of Agile and innovation are becoming core competencies. However, it is the innovation elements that distinguishes the Hospital PMO.

Collaborative PMO

The Hospital's IT PMO incorporated best practices (tools, processes, and training) and developed a project planning and delivery method. This Project Management Method (PMM) version 2.0 has matured through multiple versions and outlines critical documents and processes for technical projects. The rationale is that if the project team follows simple procedures and creates these project documents with stakeholders, then it is more likely that the "right projects are done right." The standard suite of PMM 2.0 documents include:

1. Project Requirements
2. Schedule
3. Solution Design (application, infrastructure and integration specifications)
4. Test Plan, Test Cases, and Test Results
5. Training Plan (IT teams, POCT team, and end users)
6. Deployment and Backout Plan
7. Service Operations Manual
8. Project Close Out

The required PMM documentation is mapped to project phases (Figure 8.3). The project team proceeds to the next phase when they complete the required PMM documentation. These stage gates help to ensure projects are methodically planned and executed resulting in an improved probability of project success. Those familiar with modern project management will see that this PMM approach is typical; however, the underlying philosophy has Agile and innovation elements such as co-create solutions with the customer. We believe this hybrid approach contributed to the on-time completion of the entire IT portfolio and supported the Hospital opening according to plan.

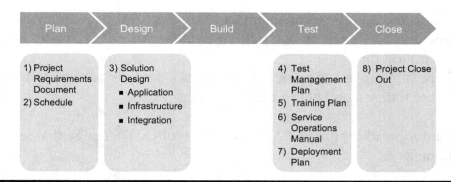

Figure 8.3   PMM Phases and Documents.

The Hospital opened on time. The systems worked as designed; while there were some stabilization efforts, the systems, processes, and people were able to support the on-time opening of more complex services for more diverse patients. During the stabilization phase, caregivers also looked forward and planned optimization initiatives such as Lab Optimization involving physicians, nurses, vendors and others in the value chain to improve patient care. The Lab Point of Care Testing project exemplifies co-created innovation. It is this case study that follows that illustrates innovation at the Hospital; but first, a look at traditional clinical testing.

Traditional Clinical Testing

Clinicians often base decision making on laboratory test results. Traditionally, testing occurred within the laboratory with specimens collected by trained caregivers for sample analysis and result interpretation. Testing results turnaround time is longer when testing takes place away from the patient bedside or point of care. Standard laboratory testing turnaround times can range from an hour to multiple days while clinicians wait for results. Long turnaround times delay patient care decision making.

Point of Care Testing (POCT) arose to address some of the shortcomings of traditional testing resulting in multiple benefits[1]:

1. POCT results are immediate, so the caregiver does not have to re-familiarize themselves with the case.
2. The results turnaround time is reduced leading to earlier decision making. Patient care can improve leading to a reduced length of stay and improved patient outcomes.

3. Testing and result interpretation can be completed by non-laboratory personnel thereby reducing staffing bottlenecks and decreased results turnaround time.

4. There is improved specimen stability since analysis occurs at the point of care rather than later in the laboratory.

Laboratory leadership at CCAD developed a POCT Strategy that leveraged these benefits.

Point of Care Testing

The Hospital POCT Strategy is a subset of the overall Laboratory Strategy that is caregiver and patient-focused to continuously improve and add value to the services offered by the Lab. The POCT team developed the POCT Strategy in the clinical planning phase before hospital go-live. The POCT Strategy addresses people, processes, and technology; planning and managing all three pillars are necessary for an effective and safe POCT service. Embedded in this Strategy are principles of Agile, Lean and innovation, and are evident when collaborating with others such as the PMO. A fundamental aspect of the Lab culture is that continuous improvement is an ongoing journey within each of these three pillars: innovate or evaporate.

People

Central to the Lab are people: patients, clinicians, collaborators, and vendors. The differentiating factor that enables innovation is how Lab caregivers work with others. Lab leadership strives to create long-term teams; that is, they provide a work environment where caregivers want to stay and be part of the Lab team. This permanence allows them to focus on common goals to delight their customers. The POCT team is self-organizing with the right amount of managerial governance. They prefer to meet face-to-face with their supply chain and other partners (e.g., PMO) and value transparency.

The POCT Laboratory team manages POCT activities ranging from training caregivers to collect specimens, to device calibration, to managing POCT documentation. All POCT caregivers require attaining, demonstrating and maintaining competence in POCT and related activities (e.g., infection control, hand hygiene, sharp object disposal, etc.). Competence is managed and documented in the organization's Learning Management and Human Resources systems.

Technology

Lab caregivers see technology as a value enabler. At hospital opening, the Lab went live with basic functionality; that is, the PMO and Lab together implemented necessary systems while supporting safe and effective patient care. Once stabilized, the Lab caregivers planned for improvement initiatives by turning on additional features to add value or to add other systems and integration to the Lab ecosystem. Thus, continuous technology improvement occurs within the Lab technological space.

Processes

The POCT team lives by the adage: "If you follow a good process, you are more likely to get a good result." (However, they are willing to break and improve processes in their continuous efforts to deliver valued services.) Therefore, a coherent and comprehensive suite of processes and policies guide point of care testing at the Hospital.

POCT Process

There are two major POCT processes: i) use POCT devices without electronic medical record integration, and ii) use POCT devices with electronic medical record integration. The Hospital opened with both integrated and non-integrated POCT devices. The Roche suite of devices was easily integrated with the electronic medical record using the Cobas application for hospital opening. These integrated POCT devices and workflows are successful and well-liked by clinicians; the POCT team learned from this experience.

The Lab team did not integrate non-Roche POCT devices with the electronic medical record due to device complexity; they left this integration for the optimization phase. The high-level workflow for non-integrated devices is straightforward:

1. The physician places a point of care test order using the electronic medical record.
2. The responsible caregiver receives the new order.
3. The caregiver performs the test at the point of care (e.g., ICU).
4. The caregiver manually enters the POCT results into the electronic medical record.
5. The ordering physician receives an alert within the electronic record that the POCT results are available.

After hospital opening, improvement opportunities became clearer. The POCT team undertook a Lean Six Sigma study to understand improvement areas and how to provide additional value.

POCT Optimization

Lab Optimization planning began before hospital opening. The Hospital opened, and the Lab caregivers with their various partners stabilized processes and systems. With these successes and learning, the POCT team and other Lab teams prioritized optimization projects. The POCT team completed a comprehensive analysis of the blood gases POCT service using Lean Six Sigma techniques including satisfaction surveys and process time measurements (e.g., results turnaround time). The POCT team identified opportunities for process simplification and results turnaround time reduction.

The POCT Strategy envisioned further device integration with the electronic medical record to i) eliminate manual results entry, ii) eliminate the potential for test results manual entry error, and iii) improve patient safety with additional positive patient ID checks. The integrated process follows:

1. The physician places an order for a point of care test using the electronic medical record.
2. The responsible caregiver receives the new order and prints the patient demographic label.
3. The caregiver attaches and scans the patient label on the specimen container.
4. The caregiver scans the patient's wristband for positive patient ID.
5. The caregiver performs the POCT.
6. The POCT device automatically analyses the specimen and sends the test results to the electronic medical record.
7. The ordering physician receives an alert within the electronic record that the POCT results are available.

The Lean Six Sigma study helped POCT caregivers understand the problems and how to improve the process. Fundamental to process improvement was device integration. The POCT leadership proposed and prioritized device integration to the PMO.

Conworx POCT Integration Solution

The technical teams integrated POCT devices with the electronic medical record with the Conworx application system. Conworx is a middleware application that integrates different vendor POCT devices and the electronic patient record. Conworx receives patient data (ADT message) and orders (ORM message) from the electronic patient record. Depending upon the type of POCT device, the demographic and orders messages flow directly to the POCT device. Integration improves positive patient ID so that the right test is performed on the right patient. Results (ORU message) then flow immediately to the electronic record for the ordering physician's attention.

Project Management Method with Agile Enhancements

The project team followed the Hospital's Project Management Method (PMM) to implement the Conworx integration solution. The PMM is a set of tools and processes used by project managers to deliver projects like the Conworx Integration Project. Traditional project documentation like a schedule, test strategy, and go-live strategy support the teams. The delivery method included Agile and the innovation principles resulting in an Agile project management delivery method.

Once the project was approved to proceed, the PMO and POCT teams continued their collaboration to plan the project and co-create the solution. They brought in other teams as required (e.g., they worked with procurement specialists early to procure devices and the Conworx software). However, it is during the transition to production and the go-live period that the PMO and POCT teams demonstrated their Agility. They acted in unison to carefully plan and manage the risks of bringing this new system into Production that would significantly change the POCT workflows.

Staged Approach: Working together with the PMO and POCT teams, they planned a staged approach to bring this new system into the Production environment. First, the Conworx technical team placed the application into Production with a detailed and rehearsed backout plan should the team need to remove Conworx from the Production system. Once in Production, the team completed comprehensive regression testing to verify Conworx did not disrupt the other applications in the Production environment. After a day of Production co-existence, the team concluded that Conworx was stable. Next came connecting the POCT devices to Conworx and the electronic medical record. The strategy was to connect the least complicated devices first, then stabilize, learn, adapt and implement more complex devices:

1. DCA Vantage Analyzer (2 devices): measuring HbA1c which aids in efficient glycemic control. These are the least complicated devices that went live without any issues. After two days, the next set of devices were scheduled to go live.
2. Hemochron Signature Elite (9 devices): coagulation testing system using k arterial or venous blood. Again, these devices went live without any issues. After a day of monitoring (rather than the planned two days), the POCT team decided to go live with the next set of devices earlier than planned.
3. RapidPoint (RP) 500 Blood Gases Analyzer (6 devices): used to test blood gas, electrolytes, glucose, lactate, and full CO-oximetry. These complicated devices were high-value devices for the clinicians, and all six also went live without any issues.

Learning: The PMO and the POCT developed a training plan for the different groups of caregivers using the system: IT Support (Level 1), Conworx Support (Level 2), POCT team, physicians, and nurses. While these formal learning opportunities were necessary, it was the informal but purposeful learning that occurred throughout the project. For example, after each piece of the POCT solution was put into Production, the team reviewed the go-live experience to see if additional training, communication or support were required. The team took their lessons learned and applied them to the next POCT devices to go-live.

Agile Teams: The POCT, PMO, physicians, nurses, vendors, and device manufacturers together committed to this quality improvement initiative. The team encouraged Agility principles throughout the value chain. For example, the core team met each day, face-to-face to align their work. The team met with physicians and nurses before go-live to answer questions and to validate the rollout strategy. When the devices were being rolled out, the PMO, POCT, and Conworx Support teams visited the clinicians to provide support, so new processes were easily followed allowing clinicians to focus on patient care.

The deployment of the three types of devices was stable with only minor configuration problems that the team quickly fixed. Given device stability and caregiver satisfaction, the PMO and POCT project leadership closed out the Conworx project early. Due to the success of POCT device integration with the electronic medical record, the POCT leadership plan further POCT device integration.

POCT Optimization Results

Now, the manual steps to enter test results into the electronic record are eliminated thereby decreasing the turnaround time and reducing the potential for human error. In Figure 8.4, one can see that the dark shaded "pain points" representing inefficiency and were reduced after integration. (Note: the graphic was sized to illustrate process improvement results indicated by the reduced number of steps and dark shaded pain points; the intention is not for the reader to read the details of the before and after processes. Nothing wrong with your eyes!) We achieved process simplification.

We would like to share two key results: POCT program success and ISO Accreditation results.

1) Point of Care Testing Success

Integrating POCT devices with the electronic patient record has yielded many measurable improvements; however, for brevity, only the blood gases results are highlighted and are indicative of the successes of the other integrated POCT devices. A critical improvement in the average turnaround time for blood gases results dropped from 25 minutes to less than 5 minutes (Tables 8.1 and 8.2).

POCT satisfaction increased for physicians, nurses, and other clinicians using the newly integrated POCT devices and process. Below are the physician results that are similar to nurses and other clinicians using POCT integrated with the electronic patient record.

Besides improvements in turnaround time reduction, integrating POCT devices provided other benefits. A significant feature of Conworx is that POCT devices can be remotely monitored and configured by the POCT Laboratory team. Remote device management saves time for the POCT Laboratory team since they do not have to go to the device should there be a technical or calibration problem; they can use the Conworx administration module in the Lab to investigate device problems. Remote device management reduces unplanned device downtime and increases caregiver satisfaction (Table 8.2).

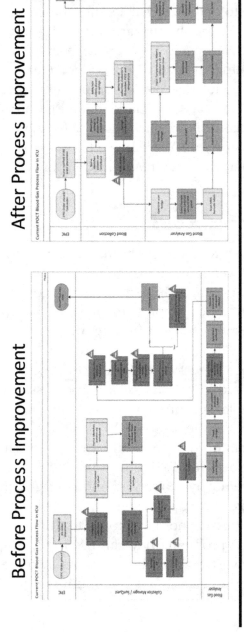

Figure 8.4   Process Improvement.

Table 8.1   POCT Turnaround Time

Modality	Turnaround Time (Minutes)
Blood gases sent to the Lab for analysis	>25
Blood gases POCT - without Conworx integration	15
Blood gases POCT - with Conworx integration	<5

Table 8.2   Physician Satisfaction

Physician Satisfaction with POCT Process	Before Integration	After Integration
Strongly Agree	11%	33%
Agree	56%	0%
Neutral	11%	67%
Disagree	0%	0%
Strongly Disagree	22%	0%

2) ISO 15189/22870 Accreditation

Achieving ISO 15189/22870 POCT Accreditation was an essential POCT strategic goal. The POCT team submitted an ISO application detailing readiness and then hosted the ISO accreditors in August 2017. The accreditors reviewed the POCT program and awarded ISO accreditation in October 2017 for eight device types including POCT Thromboelastography (TEG) devices. Accrediting the TEG POCT device is noteworthy since there are very few other hospitals in the world that are ISO 15189/22870 accredited for TEG POCT devices. The Hospital became the first lab in the Middle East to be ISO 15189/22870 accredited.

Conclusion

The POCT service at the Hospital has achieved its short-term goals: provide integrated POCT services to the caregivers' satisfaction, and to achieve ISO 15189/22780 accreditation. The work has only begun! Given the success of the POCT program, integrating additional POCT devices (e.g., I-STAT for creatinine testing) is being planned. They are adding additional Conworx functionality such as the competence management module. Here, a POCT device user will be automatically locked out of the device if their training is out of date. The competence management module will improve regulatory compliance and enhance patient safety. The caregivers expect more great things to come from the POCT program. Looking back at the project, we can identify critical success factors that begin with Agile teams.

Critical Success Factors

1. Agile Teams – Extend Agile principles across the value chain teams including vendors, device manufacturers, end users, PMO, and the POCT team. Together, they co-created solutions to add value for POCT users. The POCT and Conworx Support teams were stable in that there was the intention of "permanence" so that the momentum of success continues. These teams met face-to-face whenever possible, and it was mandatory during the critical go-live period. Indeed, during go live, there were 8 am and 1 pm team meetings to align, communicate, learn and plan.
2. Continuous Improvement – The PMO and POCT teams understand that continuous improvement is critical: innovate or evaporate! To improve they used Lean Six Sigma tools to understand problems and opportunities; then measure to improve problem understanding and results objectivity.
3. Purpose – The POCT and PMO teams had a clear sense of purpose where outcomes were measurable and objective; they formulated value-laden outcomes in the eyes of their customers.
4. Project Success – Define success regarding your customer in addition to other metrics such as delivering on time. The point is to provide products and services that delight your customer over the life of the product or service[2]; this is a bit contrary to the temporary nature of projects. However, when customer care and ongoing performance are primary indicators of value, then a constant backlog of delivering initiatives will be favored over traditional project delivery approaches.
5. Adaptable Project Management – The PMO developed the PMM 2.0 that guides project participants. It is flexible in that it can be adapted to suit the uniqueness of a project so that the focus becomes adding value (outcomes) rather than finishing on time (outputs) and perhaps not delivering a solution that delights the customer. Given the

need for ongoing performance and customer, providing value through lengthy "waterfall projects" is not always appropriate; Agile and other approaches (e.g., #noprojects) offer other delivery methods. A continuous stream of smaller Agile initiatives run parallel to large projects to deliver a continuous flow of value initiatives. This approach leads to more frequent feedback, more improvements, and increased value for caregivers and patients.

6. Innovation– Customers today increasingly demand continuous improvement and change. Meeting these expectations can be helped along through innovation. Innovation principles supported the POCT integration project. For example, a deep understanding of what the customer valued drove effective innovation. Implementing innovative solutions should be incremental and iterative.

7. Information Technology is a 'Strategic Partner' – Gone are the days where IT is just a back-office function. At the Hospital, the IT Department is a strategic partner to clinical and business functions, solving both operation challenges and developing and delivering the strategy. This forward-thinking approach ensures that IT focuses on achieving outcomes and not just implementations and support.

The POCT Strategy focusing on people, process, and technology, has been visionary, comprehensive and systematic. The POCT Strategy included attaining the prestigious ISO 15189/22780 accreditation. While achieving the ISO accreditation is outstanding, more is being planned to provide the very best patient care by a team of dedicated caregivers. The journey continues.

References

1. St. John, Andrew, "The Evidence to Support Point-of-Care Testing," *The Clinical Biochemist Reviews*, 2010 Aug; 31(3): 111–119, https://www.ncb i.nlm.nih.gov/pmc/articles/PMC2924123/. And Crocker, J. Benjamin et al, "Implementation of Point-of-Care Testing in an Ambulatory Practice of an Academic Medical Center," American Journal of Clinical Pathology, Volume 142, Issue 5, 1 November 2014, Pages 640–646, https://academic.oup.com/ajcp/article/142/5/640/1761000/Implementation-of-Point-of-Care-Testing-in-an.

2. Langston, C. (2013) Development of generic key performance indicators for PMBOK using a 3D project integration model. *Australasian Journal of Construction Economics and Building*, 13(4), 78–91. https://doi.org/10.5130/ajceb.v13i4.3658

Turning Everyday Employees into Startup-Like Entrepreneurs

Alex Goryachev
Cisco

Cisco Fosters Culture of Innovation Company-Wide

> My innovation encourages employees across all job functions and grades to tap into their inner entrepreneurs and start innovating in teams with a diversity of talents and skill

Innovation Can Come from Anyone, Anywhere

Every industry in our digital age feels the pressure to move faster and find new ways to ignite internal innovation. Moreover, the goal is always the same: inspire employees to tap into their own passions and create game-changers for customers. The road map for this disruptive journey often takes different directions.

I would like to share our method to unleash the inner entrepreneur of every employee, and transform our workforce of more than 74,000 people worldwide into a startup-like culture of constant innovation. We believe innovation can come from anyone, anywhere. Research and experience has validated this truth, especially when diverse and inclusive teams can access tools and resources.

No matter your industry or organization's size, our award-winning "My Innovation" program can help engage employees and inspire them to deliver brilliant new ideas – perhaps even the next big thing that disrupts markets with game-changing products, solutions, and services.

The Genesis of My Innovation

In early 2015, Cisco conducted a company-wide series of focus groups to get employees' ideas on how to improve the enterprise. One of the most striking themes from these focus groups was that employees wanted support for implementing innovations and a forum for sharing ideas that could shape the company's future. In response, Cisco launched a company-wide, cross-functional competition called the "Innovate Everywhere Challenge (IEC)" in September 2015. This competition provided a public, collaborative forum for employees to share, build, and invest in ideas for new products, services, and process improvements. By the end of the eight-month competition, 48% of employees across the company had participated in the Challenge. Of the 1,100 ideas submitted, seven remain active as new ventures. Moreover, the Challenge provided a space and process to discuss and build out new ideas and set the expectation that every employee can be an innovator.

The inaugural IEC became the catalyst for Cisco's company-wide support for entrepreneurship. Cisco brought all of these initiatives together under the umbrella of "My Innovation," and made this a centerpiece of the company's People Deal. To provide opportunities to build a startup mindset and skills beyond the Challenge, Cisco created an all-in-one portal for all of its innovation work, assembled a network of mentors for new business ideas, added incentives for "Angels" who supported new ideas, and gave all employees the opportunity to make investment decisions in the second iteration of the IEC. The My Innovation framework enabled synergies among Cisco's many innovation supporters and led to a significant uptake in employee engagement in innovation. Now entering the third year of its sustained effort to empower every employee to act like an innovator, Cisco continues to learn more about how to embed a startup culture in a large enterprise.

Tipping Point: The Decision to Invest in a Company-Wide Focus on Innovation

There is a widespread belief that large companies are unable to innovate at the speed needed to thrive in an era where startups can threaten established industries seemingly overnight. While many enterprises do struggle to adapt to new conditions, scale and innovation need not be at odds.

In fact, the diversity and sheer volume of employees at a large company can be an asset for sourcing new ideas if the company is able to harness and willing to act on them. The 2016 BCG Global Innovation Survey revealed that growth ideas most often come from internal sources and that the ability to tap into "employee ideation forums" was the greatest differentiator between strong and weak innovators. In other words, large companies who create the culture, space, structures, and incentives for their employees to innovate can be as effective at unleashing and harnessing new ideas as smaller companies.

In Spring 2015, Cisco held a series of focus groups across the company and discovered that employees were eager to innovate in their work but were unclear on the pathways for successfully nurturing new ideas to the execution phase. They asked for support, time, space, and money to foster and implement their best ideas for new ventures. In particular, employees wanted a central forum where they could bring new ideas, build them out with colleagues, and present them to executives and decision-makers.

Secure Executive and Peer Support

Cisco's Corporate Strategic Innovation Group (CSIG), together with partners across the company, as well as external partners began the work of mapping out how My Innovation could engage, empower, and enable *every* Cisco employee to innovate. Our first answer was the Innovate Everywhere Challenge.

During the planning phase of IEC, collaboration, research, and experience helped to garner full C-Suite commitment for the company-wide, cross-functional program. Additional collaboration with leaders across business units helped to map out goals for IEC:

- Capture disruptive venture ideas from employees and help grow them
- Develop entrepreneurship skills and culture across Cisco
- Enhance employee experience and collaboration

MY INNOVATION MISSION

"My Innovation" empowers employees to innovate everywhere and at any time.

It is our employees' innovative ideas that will accelerate Cisco's leadership in the digital age. "My Innovation" creates the environment and provides vehicles for innovative ideas to emerge, develop, and shape Cisco's future.

We disrupt the industry and ourselves by fostering a culture of grassroots cross-functional collaboration, connecting our employees with broader ecosystem of innovators inside and outside of the company, and empowering everyone to take risks.

My Innovation, kicked off by the IEC, is now one of the pillars of Cisco's People Deal manifesto with employees, championed by CEO Chuck Robbins and sponsored by Chief Strategy Officer Hilton Romanski and Chief People Officer Fran Katsoudas.

Align with Corporate Priorities

Innovation has always been part of Cisco's DNA, however, we do not innovate for innovation's sake. Our goal is to create a disciplined yet flexible approach that leads to amazing business outcomes for customers and partners. To be successful, we needed structure and focus to make sure the IEC aligned with corporate priorities.

We incorporated flexibility and discipline into our guidelines. Flexibility that we would evaluate all entries. Discipline that all entries should focus on Cisco's strategic priorities and markets. For example, we published a Table of Strategic Innovation Elements, inspired by an external best practice, to guide our employees' ideation process. The table displays key markets, novel technologies, and disruptive business models.

Through our "Operations" market, we reinforced the need to develop innovations that reduce costs, streamline processes, or improve performance within Cisco or for our customers. To discourage "science experiments," we also emphasized "business outcomes" that are faster, leaner, and just better.

In addition, Cisco leaders across the company shared where they see a need for innovative and disruptive ideas – we call these Innovation Ambitions. With the commitment from the C-suite, employees were able to watch short videos that described each of the leader's ambitions (strategic priorities) that they could align their venture ideas.

Provide Clear Path to Innovation

The Innovate Everywhere Challenge urges all employees to Team Up. Disrupt. Innovate. Win. Just like in the external startup world, IEC focuses on two personas central to creating a startup culture:

■ **Cisco Founders** create innovative ventures or join them at an early stage
■ **Cisco Angels** support innovative ventures financially or with expertise

Each IEC proceeds over eight months in four phases modeled after the life cycle of startups: ideate, validate, fund, and build. The IEC also includes a virtual investing component, giving employees the opportunity to participate in the selection process by investing free tokens (118,809 tokens invested in the last Challenge alone). These "backers" also posted 5000+ comments and ratings, which provided invaluable feedback to IEC participants.

- **Ideate:** In the first phase, all employees are invited to propose a solution to a big problem or opportunity facing Cisco. They can create or join a cross-functional team to post their idea on a collaborative platform visible to all employees. A panel of judges – as well as employee token investment – narrow these entries down to 20 semifinalists, who advance to the Validate phase.
- **Validate:** The 20 semifinalist teams have three months to work with mentors and coaches to validate their venture, prepare an investor pitch, and fill a business model canvas. (See box on how they get help.) Cisco leaders with the help of real-world angel investors chose 5 of the 6 finalist teams; employees select the one finalist through token investing.
- **Fund:** The 6 finalists have three weeks to find internal sponsors and harness support for their venture. At the end of this phase, they give a 5-minute live pitch to a panel of Cisco C-Suite executives, external angel investors and employees around the globe. The 3 winners of The Challenge are then announced at an all-company meeting and through various communication channels.
- **Build:** Each winning team gets $25,000 in seed funding, $25,000 as recognition, and the option to enter a 3-month innovation rotation program to give them the space to develop their venture. Each team also receives a corporate concierge for help with practical affairs as well as assistance from Cisco leaders in determining the most appropriate next step for its venture.

Using a workshop format, Startup//Cisco equips employees with the skills and mindset of a startup founder. Employees learn and apply innovation methodologies to accelerate new projects so they can get to stronger business outcomes faster and with fewer resources. Participants use design thinking, and lean startup innovation principles and techniques to validate ideas directly with customers. The process takes employees through designing a Minimum Viable Service (MVS), gathering feedback from customers, analyzing lessons, revising the MVS, and repeating until Cisco and the customer agree that the MVS has been perfected.

Further, if semifinalists secure an executive sponsor at Cisco, IEC matches the sponsor's funds up to $10,000, hence encouraging business adoption. Finally, IEC also rewards employees who mentored, invested their tokens smartly (i.e., in semifinalist, ventures), or more generally provided great value to ventures during the Challenge.

Excite, Inspire, and Engage the Workforce

Each IEC begins and ends with an interactive meeting broadcast company-wide featuring the CEO or other C-Suite executives who either kick it off or announce the winners. Throughout IEC, communications consistently inform and inspire employees through various multi-media, such as videos, articles, social media, presentations, and features on the progress of teams. Regular communications from corporate and business-unit leaders also reinforce key messages on the importance of internal innovation to Cisco's business strategy.

Finally, we make this serious business fun – we gamify it! Engagement levels soar when employees have creative ways to invest, root for their favorites online, hoist banners at events, search for like-minded team members, or brainstorm in online communities of their own making.

Empower and Equip Innovators All Year Round

The Innovate Everywhere Challenge is once a year. We needed something more to enable innovation year-round and constantly reinforce attitudes of innovation.

So we created "The Hub", an always on, go-to destination where employees come together to learn, collaborate, discover, and explore their innovative ideas. This interactive portal holds a wealth of resources to empower our Cisco Founders and Angels. Employees can develop their entrepreneurial skillset via playbooks and hands-on workshop, tap into a 4,000+ network to find the perfect mentor, get inspired through case studies of successes and failures, and more. The Hub is also home to IEC where our global employees can access and review the ventures at anywhere anytime.

In addition to IEC, The Hub is currently the gateway to some 40 other innovation programs.

Impact

Innovation can and should be measured. We focus on five types of metrics: engagement, participation, employee feedback, ventures outcomes, and thought leadership.

- **Engagement:** To date, 64% of Cisco employees, from all organizations and from 90 countries, have visited the Challenge website.

- **Participation:** 42% of Cisco employees have actively participated by submitting a venture, joining a team, investing their tokens, and commenting/rating.
- **Feedback:** 95% of employees surveyed would recommend IEC to their peers. Over the years, we learned from employee feedback and evolved the IEC process to what it is now. "IEC gave me an opportunity to venture outside my comfort zone and interact with people I didn't usually interact with. After 32 years in the tech industry, the Innovate Everywhere Challenge helped me to discover that there was still a lot of innovation inside me."-Doris Singer.
- **Outcomes:** The 45 top ventures from IEC1 and IEC2 have already directly yielded tangible innovations, including:
  - 16 proof of concepts
  - 4 beta products
  - 10+ patents in progress
  - 4 ventures adopted by the business
    - Example: Cisco LifeChanger has been one of the most successful and disruptive solutions to come out of the Innovate Everywhere Challenge. It is helping to create new possibilities for how employers can tap into the tremendous untapped potential of people with disabilities, and change lives. What started as a novel idea by a passionate group of employees has evolved into a movement at Cisco, resulting in a best practice for other companies to emulate. Since its inception, Cisco LifeChanger has helped facilitate the hiring of nearly 100 people with disabilities globally, across all disabilities, into a broad range of functions, including sales, engineering, technical services, employee services, customer advanced services, in addition to our general business functions.
  - Recognition and Awards:
  - Cisco LifeChanger has been recognized globally by industry-leading disability inclusion organizations, including: Disability Matters 2016 North America, and Disability Matters 2017 Asia Pacific.
  - Cisco was a recipient of the 2017 Diversity Journal Innovation Award, and the USBLN also recognized Cisco as one of the "Best Places to Work for Disability Inclusion."
  - To date, Cisco LifeChanger has also been featured as a disability employment best practice at national and global events, including the Zero Project Summit, Disability Matters, USBLN Global Employment

Summit, International Labour Organization Global Disability Summit, and the Harkin Institute Global Disability Summit.

■ **Thought leadership:** Constantly reinforcing our innovator brand is key to attract and retain talent. Since its start three years ago, the Innovate Everywhere Challenge has contributed to Cisco gaining media recognition as a "Great place to work" as well as acknowledgment from Human Resource organizations as an industry leader for our "Employee Engagement" and "Unique or Innovative Talent Management Program."

The Next Frontier: My Innovation and IEC in Year Three

In Summer 2017, the Cisco team took stock of what had been achieved since the integrated My Innovation supporters came together under The Hub a year earlier. During fiscal year 2017, 53% of Cisco's employees (more than 39,000 people) engaged in My Innovation, 23,000 of these participated actively. They came from 89 countries and all were part of Cisco organizations. This reach suggests that Cisco's innovation efforts have achieved the scale necessary for true cultural change.

Rather than resting on its laurels, Cisco has already identified two ways to strengthen My Innovation as it enters its third year. The first is supporting business owners in more clearly articulating the discrete design challenges that innovation should address. This will lead to better solutions both in the third iteration of the Innovate Everywhere Challenge as well as in Cisco's day-to-day business.

Cisco is also expanding its network of makerspaces through its thingQbator initiative. These physical spaces are dedicated to supporting hands-on learning, exploration, and prototyping and are themselves examples of how deeply the entrepreneurial mindset has permeated Cisco: the initiative started with a group of employees in Cisco's Bangalore office, and My Innovation is now helping scale it in the United States.

Conclusion

In 2015, Cisco committed to ensuring that it thinks and acts like a lean startup but scales as an enterprise. The My Innovation journey has already directly yielded tangible innovations, including seven ventures with a successful proof of concept, two beta products, and eight patents in progress. Over time, these numbers will only grow.

Accomplishments of IEC1 and IEC2 Winners (as of November 2017)

Just as important for Cisco's future success has been the change in the company's culture: employees now have the opportunity and support to propose new products, services, and process improvements and see themselves as innovators and entrepreneurs. As this expectation takes root among all employees, My Innovation will continue to evolve to ensure that everyone has the skill sets, attitudes, and opportunities to innovate.

With the Innovate Everywhere Challenge, "My Innovation" started a lasting cultural transformation. My Innovation will continue to evolve to ensure that everyone has the skill sets, attitudes, and opportunities to innovate as we launch the Innovate Everywhere Challenge 4 in September 2018.

Conclusion

What follows is less of a summary and more of an admonishment. My hope is that this is not just another book with some good stories but a catalyst for you and me. A catalyst for our industry. A catalyst to push harder and more thoughtfully along this healthcare technology journey. The beauty of the innovation pathway is its simplicity. The processes are proven and the framework widely adopted. While I do not believe there is a formula for innovation, this framework provides a solid process and pathway from which to innovate.

Blending cultures is a key place to start. You must make sure you have organizational buy-in and commitment. In cases where this is not possible, start small, gain experience, establish credibility and doors may open. I admit that occasionally, you just need to create a skunk's works of sorts and demonstrate value and ask for forgiveness later.

While it is critical to leverage technology, never start there. We are in the people business. You have to strike that perfect balance in your organization between people, process and technology. Win the confidence and heart of people and everything else will fall into place.

Some may think planning is an innovation inhibitor, but our contributors have shown otherwise. Innovation success is often multiplied when you use sound planning principles and create roadmaps. Sometimes innovation just happens as needs arise, but roadmaps have a stronger track record.

John Maxwell says that "one is too small a number for greatness." I agree. Very few innovations come from a single person. They come from a team of teams or an agile environment where collaboration and communication dominate the culture. I do not recall any innovation that I have been involved with that emanated from just one person.

One of the key tasks of a leader is to eliminate barriers. Some of the contributors highlighted roadblocks to innovation and how they overcame them. Whenever you pioneer you naturally encounter barriers. Accept this fact, do not be discouraged. Rather, see barriers as signs you are on the right path. Then relentlessly eliminate them.

A primary key to Apple's success has been the diligent pursuit of simplicity. Too often we complicate matters which in turn reduce our opportunity for success. Always seek to simplify the complex. The more focus, the sharper the solution. Innovation dies with complexity.

It's human nature to be driven by recognition and reward. We have a propensity to repeat those things rewarded. Create programs and incentives for innovation. It will eventually become the fabric of you and your organization. Celebrate failure.

Just as you seek to collaborate within your organization, consider including other key partners. Many of the examples in this book were instances of supplier and prover collaboration. Provider and patient collaboration is powerful as well. Often, a collaborator will have the missing piece for you to complete or enhance your innovation.

Now that you have completely read the book, I want to leave you with what I believe is the single biggest key for successful innovation: You. To be innovative *you* must be innovative. You can take the innovation pathways framework and adopt it in your organization. As the stories demonstrate, when the framework is adopted well, it will work. If you want to get to the next level, work on yourself. Seek to be an innovative person if you are not already. Too often, I speak with people who are frustrated because of a lack of innovation in their organization. The first question I ask them is how do they make sure they are personally innovative. If they are still using kiosks at the airport, probably not innovative. If they still have a printer in their office, probably not innovative. If they are still going to their local bank or grocery store, probably not innovative. If they have the same hobbies as they did 10 years ago, the same clothing and music styles... probably not innovative. If they don't routinely read and study inside and outside of their expertise, probably not innovative. Same phone forever? Same glasses? Same drink? Basically, if you are limiting your experiences, you are unable to take advantage of all the diversity in science, nature, tech, arts, and philosophy. It is the combinations of these inputs that make one innovative.

So if *you* are not innovative, you will struggle to innovate.

The solution is simple and pragmatic. Do new things. Constantly introduce change into your life. Consume diverse news and listen to contrarian viewpoints. Activate Twitter, Snapchat and Instagram. Download new music. Learn a new dance or hobby. Go back to school. Use all the tech in your car. Grab a mentor who is a generation or two younger. If you are a technologist, learn art and vice versa. I guarantee that as you become innovative, everything else will follow. And we will change the world.

Index

and PACS, 115
Yale New Haven Health, 120
Epimed Solutions, 80
Establishing culture of innovation,
    eliminating barriers, 146–149
  communicating openly, 148
  Electronic Health Record system
    adoption of, 147
    implementing, 148
  Electronic Practice Management, 148
  healthcare IT field, 146
  IT
    as expensive overhead, 149
    as one-off solution provider, 149
    as partner, 149
    as utility, 149
  service-oriented team, 148

Fast Healthcare Interoperability Resources
    (FHIR), 24, 42, 43, 44, 117
FHIR, *see* Fast Healthcare Interoperability
    Resources
Financial catalysts, 45

Game-changers, 58
Global Cardiovascular Innovations Center
    (GCIC), 2
GlobalMed (company), 132, 134, 135,
    137, 139
  ClinicalAccess Station, 136
  Transportable Exam Station (TES), 136
Google, 59, 87, 140, 190, 195
Governance, 63–64, 65, 67, 117, 217
  managerial governance, 232
Guiding behaviors, 176

Health Insurance Portability and
    Accountability Act of 1996 (HIPAA),
    26, 27, 28, 59, 91, 150
  Information Security Risk Assessment, 153
  Police, 150
Health systems in leveraging technology, 121
  Bluetooth enabled scale, 121
  Cleveland Digital Patient Engagement
    Model, 124–126
    components, 124
    digital inclusion organizations, 125

consumer health technology adoption, 121
digital health tools, 122
health care system, 122–123
  to address risk factors, 122
  Precision Public Health approach, 122
MetroHealth System, Cleveland, Ohio,
    123–124
  digital redlining, 123
  digital skill training, 123
Healthcare Information and Management
    Systems Society (HIMSS), 24
  EMRAM Level 7 certification process, 189
  Innovation recommendations, 111
  memberships in, 154, 189
  Wolf III, Hal (CEO), 213
Healthcare information technology (HIT),
    stressing simplicity, 173–175
  emergency desktop notifier, 174
  mobile application, 174
  redesigning of IT services, 173
  specific documentation, 174
  value-based reimbursement model, 175
Healthcare innovation, blended cultures
    in, 1–2
  blending big and small company
    cultures, 4
  blending Japanese and American
    business cultures, 3–4
  Cleveland Clinic, 2–3
  concept of Shaze, 3
  Murata Manufacturing Co., Ltd., 2–3
  Prevent Biometrics, 5
Healthcare Partner Council for Cleveland
    Clinic Information Technology,
    104–105
  Main Campus Voice of Patient Advisory
    Committee (Main Campus
    VPAC), 104
  Our Voice: Healthcare Partners (Our
    Voice: HCP) program, 104, 105
Healthcare without borders, *see* Innovating
    for global impact
HIMSS, *see* Healthcare Information and
    Management Systems Society
    (HIMSS)
HIPAA, *see* Health Insurance Portability and
    Accountability Act of 1996 (HIPAA)

Printed in the United States
by Baker & Taylor Publisher Services